PRAISE FOR

PIGLET

Named one of the best feel-good books of 2021
by *The Washington Post*

"A puppy with a purpose, Piglet teaches us the power of love and
kindness."

—*Good Morning America*

"A little dog with a big following, helping students learn a powerful
lesson about acceptance."

—Lester Holt, *NBC Nightly News*

"Piglet—a pink, blind, and deaf puppy—inspires others to overcome
the odds."

—*CBS News*

"Piglet is a social media superstar. But before that, he was a two-
pound, deaf, blind pup without a home. Shapiro, a veterinarian, took
him in and fell in love. This sweet story details Piglet's transformation from a traumatized, anxious puppy into a confident, spirited
pink dog and his new family."

—*The Washington Post*

"Piglet is just getting started on his quest to make the world a better
place."

—*People*

"Shapiro's personal tale will inspire even the most time-pressed among us to take time out for the pups—and people—that matter."

—Zibby Owens, *The Washington Post*

"[Piglet's] journey to love and communication inspires students, teachers, and everyone who meets the spirited six-pound Chihuahua-dachshund mix to change the way they think about overcoming obstacles, meeting challenges, and interacting with those who might appear to be different but have the same need for love and acceptance as everyone else. Piglet and his people are making the world a better place and inviting us to join them."

—*StarTribune*

"The heartwarming journey of how Piglet gained confidence and now helps others face their own challenges. Each page of Piglet's story shows the power of empathy, love, and kindness—it's a joyful respite that is certain to inspire."

—*Woman's World*

"Educators and their students, animal advocacy groups, his legion of social media friends, and now readers of this book will continue to be inspired by Piglet and his pack facing each new challenge with resilience. Including serious factual details as needed while creating an emotional bond with touches of sorrow and joy, this book will rightly gain its canine influencer new followers."

—*Booklist*

"Shapiro and Piglet's uplifting odyssey, cowritten by Eichler Rivas (*The Pursuit of Happyness*), is touching, emotional, and not to be missed."

—*Library Journal* (starred review)

"Shapiro's inspirational memoir—candid details of her veterinary career, her family, lovable Piglet and his incredibly sweet, resilient spirit—will win hearts."

—*Shelf Awareness*

"Such a beautiful, inspiring story of Piglet, and his loving, patient human mom and veterinarian, Melissa Shapiro. This story will warm your heart and brings to life how this beautiful dog came into the Shaprio family with his own purpose. Through sheer love and dedication, Piglet no longer lives in a world of total darkness. This story touched my heart and soul in such a profound way, as it reminded me how my sweet, blind, and deaf five-pound poodle, Emma, is happy, content, and loves her precious life too."

—Laura Schroff, #1 internationally
bestselling author of *An Invisible Thread*

"I never thought I would call a book about a dog and their caring and compassionate humans a page-turner. However, I was wrong and pleasantly surprised that Melissa Shapiro's riveting Cinderella story of a tiny deaf blind pink pup called Piglet, who surely would have died had not human hands and hearts intervened, took me on this unexpected joyride. Suffice it to say, *Piglet* is a beautiful and inspirational story about a beautiful and inspirational dog and his beautiful and inspirational humans who all can be viewed as poster beings who enrich our lives by embracing kindness, compassion, and love when the easy way out would have been to say something like, 'This is hopeless.' Feeling hopeless? Pick up this book, savor its heartwarming messages, and share it widely. It is *that* good."

—Marc Bekoff, PhD, author of *Canine Confidential:
Why Dogs Do What They Do* and *A Dog's World:
Imagining the Lives of Dogs in a World Without
Humans* (with Jessica Pierce)

"I worked with Lassie for many years, one of the most heroic dogs the world has known. I never thought a profoundly disabled, one-pound pink puppy could rival her. But little Piglet does just that, overcoming enormous obstacles to raise awareness for fellow animals in need of rescue. Vet Melissa Shapiro's story of adopting and training Piglet is sweet, funny, very emotional . . . and, above all, entertaining. And just like my adventures with Lassie, Piglet's tale is a love story. Knowing him will enrich your life."

—Jon Provost, actor who played Timmy on
Lassie and author of *Timmy's in the Well*

"Sometimes we need a little inspiration to remember to never give up. . . . And a little deaf and blind puppy named Piglet is just that inspiration."

—theanimalrescuesite.greatergood.com

PIGLET

The Unexpected Story of a Deaf Blind
Pink Puppy and His Family

MELISSA SHAPIRO, DVM

WITH MIM EICHLER RIVAS

ATRIA PAPERBACK
New York London Toronto Sydney New Delhi

An Imprint of Simon & Schuster, Inc.
1230 Avenue of the Americas
New York, NY 10020

First Atria Paperback edition June 2022

ATRIA PAPERBACK and colophon are trademarks of
Simon & Schuster, Inc.

For information about special discounts for bulk purchases,
please contact Simon & Schuster Special Sales at 1-866-506-1949
or business@simonandschuster.com.

The Simon & Schuster Speakers Bureau can bring authors to your
live event. For more information or to book an event, contact the
Simon & Schuster Speakers Bureau at 1-866-248-3049 or visit our
website at www.simonspeakers.com.

Interior design by Suet Chong
Illustrations by Ellie Snowdon

Manufactured in Italy

1 3 5 7 9 10 8 6 4 2

Library of Congress Control Number: 2021937324

ISBN 978-1-9821-6716-5
ISBN 978-1-9821-6718-9 (pbk)
ISBN 978-1-9821-6719-6 (ebook)

To my parents—for your encouragement and commitment to helping me achieve my childhood dream of becoming a veterinarian.

And to Pretzel, April, Baby Bird, Susie, and all my other dogs, birds, rodents, and one tiny ferret—for enriching my life with your own unique love and devotion.

We who choose to surround ourselves with lives even more temporary than our own, live within a fragile circle; easily and often breached. Unable to accept its awful gaps, we would still live no other way. We cherish memory as the only certain immortality, never fully understanding the necessary plan.

—*Irving Townsend, author and record producer*

CONTENTS

A NOTE FROM THE AUTHOR

This is a work of narrative nonfiction in which I recall interactions with others and re-create dialogue from remembered conversations. Although these exchanges are not presented as word-for-word exchanges, I have endeavored to write about events in the true spirit in which they took place and with which the words were spoken.

Additionally, it's important to note that though I've included information in this book that comes from my expertise and experience as a veterinarian and animal welfare advocate, as well as my own approach to dog training and advocacy for animals with disabilities, this book is by no means a comprehensive guide to treating and caring for our pets. For questions and guidance as how best to care for your beloved animals, please consult with veterinarians and animal welfare professionals in your area.

PIGLET

PROLOGUE

A MOST UNEXPECTED, VERY SPECIAL GUEST

"We're almost there!" I announced with a small sigh of relief as I caught sight of the street sign that promised we were nearly at our destination.

"Almost there," I repeated a little louder, turning around from the passenger seat to reassure our canine population in the back—two of them buckled in on the seat, and the littlest two, each asleep in their own carriers on the floor, that "as soon as we get there, everyone gets to go pee!"

Our two back-seat passengers both pricked up their ears, each turning their heads in my direction with their version of dog smiles.

From as far back as I can remember, probably as young as five or six years old, I have always talked—and listened—to animals. That was around the same age that I realized with lasting certainty that when I grew up I was going to become a veterinarian. For some it's a profession, for me a calling—the only one thing I ever wanted to do.

My husband glanced over to give me a skeptical look, as if to ask, *Didn't you say we were almost there about fifteen minutes ago?*

After a beat, Warren—whom our three kids and I all think kind of looks like Will Ferrell if he wore glasses, only more athletic—shook his head and laughed, being the good sport that he almost always is. This was not how he'd hoped to spend a Thursday during one of the more demanding times of the year for his high-pressure job working at a major bio-pharmaceutical company.

With a hopeful nod, I promised, "You'll see, this will be fun. It's gonna be worth it."

The two-and-a-half-hour trip from our house in Westport, Connecticut, to Plainville, Massachusetts, to pay a surprise visit to a classroom of third graders had looked like an easy drive on our GPS, but we had hit a few traffic snarls and the trek was now taking forever. The day itself had begun gloomily with overcast skies, but the dogs don't change their routines just because there's bad weather. We still started the day as we always did, making sure that all seven members of our dog pack were up and out to do their morning business—in two groups—and were fed and accounted for before we loaded up the van.

Our morning routine is elaborate, though pretty well set, and everyone knows the drill. Unless the weather is irresistible, we don't do too much playing in the mornings—especially not on a day when some of us have to get on the road by nine. On this particular day, once inside, everyone lined up to be fed, each in her or his self-proclaimed spot. After eating, the dogs waited at attention while I prepped food for my birds—each canine watching intently as I cut up the birdie veggies and pieces of cooked eggs. The little scrambled egg "pockets" that I use for dispensing pills to the different dogs who need them were, as usual, the featured delicacy of the morning. Moving faster than normal, after I fed Lukita, our blue parakeet, I ran up the stairs, cleaned the cages of the three rescued house sparrows—Sunny, Betty, and Blind Boy Willie—and filled their dishes with fresh food and water. Before it was time to leave, I let everyone out again, all the while talking to them and letting them know the agenda for the day.

I'm always amazed at how the dogs pay full attention to me when I'm talking, carefully listening for words they recognize. On such hectic mornings as this one, I do sometimes wonder whatever happened to our "two-dog MAX" (as in maximum) rule. Somehow we make it work.

The hardest part this day had been reassuring the animals who weren't coming with us that we'd be back before too long. Each of our dogs has a job, and one job they all share is to support one another, as I reminded Dean, Annie, and Gina. Dean is our handsome Lab mix who loves car rides but also enjoys being a couch potato. Annie is our exceptionally sweet, shy, tan terrier mix. And Gina is our beautiful white Australian shepherd/border collie mix, who is deaf in one ear and has vision deficits, along with separation anxiety when I'm not nearby.

Each of the three watched me go with stoic resolve while Lukita, chirping away, put in his foreign-flavored two cents as I ran out the door into the morning mist.

Once on the road, the clouds finally began to lift, and the sun broke through by the time we exited the highway. We picked up speed briefly, but as soon as we made it to the local streets of Plainville, we hit a maze of stop signs, right turns, left turns, and wrong turns. Just when I started to get nervous that we might never arrive, we came around a corner and spotted the elementary school.

"We're here!" I announced as we pulled into the crowded parking lot and began to scout around for a vacant space. A couple of tails began to wag. Susie, our gray terrier, the sweetest and most senior of our seven dogs at twelve years old, shook herself into an alert position. She understood that it was time to go to work. Next to her, Evie, our five-year-old vivacious white poodle/terrier mix, also seemed to beam, craning her neck to look outside and confirm that I was telling the truth about our arrival.

Before I'd gotten a chance to get the littlest ones out of their carriers, I realized that there were other cars parking and excited-looking adults hurrying toward the entrance to the school, many of them dressed in some shade of pink.

Pink? For a split second, I thought that was odd, maybe just coincidental. Was there something else happening at school that day besides our planned surprise visit to the classroom of Tricia Fregeau? As I glanced down at my own pink T-shirt, it occurred to me that the other adults in pink could be connected in some way to our arrival. Well, not *our* arrival, so much as that of the very special guest of honor.

"Hmmm?" I heard Warren say from outside the van, where he was pulling out leashes and setting up the stroller, clearly having the same thoughts as me. From inside her carrier, Zoey, a six-pound three-year-old chocolate Chihuahua/Yorkie-Maltese mix, let out an eager bark, which sounded close to *Let me out! I want to play and be part of the action!*

Last but not least, I opened up the carrier holding tiny Piglet, who yawned and stretched, waking up from his beauty sleep. With a gentle tap—over his shoulders and back—to let him know it was time to go out and find a spot for peeing that was to his liking (never easy), I couldn't resist getting in a couple of kisses and snuggles. Even though I am keenly aware that he can't hear a word that I say to him, and though I know he will never be able to see me, I have always talked to him out loud with gestures and expressions. In his own way, I am convinced, he understands.

"Piggy Lee," I asked, using one of my umpteen nicknames for him, "ready? Everyone's waiting."

If a dog could shrug, that's exactly what Piglet did, with a kind of amazing confidence that made me imagine him saying, *Ready? I was born ready!* And then, holding his leash as I set him on the ground alongside Zoey, we started to follow Warren, who was pushing the stroller and holding the leashes attached to Susie and Evie. We turned toward the main entrance and I watched the five-and-a-half-pound Piglet—handsome in a striped, collegiate kind of red-white-and-blue T-shirt—pause, take a moment to compose himself, and then let loose with a twirly, wiggly dance.

Unbelievable. He almost seemed to know he was a rock star and that this was his day, that he had come on a long car drive with three members of his Inclusion Pack (as we later dubbed it), with his human Dog-Mom, me, and his Favorite Dad, to put smiles on the faces of children who had no idea that they were going to get to meet him in person.

Like everything else that had happened over the previous fifteen months since the tiny, one-pound, deaf blind pink puppy had entered our lives, this entire outing had come about in the most unexpected of ways. After having Piglet for a very short time, I had started posting videos and pictures of him on my Facebook page. Within a month, at the suggestion of friends and family, I created his own page and called it "Piglet, the deaf blind pink puppy." One of my main goals was to get the word out about the importance of fostering, adopting, and caring for special-needs animals and about the little-known condition that had caused Piglet's disabilities. As a Chihuahua/ dachshund mix, Piglet was the product of two dapple-colored (multicolored or splotchy) parents. Dapple-to-dapple breeding results in a twenty-five percent chance of the offspring being born "double dapple"—a mostly white color pattern linked to congenital ear and eye defects that commonly result in partially or completely deaf and/or blind puppies.

To my surprise, the Piglet posts gained a lot of traction. There was something about him in his pictures and videos that gave complete strangers a feeling of connection and license to express their emotions in text. There were dozens of comments on any one post, and I took the time to read each and every one. I got to know many of Piglet's followers quite well. One comment by Tricia Fregeau stood out, and I felt compelled to respond.

TRICIA:
The fact that Piglet is able to be successful in spite of his limitations is a testament to the patience and hard work of his human parents. Thank you for taking such good care of him and letting him see this side of humanity rather than the side that he started life with! I can't wait to show Piglet videos to my third-grade students so they can see the

amazing things that can be accomplished no matter who or what stands in your way!

PIGLET, THE DEAF BLIND PINK PUPPY:
I can provide you with a personalized video for your students if you'd like.

TRICIA:
I would love that!

A short time later, in the fall of 2017, I created a PowerPoint presentation called "The Story of Piglet, the deaf blind pink puppy" and posted it as a video on YouTube so it was easily accessed by Tricia and eventually other teachers. I had no idea exactly what Tricia had planned until she reported the response to the video:

TRICIA:
They love him!! We finished his story this week and the students brainstormed about Piglet's mindset in overcoming challenges. Thank you! We love our little pink mascot!

Soon after that, I received a photo from Tricia that showed me what her third-grade students thought about Piglet and his mindset. On a large white poster with a photo of the deaf blind pink puppy in the middle of it and a caption at the top reading, "A Piglet Mindset is . . . ," words and phrases suggested by students were printed out in bright pink marker:

POSITIVE—FRIENDLY—PROUD—BRAVE—TRUSTING
OPTIMISTIC—NEVER GIVING UP—HARD-WORKING
CONFIDENT—UNIQUE—COURAGEOUS
SMART—STRONG—EXCITED ABOUT EVERYTHING
LOVABLE—ENERGETIC—HAPPY—LEARNING NEW THINGS
MAKING THE MOST OF WHAT YOU HAVE—PRODUCTIVE—KEEP TRYING
NEVER STOPPING—FOLLOWING DREAMS

Their creativity inspired mine. Over the course of the school year, I created three more PowerPoint videos to illustrate specific examples of Piglet's positive attitude toward facing his challenges. The students and Ms. Fregeau would often send messages together with questions and comments about how Piglet had made a difference in their lives and how he was helping them believe they could make a difference for others. She kept a basket in the classroom filled with handmade soft pink, floppy Piglet ears on headbands that the children could wear to get into a Piglet State of Mind. Parents loved the program. One mom reported that whenever her daughter was acting out, she'd overhear her asking herself, "What would Piglet do?" and that would calm her down long enough to come up with her own way to cope with whatever was bothering her.

Tricia offered to let me share her lesson plans and aspects of her program on Piggy's pages, which in turn inspired other teachers to introduce Piglet to their students. As the daughter of a teacher, I was thrilled to honor my mother's passion and talent this way. We began to discuss the possibility of a visit to the classroom from Piglet and me. As a backup plan—because schedules and logistics could always change last-minute—we settled on the idea of a Skype session. The closer we came to the end of the year, though, the more determined I was to make a live-and-in-person visit happen. Soon the elements for the surprise came together, along with the added idea of throwing a Pink Party to celebrate everything the students had learned from adopting a Piglet Mindset.

There would be pink balloons and pink refreshments, and all the students in the class would be encouraged to wear pink. Naturally, for the Pink Party, all the third graders could wear the pink felt Piglet ears in solidarity with their tiny pink mascot. Tricia would inform her class that they were going to do a Skype call with Piglet for them to watch on the SMART Board—a projection screen—in order for them to include him in their party.

We devised a plan for the students to be seated on the carpet in front of the SMART Board, waiting for us to appear on-screen, so that we could discreetly enter from the back of the room and call out, "Surprise!"

From the minute we approached the main entrance to the school, it was clear that every adult—from the administrators, teachers, and staff to parents and other special visitors—was in on the surprise. With Piglet posed in a proud, seated position in his stroller, lined with plenty of cozy blankets to make him comfortable, you would have thought that royalty had just arrived at the Jackson School in Plainville. A handful of parents and office staff were right there in the lobby and gathered around to have their own viewing, some of them snapping selfies with the little pink celebrity and with the other dogs too.

When I checked to see how Warren was enjoying himself so far, I could tell he was warming up to the experience. But nothing could have prepared us for what happened next, when we were shown to the door of Ms. Fregeau's third-grade classroom.

There were parents and teachers standing all around the perimeter of the room, holding up their phones to capture the kids' reactions. And there was Tricia Fregeau, who was in the middle of announcing that the Skype call was about to start when she signaled to us to enter.

Every adult in the room called out, "Surprise!" as Piglet rolled in, sitting up at attention in his chariot. While I pushed the stroller, the three dogs—Susie, Evie, and Zoey—bounded in with Warren in tow. The reaction was unlike anything I'd ever experienced before or since. Warren said it was as close to the first time the Beatles came to America as anything he had experienced in his own life.

Every single child, and almost every adult, in the room began to cry. I cried. Ms. Fregeau wiped her tears. All the parents cried. Warren did his best to maintain composure, but he joined the tear fest as well. It was one of the most breathtaking, heartwarming, tear-jerking, and unexpected experiences that we had ever had. That is saying a lot because Warren and I have three children, now college-age and starting their real-world lives, who are each extraordinary in their own way, and who have given us untold numbers of proud moments.

As the visit went on, I felt a level of pride that could not be put into words. Throughout our time in the classroom, Piglet was calm and regal, demonstrating with poise and elegance all the things he could do. The Piglet Show, as we call our performance of tap-signal tricks, was a smash hit. His three sister dogs, whom I would always prep by telling them, "You're going to be in the show today!" really got into the scene.

The children stayed seated in sheer amazement, barely making a sound, so as not to miss anything. We began with the basics, demonstrating "sit"—which each dog would do, one by one. I would say, "Zoey, sit!" and she would. "Susie, sit!" and "Evie, sit!" Next, I said, "Sit, Piglet!" even though we all knew he couldn't hear me, but at the same time I tapped him lightly on his lower back, right above his tail. Piggy responded to this familiar tap signal with an impeccable sit, lifting his head for the cookie that he knew was coming.

"Piglet can do just what the other dogs can do!" one little boy exclaimed. A chorus of agreement followed.

We moved on to demonstrating "wait" and how I could call each dog to come to me by name—Susie, Zoey, and Evie. Piglet sat waiting until I offered his tap signal to come to me, a gentle swipe under his chin. He came right over to join the other three dogs in a sit, at which time each got their treats. Next, we did a brief Q&A; I could not have been more impressed by the thoughtfulness of the questions from the third graders. Hands shot up in the air, and each question showed a striking amount of empathy and the desire to know about what it was really like to be Piglet. All four dogs sat looking out at the children, as though they were answering questions right along with me.

After the Q&A, I sat in a chair with Piglet in my lap, wrapped in a blanket, and all the kids lined up so they could come and meet him—one by one. Each child had a story to share. "I have a blind dog too." "We just adopted a puppy from a shelter." "He's very smart!" One of the last children to approach us was a little boy with a blond crewcut and a big smile. He put his hand on Piglet's head and then on his own. I asked, "What are you doing?" and he said, "We have the same haircut."

Toward the end of this amazing day, I thought of something our daughter Rachael had said the first time she met Piglet when he was so much tinier, and so anxiety-ridden, and so very, very pink.

We had gone to help her move from one apartment to another in New York City, and we had brought Piglet along. Rachael, brilliant and beautiful, and a formidably gifted pianist, who was getting ready to start a promising career in the field of investment banking, had lovingly taken tiny baby Piglet in her arms. She looked down at him all snuggled in her coat and then looked up and said, "I feel like I gave birth to him."

I totally understood how she felt. Holding him and caring for him is unlike my feelings for any of my other dogs. It's not that I love him any more. It's that I actually feel the tug of protectiveness and pride that I can only associate with motherhood. It's just an inexplicable, almost embarrassing emotion that he elicits.

That was what I was feeling during the end-of-the-year Pink Party for Ms. Fregeau's third graders. It was a rite of passage for Piglet, the deaf blind pink puppy. He had come so far, unexpectedly, and had touched so many lives in ways I never would have imagined.

In those moments, I like to think this book was born—a reminder to the world of how much we can accomplish by caring for our fellow beings, human and nonhuman, whether disabled or not, or simply an individual searching for a little extra consideration and kindness. There will always be too many abandoned and neglected animals in need of rescue or just overlooked and unwanted. But Piglet definitely came into our lives to teach us lessons. Just when you think you can't open your heart any more than you already have, something can happen to help you discover that you have more to give. And what you get from being open to the unexpected in animals and in humans is the greatest gift you can ever receive.

There's a Buddhist saying most of us have heard at one point or another that "when the student is ready, the teacher will appear." In my experiences and observations—certainly with musical training and in my educational/professional journey—that proverb has been right on the money. But with Piglet, the unexpected twist was that ours was a case of "when the teacher is ready, the student will appear."

Piglet, the deaf blind pink puppy, was that very student who showed up with such a capacity to learn, he put me on notice.

How did it happen? How did Piglet make his way into our lives, and how was he now getting ready to spark a global movement? The craziest part of the story is that, statistically speaking, it's a miracle that he even made it into our care alive.

That's the story I decided to write that day in Plainville—about a miracle puppy who dared to live.

PART ONE

RESCUE

Chapter 1

MEET THE SHAPIROS

"Why say no, when you can say yes?"
—Harold and Arline Foodman

SATURDAY, MARCH 4, 2017
MILFORD, CONNECTICUT

There is very little I've forgotten about the winter day in early 2017 when I drove the twenty-five minutes or so from our house in Westport up I-95 to Milford, Connecticut—to the local Petco, where a pet adoption event was underway and where I'd promised to arrive around ten thirty in the morning.

Compared to how Saturdays usually go in my line of work as a house-call veterinarian, my list of concerns for the day was short and the schedule of things to do was relatively light. That may be exaggerating. Let's just say as a mom of six dogs, four birds, and three human kids—ages seventeen to twenty-two whose well-being I tracked on a consistent basis—I recall greeting the day with an unusual sense of calm.

There was still snow on the ground from weeks of on-again-off-again heavy snowfall. From the moment I got out with the first three dogs of our six-pack—Susie, Annie, and Zoey—it felt like the temperature had dropped from earlier in the week. As they explored the backyard, even though it's fully fenced in, I kept a watchful eye on each of them, as is my habit. The secret for tracking the six dogs and varying number of indoor birds that I have found most effective over the years is to count them. Literally, I count our dogs, naming them too, numerous times during the day and into the evening to be sure everyone is safe.

Outside—whether on a walk or in our fenced-in yard—I keep myself from being distracted by doing periodic head counts. That Saturday morning, cold as it was, nobody seemed to mind if we didn't stay out super long, but they were also dawdling and sniffing around. What were they so interested in? I had to go check. We had been getting a lot of deer coming into the yard and leaving messes that our dogs considered a delicious delicacy. In the winter, the deer would come right over the fences as if they were on the track team doing hurdles. Easy in and easy out for them, while the dogs chased the deer like a pack of wolves.

There were plenty of hidden dangers that kept me on the lookout, especially with the smaller dogs who could suddenly be hauled off by one of the hawks or coyotes that were often spotted in the vicinity of our woodsy neighborhood. In late spring and summer, any one of our dogs might eat the highly toxic mushrooms that we could never fully banish from our grassy yard. That's one reason why I began taking them out in two groups—to make sure they were supervised, and then when it was time to go inside, nobody would accidentally be left outside in the yard.

Lately, I had been keeping an extra eye on Susie, our scruffy gray terrier mix, who just seemed to be moving a bit more slowly. When I had first heard about Susie, ten years earlier, I was actually looking for a puppy for a client and had connected to Pet Matchmaker Rescue, run by Morgan Sokolow Gall, the daughter of a longtime client of my vet practice. It is common for Northeast rescue groups to partner with rescuers and shelters in the South, where the dog and cat overpopulation is exponentially worse than it is up North. Some Southern rescues have partner rescue groups all over the country. Morgan's rescue organization, which was based in New England but later moved to California, worked with a number of rescuers and shelters in Tennessee. When I called, she told me about a volunteer named Trudy, who'd heard about a little scared gray dog that had been spotted hiding under a barn next to a kill shelter. After five days, Trudy—who named the terrified terrier mix Susie—set out to capture her. Trudy lay on the ground singing for hours until Susie, starving and covered with burrs, finally came out of hiding. Susie never made it into the shelter. Instead, Trudy put her in her car and took her home to foster. She cleaned her up, fed her, and weeks later, sent her off on a transport to Connecticut, where Morgan was holding a dog adoption event.

Five months earlier, we had lost our black Lab, Edie, which left us with two dogs—Lucy, a deaf border collie, and Wendy, a whippet. After some discussion, Warren and I had decided that we were happy with two dogs and with abiding by the so-called "two-dog MAX rule." We were busy, my list of veterinary patients was growing longer by the day, we had a full house of very active kids and fragile birds, and two dogs was a good balance.

But after hearing Susie's story, despite Warren's insistence that we had to stick to the rule, I couldn't resist going to see her at Morgan's adoption event—held in front of her aunt and uncle's liquor store near the train station in Darien. Just to get another opinion, I took our eight-year-old daughter Ellie with me. The moment I met Susie and saw how she interacted with people and other dogs, wagging her tail nonstop, I fell in love with her—and so did Ellie. There was no question. She was meant for us. Ellie and I couldn't imagine driving home without her.

Warren was not receptive when I texted him on my old-school flip phone. He emphatically said, "NO! Do not bring another dog home. I do NOT want three dogs!"

Certain that Warren would fall in love with Susie as we had, Ellie and I decided to bring her home anyway. And of course—he fell for her pretty much instantaneously. Susie was the small, sweet, adorable terrier he and I had secretly been looking for—just not admitting it because we were trying to be practical.

The three dogs were all great friends. Whenever we went out, the three would go downstairs in the den to lie on the couch together and keep each other company. Lucy the border collie, Wendy the whippet, and Susie would often come to work with me. Sometimes when I'd bring just Susie alone, she'd miss the other two. Years later, when Lucy died during the summer while the kids were away at camp, Susie bonded even more closely with Wendy, who was already fourteen and not doing well. Just two months later, we lost Wendy, leaving Susie, a pack dog, very depressed. She moped around all day, only perking up when she met another dog. Clearly, Susie didn't want to be an only dog. So, after two months of watching her pine for companionship, Warren finally said, "It's time to add dog number two." That turned out to be Gina, a white Australian shepherd/border collie mix who was deaf in one ear and had mild vision deficits.

Gina had come from a rescue organization in Georgia run by veterinarian Dr. Gloria Andrews. At four and a half months old, Gina was wild and skittish. In addition to not being able to hear out of one ear, which led to her not being able to tell where sound was coming from, Gina had been through a terrible ordeal before we adopted her. Susie seemed to understand that Gina had disabilities, or at least that she needed extra patience and loving attention. It was so sweet to see our little gray Susie taking such good care to make the bigger white dog feel comforted and at home. They played together, slept next to each other in dog beds and on the couch, and were nearly inseparable. Susie was so nurturing to Gina. It was nice to witness their friendship, which was so important to little Susie. I felt very happy with our two dogs—the little gray eight-pound terrier mix and the (eventually) thirty-two-pound, tall, white herding dog.

The next four dogs arrived in much different ways. We weren't necessarily looking, but each of them found us anyway. Dean (a thirty-five-pound black Lab mix) joined the family after Gina, and then there were three. Annie (our tan twelve-pound terrier mix) and Evie (another twelve-pounder and a white poodle mix) came next, followed by Zoey (the tiny chocolate Chihuahua/Yorkie-Maltese mix), giving us a total of six. Susie was the heartbeat of the pack, more like a den mother than an alpha leader. Still, as far as I was concerned, she ruled the roost.

As I count the dogs—as I did with the second group that morning of Dean, Gina, and Evie—I typically give them the plan for the day, letting them know, for instance, "Okay, everybody inside. I'll be going out to do errands, but I won't be gone long." How much of this they understand from language alone, I never know, but they pick up a lot from paying close attention to subtle nuances in my tone and behavior. It's amazing to me that I might say something like, "I'm just going to cut the dogs' nails before we go for a walk," and Gina, who actually hears well despite being deaf in one ear, deciphers the conflicting pieces of that message—*walk* and *nails*. Any mention of a nail cutting is enough for her to go running for cover, forgoing the walk proposal until it's safe.

While I waited for the dogs to finish up outside on that March morning, I did a casual head count. *Do you know where your dogs are?* is a mantra worth adopting to be sure everyone is where they need to be during transitions throughout the day. It's helpful to visualize them when you leave your house and when you return. Whenever I leave the house, I give everyone a treat as a way of making contact with each, knowing where everybody is in the house, and I do the same for whoever is coming with me in the car. Once I return, we all get to go out in the backyard again, which gives me a chance to make sure everyone is home safely.

Counting can prevent dogs from getting lost or running off, or even the tragic consequences of being left in the car in the driveway on a hot day, a horrifying experience that has happened to more than one of my patients.

You'd think that living as we do in a modest home for the area, it would be easier to keep tabs on all of our residents, but that's not the case. I have no idea what was in the minds of the builders of this older style of grayish clapboard split-level house. The layout alone is confusing enough that anyone could get lost in it. There are stairs everywhere, going this way and that, five steps down and four steps up. Also, though there are not too many obvious hiding places—the rooms are all small, and there's no closet space—that makes it easier for a dog or a bird to get stuck somewhere that isn't the first spot where you'd go looking.

The house is always very clean, thanks to Warren, who genuinely loves to vacuum. With all our dogs and birds, we are well stocked with an absurd variety of vacuum cleaners, carpet steam-cleaning machines, and floor sweepers. Keeping up with the dog hair and bird feathers became an early priority not just for aesthetic reasons but out of necessity, because it turns out that most of us human Shapiros have allergies to the dust that can accumulate in too much clutter. My big complaint, no matter how disciplined we are, is that the clutter always wins. It's like pestilence. Somehow little things like mail and random books or semi-important papers take up residence on our kitchen counters and never leave, while other surfaces and corners pile up with dog toys and beds, and lots of work files and supplies.

Living in a household with so many big personalities, human and otherwise, requires compromise, collaboration, and consideration for one another. Years earlier, in order to navigate the perils of our tight quarters and to offer lasting sage advice to our then-elementary-school-aged kids, Warren worked with Rachael and Daniel to come up with a list of helpful hints that were actually serious family values. These were soon dubbed the "Shapiro Rules." Some of the rules were only to reinforce actions we were already taking—like making sure that young musicians practiced a certain amount of time every day and, in preparation for the working world, reminding the kids, "Never quit a job before you have a new job." My only rule, and it was more of a gentle nudge than anything, was to say to the kids, often when they weren't busy and didn't seem to be motivated, "If you're gonna do nothing, do something . . . for someone."

To the best of my knowledge, we lost the printout of the Shapiro Rules and, slowly but surely, with important values in place, we went back to being the much-loved and -counted five humans, four birds, and eventually six dogs—in defiance of the "two-dog MAX" rule.

Overall, I'd come to feel that our house had its unique charm. I gave up worrying about things like whether the sheets matched or the towels were all part of a set in the bathroom. The fenced-in yard was exactly what we needed, and a view of the tall oak trees in the woods behind the house let us feel we were perched in the midst of nature. Who really cared that there were no curtains on the back windows (even though I'd been promising to hang them since 1993)? My favorite thing about where we live has always been the proximity to the beach, a happy place for all of us.

For the most part, I remember thinking that Saturday, that we were making all of it work, mainly with a lot of good humor. That was a Shapiro thing. Even the dogs were funny. The last thing that I could have even been tempted to do was to add one more personality to the mix at home—and definitely not on a permanent basis.

When I backed out of the driveway, I spoke to the three dogs accompanying me for the day—Gina, Evie, and Zoey. All were secure in their crates or harnesses, comfy in sweaters and buffeted with extra blankets. "Okay, we're on our way. We're going to get a tiny little baby dog." I paused before adding, "Don't worry, he's not staying."

I shifted my focus away from the dogs and onto the route we were taking to the Milford Petco. The veterinary house-call business I'd built over almost thirty years had taken me to every city up and down the southwest coast of Fairfield County, Connecticut.

I loved driving the streets and passing by the houses of families whose dearest pets had come into my care through the years. Having my own practice was a great fit for me, full of hilarious, poignant, and moving experiences that came from visiting my patients in their own homes. My "fly on the wall" perspective allowed me to see the sometimes outrageous setups people concoct for their new puppies, to meet neighbors and the in-laws, and to learn about the most personal aspects of my clients' lives, all while giving rabies vaccines to their dogs. I'd get to see issues that could only be addressed by visiting homes. For example, frequently when I walk in the door I find an old arthritic dog slipping all over the beautiful wood floors, and I can then recommend covering them with cheap yoga mats to provide better nonslip footing. I'm also able to identify danger zones where a simple gate could be lifesaving for a blind pet.

Being the veterinarian for dogs and cats who have lived long lives, I've also witnessed the growth of their human family members. My clients' children, whom I watched grow up, have gone on to graduate college, get married, and have kids; many of them have eventually called me to be their veterinarian for their first pets! And some of my clients have known me since I was a kid, obsessed with becoming a veterinarian—including my beloved kindergarten teacher, Mrs. Lalime, whom I'd stop to see now and then. Her daughter's dogs and cats were my patients too.

Every day as I drive through the area, I pass a familiar address and revisit memories of having been there on a call. In these homes, I have guided my clients through the happy, emotional, and, over time, heartbreaking stages of their pet's lives. Being witness to that intimate journey—a partnership that starts on a joyous day and inevitably ends in sadness and loss—is a humbling experience. Many of the patients I've treated have been foster animals, and I'm always grateful to the families willing to provide shelter and love to a dog or cat or other animal to whom they aren't necessarily planning or able to offer a forever home.

Once we hit the number-six dog at our house, I was not concerned about being tempted to adopt again. We continued to foster dogs for brief stays; because I had long been interested in taking care of special-needs pets, I was open to taking in a new rescue in need of professional care at least for a couple of weeks. In the past, Warren might have been concerned that I'd be tempted to want to adopt yet again, but I think he knew that at this point even I had reached my limit.

Before I'd even ventured out the door earlier with three of our canine six-pack, I'd called out, "Drive safely!" to Warren and our youngest, Ellie, a senior in high school, as the two dashed out the door to hit the road for NYC. Ellie attended classes every Saturday at Juilliard's competitive Pre-College program. Twenty-year-old Daniel had also attended Juilliard Pre-College. Rachael, twenty-two, had studied and participated in other intense New York music programs.

For the past decade, Warren and I had taken turns making the one hour and fifteen minute drive to New York City with a kid or two in tow. The trips were a regular feature of our weekly lives.

All three of our kids had become highly accomplished musicians. When all three were practicing at the same time—Rachael on piano, Daniel on French horn, and Ellie on violin—our house sounded like a music conservatory. Whenever they indulged us and agreed to play together, after the usual arguing, the music that filled the entirety of our house was always arrestingly beautiful.

Even though Ellie had already been accepted to attend Princeton in the fall, she was powering through to the end of her senior year of high school, studying intensively for her remaining AP classes and exams. Warren always said that I was the most disciplined person he'd ever met. Then we had Ellie, and she grew into the most disciplined person *I* have ever met.

My hunch was that after dropping Ellie at Juilliard for the next several hours, Warren might have a chance to check in with Rachael—maybe grab lunch at one of our favorite Chinese restaurants. Rachael had graduated from Oberlin College the previous summer and was acclimating well to the career path in finance that Warren and I hadn't seen coming. Happily, she was only an hour away by train and came home for quick visits on a fairly frequent basis. Rachael was also close enough for us to visit her, and, conveniently, Daniel, an undergrad at the Manhattan School of Music, was in NYC too.

Daniel, lately, had been coming home a lot on the weekends to play the horn with the Norwalk Symphony Orchestra and the Norwalk Youth Symphony. Norwalk, right next door to Westport, was where I grew up, one of three children born to my parents, Harold and Arline Foodman. Daniel had started playing with the Norwalk Youth Symphony, recognized as one of the best youth orchestras in the region, in the sixth grade and stayed through his high school senior year. Before his last concert, aware that they would be short of horn players, the program director, Sara Watkins, discussed his returning as a "ringer," a paid position—which meant we would get to continue to see and hear him play locally.

As I drove to Milford, I received a call from Daniel, to say he was going to be at a rehearsal at the Norwalk City Hall. He asked me to stop by and hear him play his new horn in the Concert Hall, known for its exceptional acoustics.

"Daniel, I don't know . . . I'm going to have this foster puppy and three other dogs in the car with me."

"Just ten minutes, Ma. I really want you to hear me play."

How could I disappoint him?

Then I thought of the example my parents had set for me. Their attitude with me and my brothers was a consistent: "Why say no, when you can say yes?" City Hall was only minutes away from the Norwalk Veterinary Hospital, where I'd already planned on stopping by to pick up some medical supplies.

It was about 10:10 a.m. as I made the turn onto the road leading to I-95 North. I felt grateful and relaxed, knowing that everything for the day was well planned and could be counted on to go smoothly. Right before I merged onto the highway, though, it suddenly dawned on me that maybe I should have deliberated a little longer when a request came in four days earlier.

The truth is I tried to say no.

"Lethal white chi/*each* mix" was the somewhat confusing subject line of the email that came in on Tuesday, February twenty-eighth, from Dr. Gloria Andrews, my friend and colleague who was the founding director of Colbert Veterinary Rescue Services in the tiny town of Colbert, Georgia, not far from Athens. Six years earlier, I met Gloria when we adopted our beautiful white Aussie/border collie Gina from her rescue organization. Warm and kindhearted, Gloria Andrews proved to be a kindred spirit, a vet with her own hospital, and one who rescued animals from sometimes horrific situations. She was relentless in finding them loving homes—in many states across the country, including Connecticut.

Normally, I would have opened the email instantly, but the phone was ringing and the dogs needed attention. Because we had just gotten back from a cross-country ski trip (the last vacation, unbeknownst to us, that we'd enjoy for some time), there were other more urgent emails to open.

When I finally returned to Gloria's email, I stared at the subject line again before opening. Hmmm. Oh, then it hit me. This was probably an autocorrect typo and that she had meant to say, "chi/*dach*" mix. A Chi/doxie. A *lethal* white Chihuahua/dachshund.

Now I was intrigued. Still, I had to laugh at a subject line meant to warn me and tempt me at the same time. With that, I thought, *Oh, I'm so not worried about extra dog temptation right now*, and I opened the fateful email.

> Good morning Melissa. We have this precious little fellow who came with his litter from a hoarding situation. He has microphthalmia and is not visual. The dachshund mixes that came to us from the same place are dappled and mom is dappled as well so this is likely how he came about. He is 1 pound now at 6 weeks and he will be a special placement. Know anyone who may be a good fit for him?

First I looked at the photo of the one-pound ADORABLE puppy cradled in her hands and thought, *Oh my God, he's TINY. He's PRECIOUS. And he's PINK!*

Then I read Gloria's email again, which said he was blind and had a condition affecting the size of his eyes, most likely caused by birth defects and generally the result of "double dapple" genetics (suggesting that he was probably deaf too). As Gloria was aware, I had a particular desire to care for and help place animals with special needs.

In hindsight, I think it's hilarious that Gloria asked, *Know anyone who may be a good fit?* Even more hilarious is that my immediate response was to write back and say, *No.* For about two minutes I felt strong and decisive. My "no" was grown-up and responsible. The thought of spreading myself too thin, with a full house and busy vet practice, was enough to make me feel good about my boundaries.

But then I looked back at the picture. This could be a problem for me. True, this was not my style of dog—practically hairless. My dogs are all fluffy. But he was PINK! And deaf and blind!

I was concerned about the reference to the hoarding situation. The accounts are upsetting to hear—overcrowding and animals confined in numbers to cages, many kept outside in the elements, or hidden under piles of various hoarded belongings, in barns, old cars, or in horribly unsanitary conditions in people's homes. Studies had documented how the accumulation of urine and feces could cause fumes strong enough to kill young dogs, cats, and other animals, or severely damage their development. Starvation is a common effect of hoarding when so many animals have to compete for a scarcity of food, and only the strongest survive. Whenever police are called to investigate hoarding situations, they commonly find dead animals strewn throughout the collection of suffering.

After about three minutes, I wavered, and then launched completely into *I have to help!* mode. All I could think about was what it was like when we got Gina—who had come from Colbert Veterinary Rescue Services through similar circumstances, except she had been at the rescue for two months before Gloria got her up to Connecticut for an adoption event. Gina's level of anxiety was off the charts. As an Aussie/border collie, Gina's disabilities were in keeping with a genetic condition that afflicts Australian shepherds and other herding breeds called "double merle"—resulting in a mostly white coat, deafness in one or both ears, and potentially serious structural eye defects that can cause vision deficits and blindness. Disabled puppies like Gina and the pink puppy in the email needed an extensive amount of care and supervision that is hard to offer in most rescue settings.

Of course, I had to help. How? Well, the most obvious answer came to me—we could foster! We would only need to help for a few days. Two weeks, max. In a nanosecond, I shifted right into high gear with the expectation of how much fun it would be to take care of and work with a deaf blind puppy. My long-term plans, further down the road when we weren't so full up at the inn, had been to adopt a dog with those disabilities. Specifically, that plan was to adopt a deaf blind herding dog later on, not a tiny Chi/doxie mix.

But I got excited contemplating how much I could learn from such a profoundly disabled dog by taking him in for a little while. He was so cute, Gloria and her people would have no trouble finding him a permanent placement.

In addition to many years of observing the fostering process with my clients, as a family we had experience with fostering a number of dogs and birds in the past. We approached the undertaking with the recognition that they came to us so that we could care for them, help them settle down, take care of their medical issues, and then send them on their way to a wonderful life with a loving family. Each came with a different backstory, but all needed some time to decompress, heal, and feel love. Foster parents to dogs, cats, birds, and others have very mixed emotions that vary with each experience. Some fall so madly in love with their foster pets that they end up adopting them. Some are resolute that they are there to foster, not adopt, and help one animal after another. We all know that for each pet we foster, we save that individual, but also open a space up in a shelter for another homeless pet to enter. So we actually save two for every one we agree to foster.

Back in the summer of 2013, we had fostered three dogs in succession—Axel, Tommy, and Olivia. Each one presented different fostering challenges. Axel was a young adult, a cute-as-could-be black Chihuahua/Yorkie mix who had a severe blood disorder and who I was able to stabilize. During the time he lived in our house I fell madly in love with sweet little Axel and couldn't believe I managed to give him away when the time came to deliver him to his forever home. Axel was followed by the very anxious Tommy Touchdown, a Maltese/poodle who had been abused before being rescued. He wanted to pee all over our house, something that was not easy to address after his earlier trauma. Right away, I put a belly band on him to solve that problem, even though I knew that he would require a tremendous amount of work from whatever family was found for him. Actually, his next home was another foster placement, and when I went to drop him off, two hours away, I again warned Tommy's new foster mom about the peeing, asking her, "Are you sure?"

She was sure, letting me know that she and her four delightful daughters—whom I met—would give Tommy lots of love and attention, and they were all committed to fostering him until the right forever home was found. Sure enough, four months later, Tommy's long awaited placement turned out to be his very own happily ever after.

Our third dog that summer was Olivia, a six-week-old goldendoodle, a midsized dog who needed urinary tract surgery for a problem that caused her to continuously leak urine. She was none too pleased with the diaper I had put on her and frequently ended up running around with it in her mouth, like a toy! One of my clients generously donated the $12,000 for the surgery and Olivia recovered beautifully, new and improved. She ended up finding a wonderful family who was ecstatic to bring her into their home.

Those three experiences, in addition to others, gave me every reason to think I could help out with Gloria's tiny rescue puppy, without being tempted to keep him.

Before I signed on for sure, I forwarded the email to Warren, with a quick question, *Foster project?* Maybe it was more like giving him notice. Fortunately, he came back with an affirming *Fine*.

We talked later that night when he came home from work, though not at length. We were both completely set on not adopting any more dogs, so there was nothing to worry about. Besides, we assured each other, "How much trouble can a one-pound puppy be?"

Gloria and her team were planning to transport dogs from Georgia up to Connecticut for an adoption event a few days later. "Go ahead and bring the baby up for us to foster," I told her, and agreed to pick him up on Saturday at the Petco around ten thirty.

It was then that she told me the dog's name: Bart. Gloria filled me in on his story. There had been three people with three dogs who were not spayed and neutered, all living in a small apartment. The dogs bred uncontrollably over a period of time until there were about thirty dogs. When they were evicted, the humans listed the dogs on Craigslist. By the time the rescue group found out about them, they had already given many of the dogs away.

This is an upsetting scenario to anyone who is familiar with the fate of the many animals that are given away for free through Craigslist ads. It's always advisable to go through rescue organizations before bringing a pet home or for giving one away. Without thorough, skilled screening, it is very difficult for an average trusting citizen who is desperate to "get rid of" or sincerely place an animal to differentiate between good and bad people coming to take pets. Some people are forced to rehome their pets due to circumstances out of their control. They look for a loving home for their beloved pet. Potential adopters can dress themselves up to be whatever they want to come off as—kind, caring—but some are cruel animal abusers who pose as interested new pet parents.

For these reasons, I leave placing my foster dogs to the experts associated with reliable, reputable rescue organizations. Now and then, I hear complaints from potential adopters who claim to have been scrutinized more carefully than if they were adopting a child. This is all out of love for the animals into whom rescue groups invest a great deal of time, money, and emotion. The bottom line is: Don't give dogs away for free. Don't get them for free from ads. Go to rescue groups. Call local veterinary hospitals, or visit reputable online listings like Petfinder and Adopt-a-Pet that will lead you to reliable rescue groups in your area who have pets in need of homes. Or attend in-person adoption events. The donations you make to rescue groups help them continue the lifesaving work they do.

Gloria described aspects of this particular rescue process that sounded unfortunately familiar—how they met in a gas station parking lot and about nine dogs were handed over, including Bart's mother, Abigail, two-week-old Bart, and his three littermates.

Although they didn't know which dog was the dad, Gloria assumed that both of Bart's parents were dapple—the marbled color pattern seen in dachshunds. In herding breeds and bulldogs this marbled color pattern is called "merle," and in Great Danes it is called "harlequin." Gloria felt the breeding that led to his double-dapple complications had not been intentional. Some breeders intentionally breed two dapples together, hoping to get very splashy-colored puppies. But this results in a twenty-five percent chance that each puppy will get two of the dominant dapple genes, which is linked to a predominantly white coat and congenital eye and ear defects. In Bart's case, the original three parent dogs weren't bred intentionally for color; they were negligently not spayed or neutered. Some of their offspring carried the dapple coloring gene, so when they bred, the dapple gene was again passed on, until eventually two dapple-colored dogs bred—producing a litter that included three out of four double-dapple puppies. Bart was the tiniest and the only one who was pink. It was a miracle that he survived those precarious first two weeks of life, but what came next was just as traumatic—his canine mom, Abigail, rejected Bart when they arrived at the rescue. Gloria hand-fed him until a few weeks passed and he gained enough strength to push his way back to Abigail.

The other puppies, Gloria said, were twice his size and better adjusted. Two, a male named Barrett and a female named Belinda, were also white coated, deaf, and had vision deficits. A fourth puppy, Blaze, was brown and white and was not disabled.

At the parking lot of the Milford Petco, I pulled into a spot and made sure everyone in the car was warm and snug before I hopped out and hurried inside, excited to meet the adorable baby boy dog. For just a beat, I wondered if I'd downplayed the challenges of caring for Bart. But my own refrain interrupted me: *How much trouble can a one-pound puppy be?*

I was about to find out.

❧

As I approached the check-in desk at the adoption event, before I could say anything, one of the two volunteers who recognized me said, with great enthusiasm, "Thank goodness you're here."

I was about to ask where Bart was but was interrupted by the most grating, ear-piercing, banshee-sounding scream. It went on, and on. As I turned to my left, I saw a tiny pink dog sitting on a cushion in a small crate, all by himself, literally screaming at the top of his lungs. How he managed to get so much sound out, as minuscule as he was, I had no idea. His voice had a nasal rasp at times, like a goose, and at other times it rose up the scales as if he were being murdered. Bart was disrupting the adoption event and the whole store. I ran over to him and picked him up, expecting that he would stop. But no—he continued to wail. So I wrapped him in a blanket, grabbed his yellow records envelope, and ran out of the store.

It only occurred to me when I got into the car that I hadn't even said hi to Gloria.

It took a few minutes for him to calm down in the car, as I petted and reassured him. He started to chew on some new puppy toys I had ready for him. After a few minutes taken to calm myself, I finally paused to get a good look at him. Bart was the size of a rat, even pinker than in his pictures, and extremely adorable.

He became quiet. I exhaled. And I gently put him in his car crate. As soon as I closed the crate door, Bart began to scream bloody murder again. Pretty soon the other dogs in the car, usually so well-behaved, started letting out little confused barks of their own. *Who is this guy?*

Dogs often become alarmed when they hear an animal in distress. Their responses are different, of course, based on their breed type, temperament, experiences, and the nature of the distress. My dogs were in my car with me. As horrible as the screaming was, because I was outwardly calm, the dogs could assume things were under control. As the screaming continued, Zoey was the first to become vocal, no doubt wondering what was going on with that little baby pup. Our dogs tend to egg one another on in situations like these. Zoey and Evie commonly get going together, and so it wasn't long before Evie decided to join in on the barking, less out of concern and more because it was fun. Gina stayed relatively quiet, but I knew she didn't like dogs that barked. Gentle and sensitive, Gina understood that she was bigger than most of our dogs (except for Dean), but rather than go up in volume she would react with a firm look and emphatic lunge toward the barker to express her displeasure. I knew the plaintive wailing of the puppy would upset Gina—a herding dog, who prefers for everything to be orderly and organized.

Before I could back out of my parking space, I realized he was screaming because he had to poop—which was what he was doing. Turning the car off, I leaned over to clean him and the crate, got him quiet, and put him back in. Then he pooped again as he screamed some more. Again, I cleaned him and the crate, and got him quiet. For a minute, I sat there in the driver's seat, caught my breath, and finally pulled out of the parking lot, at which point he started to scream louder than before.

The anxiety and fear he had to be feeling—unable to see or hear— broke my heart. Maybe, I hoped, he'd tire himself out soon. Nope, the screaming continued the entire thirty-minute drive to the Concert

Hall in Norwalk. Once I parked, Bart's screams subsided, and, to my surprise, he then fell asleep, apparently exhausted.

Inside, I jogged into the auditorium, where the rehearsal was over. Daniel was waiting and happy for me to hear him play. For those ten minutes, I was rejuvenated, revived. My ears needed a reprieve. I loved listening to Daniel play his horn in that hall. His beautiful tone was always recognizable and comforting. When he was finished, he walked back to the car with me to see the new foster puppy.

As I opened the door carefully, expecting a blast of dog screams and barks, to my surprise, all the dogs were fast asleep.

"Well," I whispered, not wanting to wake the baby and giving Daniel a quick hug goodbye, "you'll meet him next time."

With that, I got into the driver's seat and hoped for the best.

Maybe there was something about the motion of the car that unnerved Bart, or maybe he had just tired himself out before and was now rested enough to scream some more. He was a seven-week-old puppy, after all. In silence, I willed everyone else to stay silent too as I pulled out of the Concert Hall parking lot. Bart let out a guttural howl, rousing everyone else, and kept it up at top volume for the whole ten-minute trip to the vet hospital.

This was not the way that I had hoped to introduce our new foster dog to my vet hospital friends, but by this point, upset and concerned as I was for him, I recognized that he was reacting to his fear and to the trauma of being cut off from the only familiar bonds of his earlier life. My hope was that someone at Norwalk Veterinary Hospital—aka NVH—could help me get him calmed down. Bart screamed all the way up the sidewalk and into the side entrance. He was still screaming as I carried him into the hospital treatment area, where everyone was surprised to see—and hear—my new baby foster dog.

That's when we found Monica, a vet tech, who came right over, took him from me, and began to sing to him and speak softly in Spanish, kiss him, and pet him. Before he could make another peep, she stuffed him down her shirt. He was in heaven. Bart fell asleep immediately, and the bond he formed with her that day was instant and forever! We didn't know then, but we know now that he was connecting with her through the smell of her breath. We would soon learn that this was how the tiny pink boy would identify and recognize people and other dogs. Monica had breathed him into being a contented, not-so-terrified one-pound puppy.

It was a huge relief to finally see him calm and content. I gathered up some puppy meds and other supplies that I needed, and then was ready to head back to the car.

"Here you go," Monica sang and breathed to Bart, handing him back to me. Of course, being taken away from his new BFF and back in my arms, he started screaming at the top of his lungs all over again.

That guttural screaming, both low- and high-pitched, lasted the whole twenty-minute ride home. As soon as we walked into the house, suddenly the screaming stopped. Like a howling wind that had ceased to blow. I put him on the kitchen floor and let all the members of the six-pack come check him out.

As they did, Bart was quiet and stood very still. And then his tail began to wag.

Chapter 2

BORN THIS WAY

Human beings are a part of the animal kingdom, not apart from it.

—Marc Bekoff, biologist, ethologist,
behavioral ecologist, and author

Sitting in the middle of the kitchen floor, as I watched the six canine members of the household sizing up this tiniest of puppies, I felt a wave of joy that brought with it a series of memories and realizations. One of the clearest images of that same immeasurable feeling of happiness came when I was about six years old, as my family welcomed home a mini schnauzer puppy, whom we named Pretzel Bitsy.

A couple of weeks earlier, we had paid a visit to a pet store in Queens, just outside of Manhattan—where I'd fallen in love with a dachshund puppy. Up until this time, my mother always had to be the bearer of the news, "Melissa, we know how much you want a puppy, but we can't have one because of Daddy's allergies."

My father's allergies were very severe, so that was pretty much the end of the conversation. But I wasn't a child used to giving up once I had my mind set on something. I knew nothing about treating aller-

35

gies or about how certain dogs were thought to be less or more aggravating to allergies. What I did know was that my parents loved me and my two brothers, and that they would figure out a way for us to have a dog—under the right circumstances.

My parents, Arline and Harold Foodman, who both grew up in Brooklyn, New York, but who made their way to Connecticut once they'd begun raising a family, were the absolute most supportive mom and dad that I could have ever wanted in life. They were the original enablers.

Whatever it was that looked to be of interest to the three of us kids—all born within four years, starting with me, followed by brother Marc (in the middle) and then Bruce, the youngest—my parents actively encouraged and enabled those interests and capacities.

Before I was even two years old, as the story goes, I was drawn to animals of all kinds. Right from the very start. One of my favorite old family pictures that crops up here and there shows me at about eighteen months pointing at a group of deer in a park. It didn't matter what type of animal it was, I wanted to stop to meet them. Because of this attraction, my parents decided we should visit every animal farm they could find, every nearby petting zoo, and the Bronx Zoo on a regular basis. Now the thought of how animals were really treated at many of the zoos makes me cringe, although my happy early memories are full of images from weekend trips to Tony's Pet Shop, and frequent stops at the Nature Center in Westport—where there was an animal hall that I never tired of visiting.

The Nature Center offered an assortment of beautiful trails for hiking and other expeditions in the woods that fed my early love of being outdoors. There was a statue of a mama bear and her two babies that we'd excitedly run toward upon our arrival and climb all over before our hike. After tackling the trails, we would head inside to visit the animal hall. There were injured hawks, owls, snakes, turtles, rabbits, and others who served as animal ambassadors for children to learn about wildlife and how we coexist. These were the first rescued animals I had ever met.

The program was innovative, so long ago, when there was much less concern for the environment and wildlife protection. Almost a lifetime later, I'm still amazed at and thankful for the lengths my dad would go to expose me to animals in various settings.

In our neighborhood, I saw other homes where dogs were exalted as family members. Some neighbors even had two dogs, in addition to cats, fish, and birds. Even though my parents gently explained that my father's allergies made it impossible for us to bring a dog into our home (much less a cat), I refused to accept that impossibility. Somehow the words "no" and "can't" didn't register when it came to my quest to bring animals home.

That was how, one day when I was six years old, I managed to convince my parents that getting a dog would be the solution to an urgent concern. My four-year-old brother, Marc, had become ill with a GI salmonella infection. The medicine must have tasted awful, because no matter what my parents did to cajole, persuade, tempt, or convince him to take it, Marc just refused. Desperate, my mother finally proposed, "Marc, if you take your medicine, we'll get you a present, something you really, really want."

That got Marc's attention. He nodded his head slowly, agreeing to the deal, and took his medicine with a grimace. My parents praised him for his bravery.

"Well?" my father asked.

Marc hadn't thought this through. He hesitated, unsure. This was my shot. "A puppy!" I volunteered. "Marc wants a puppy. He needs a puppy."

No one questioned my authority as to what Marc wanted and needed in exchange for taking his medication. My excitement must have been so contagious, though, because he immediately agreed, echoing, "A puppy! I want a puppy."

My parents couldn't argue, so instead they started to do the research about the breeds of dogs alleged to be hypoallergenic. There is no such thing as a purely "hypoallergenic dog," but there are breeds that are much less allergy-provoking than others. Armed with that list of breeds, we went to the Queens puppy store owned by a friend of my aunt and uncle—which was where I fell madly in love with a little brown dachshund.

As badly as I wanted that doxie, she wasn't on the list. But while I was preoccupied with her, my father spoke with the owner of the store about ordering a mini-schnauzer. And that was how, a few weeks later, my father brought home Pretzel Bitsy, who marked the opening chapter in the book of dogs that were to change and shape my life. Pretzel slept in bed with me every night, and I walked her and doted on her. She ran around with us kids outside, rode in my go-kart with me, and was loved by the whole family. Marc got better and was happy for me to take care of the dog brought home to help him heal. My dad built her a custom puppy pen—a foot high, made of Sheetrock, with newspapers on the floor and a bed in the corner. My mother kept her clipped and groomed, making sure my dad's allergies weren't aggravated. Pretzel was always sweet, playful, and friendly. She was a perfect first dog.

Bringing home a new puppy meant that we needed to find a veterinarian. My mother chose the nearby Norwalk Veterinary Hospital—housed then in a small building set back from the main road. A newer, bigger, more visible hospital was built a few years later. Pretzel's first visit was with a younger associate, Dr. Donald Hartrick, who would come to epitomize the kind of caring veterinarian I wanted to be when I grew up. He was gentle and kind as he examined her and gave her puppy shots. He explained every aspect of the exam to me, and I ate up every word. He handled Pretzel with such care, it was obvious he loved what he did.

Later, Dr. Hartrick would go on to become the owner of NVH, and a lifelong connection for me. By the time I left for college, he had ministered to a series of dogs, birds, rodents, and other animals I convinced my parents to let me bring home.

Despite his allergies, my father was happy with the menagerie that came in and out of our lives once Pretzel had shown him and my mother that we could be a home with pets. Initially, my dad said no to the eighth-grade science-project mouse I wanted to keep, but relented once he saw how much I loved her. My mother was always supportive, even if she was the one who had to help with some of the caretaking. My brothers both loved Pretzel and all the dogs that followed. As adults, they both have families that include dogs.

Pretzel, my first dog, was also the first disabled pet I'd known.

She had slowly progressive cataracts that led to complete blindness by the time she was six years old. Pretzel adjusted and adapted so well that most people who visited had no idea she was blind. Of course, we were aware of her need to be kept safe inside and when she went out to play.

Back in the day, dogs were often let out of houses to roam on their own. No matter how many times I begged my family members not to let Pretzel go walking unattended, she'd slip through a door and take herself out for walks. Thanks to her highly developed sense of smell and her ability to map the neighborhood, she usually made it back safely.

Those times when she didn't return from one of her jaunts—like the time when I was about twelve and got home from school to find her missing—I'd run at top speed looking for her, covering quite a distance, calling her name at the top of my lungs, "Pretzel! Pretzel! Pretzel!!!!"

On one of those days, tears streamed down my face as I recalled images of dogs who had been hit on the street. The thought of seeing her splayed on the pavement fueled my desperation. Suddenly, after having scoured the far reaches of the neighborhood, I spotted interesting movement underneath the neighbor's porch only three houses down. It appeared to be a big black garbage bag that was moving on its own. Obviously, there was something or someone inside it. And that someone was Pretzel—happily feasting on the neighbor's leftovers from the night before. As I grabbed her up, my relief at having found her was overwhelming.

Pretzel shook her filthy, garbage-soiled, gray-and-white beard, and gave me the equivalent of a dog smirk, as if to say—*You interrupted my dinner!* I just hugged her tighter.

Pretzel Bitsy changed our world, proving to my father that he wasn't as allergic to all dogs as he had once believed. So much so that I convinced him we needed to get a second dog. We brought home a standard schnauzer named Tyke, who turned out to be a fierce, biting dog. She went back to the breeder in exchange for another standard schnauzer, a puppy named Zigfried, who was one of the worst dogs I've known. Over his fifteen years, the fifty-five-pound Zig took bites out of many of our friends. Why my parents kept him all those years was a mystery to me for the longest time. He was a very good watchdog, which seemed to give my parents some comfort when my father was away on business trips. I'm not sure the tradeoff was a wise one.

I think my mother and father embraced their own love for animals that was there all along. They gave up trying to say no. However, my parents were both so allergic to cats that there was no discussion about bringing any felines into the house. We did at different times have gerbils, guinea pigs, a rabbit, parakeets, turtles, a mouse, snails, and more. The line was drawn when it came to a snake. That may have been the only time my mother said no to me. After all, I was planning to be a veterinarian, and that was essentially a family effort. My parents did everything possible to encourage me and support my animal experiences.

They never questioned my determination. Even back at age six. "When you made up your mind about something," my dad always says, "there were no ifs, ands, or buts."

As a parent myself, I know this kind of approach was not necessarily how every parent might have reacted to a strong-willed child. But my father would literally do anything for me and my brothers. Anything. My mother would as well, though she did so in a style of her own. Dad, an electrical engineer with multiple degrees in subjects that included math and history, was hands-on with everything. He planned and then took part in every outing or project that he believed would appeal to our sense of fun and curiosity. My mom was in on the plans as well, drawing from her path as an educator—a career that would span fifty-plus years of teaching pre-K, elementary school, and religious school, and later, working as a supervisor of student teachers.

My mother practically invented the basics of "enrichment" without using that term. We had lessons for everything. For me there were piano and violin lessons. For Marc there were cello lessons, and for Bruce there were drum lessons. We attended cultural events, took swimming, skating, and skiing lessons, and were enriched by whatever else our mom deemed worthwhile.

My mother went all out, passing on to me the lasting belief that if you're going to do something, why not strive to do it exceedingly well? She schlepped me to ice-skating lessons and practice sessions all over the county as if I were going to become an Olympic skater. Gliding over the ice with ease appealed to me, but I never thought my destiny was to become the next Dorothy Hamill—who, coincidentally, trained at the same rink as I did. It was clear to me from watching her who was going to be the professional skater and who was going to be the veterinarian! In high school, I decided that it was necessary to give up skating so I could focus instead on running track and cross-country. My mom was willing to go along with my decision but first asked me, "Are you really sure you're ready to give up skating?"

"Yes," I answered, fully committed, explaining, "it's expensive and time-consuming, and it's time to stop. I love running." She heard me and agreed that it was time to trade in ice skates for track shoes.

My parents were my top fans and led my small cheering squad whenever they could attend meets. They genuinely enjoyed helping and being part of all our learning experiences. Mom spent so many years creating posters, bulletin board displays, and other art projects for her students that she couldn't resist helping me with mine. Much to the later amusement of my three kids, she passed that habit down to me. Whenever my three were assigned poster projects in school, all the way up through high school, I'd happily set aside time to add borders to the posters—after they had gone to sleep. With all my colored markers, I'd outline their poster boards in various matching colors. The process was relaxing and fun for me; the kids were delighted. It got to the point that they would confirm with me that I was going to do it when they went off to sleep. After a while, I'd actually feel guilty if I didn't spruce up their poster borders in the very late hours of the night.

More than anything, my parents taught and enabled us by example. The offspring of immigrants, they embraced the ideals of the American Dream, emphasizing the importance of hard work, education, family, and community. They chose to live in a newer part of Norwalk that was diverse and inclusive. Our neighborhood was packed with kids our ages. We walked to school together and played outside together. We were very lucky to grow up with such a tight-knit group of friends. It was like going to camp every day after school. We went to local public schools, where we had friends who came from cultures and backgrounds that were vastly different from our own.

Later, when I met Warren, I described to him those fun summer nights of kickball, jump rope, tag, and just running around. As I was telling him about some of my friends whom I still keep in touch with, I mentioned a kid we knew as Little Maurice Vaughn—Maurice's mom was a teacher who knew my mom from the Norwalk school system. Little Maurice visited our neighbors often and joined our full neighborhood games. When it was time for him to go home, his mom would call to him, "Maureeeeeeece!"

I added, "I think he became a pro athlete. I think he ended up playing baseball?"

Warren busted out laughing and said, "You knew Mo Vaughn!?" He then informed me that Mo Vaughn had been a three-time All-Star with a reputation as a fierce competitor and a powerful home-run hitter as the first baseman for the Boston Red Sox. As a professional athlete he was known for many things but none of them was for being "little." I had no idea!

During the summer months the neighborhood games would continue on after dark. Once the school year started, though, my brothers and I were always the ones being called home first. We had a ridiculous bedtime of seven thirty every night—except once a week when *Lassie* came on. I lived for that show. Otherwise, aside from getting enough sleep, there were very few rules in our household. The toughest requirement, enforced by my mother, came from her belief that we should never miss school unless we were sick. Her own work ethic was such that she almost never missed a day of work unless she was sick, and that was a rarity.

A huge priority for my parents was putting each of us through college and grad school, making sure we graduated with no debt. This was a tall order to provide for three kids with advanced degrees paid for in full. It was a great gift to be able to get through schooling and begin my career without being saddled with loans for the rest of my life. With my own kids, this became a top priority for me as a parent.

My father adhered tightly to a fairness doctrine. Both he and my mother wanted us to know that we were each loved and supported equally, not only when we were young but later, when the time came to start our careers and family lives. By their examples, they definitely helped to enable our eventual success.

My father's professional journey began as a design engineer that led to tenures with RCA and CBS Labs, and work in the space program. From there he went on to become vice president of a manufacturing company before starting his own firm, which pioneered computer technology. His business, Data Service Company, developed and sold turnstile ticket and cash register systems that were used in major entertainment attractions in the United States and around the world—glamorous places for us kids like Disney World, Six Flags, and many of the major baseball stadiums. My father also manufactured and sold all kinds of time clocks used in large installations, among lots of other products.

Arline and Harold Foodman were never the *do as I say* kind of parents who ask that their children grow up to fulfill their dreams and expectations. They truly parented by example, demonstrating their values by their deeds. Both were constantly volunteering in different capacities. My mother was the president of the PTA, a major commitment, and she held other offices when she stepped down from the presidency. She and my father were active in philanthropic and civic organizations and volunteered for good causes through our local temple. Whenever my mother heard of a student who was struggling (in her own classes or in someone else's), she'd make the time to see how she could help find the resources needed. My father was available to anybody who needed anything. He volunteered for an organization that served disadvantaged youth, and he even agreed to become a Boy Scout leader, even though my brothers weren't in the age group that needed a scoutmaster.

When I asked him what prompted this gesture, his answer was a predictable "They couldn't find anyone else to do it."

 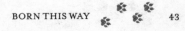

My parents enjoyed helping others. Not because they wanted to be heroes or call attention to themselves but because they genuinely liked being kind and making a difference in someone else's life. But despite their giving nature, my parents both had their limits now and then. The Boy Scout leader job came to a premature end after one of their meetings in our garage got out of hand. Apparently, my father had brought in donuts for a snack and instead of taking a relaxing break from their project, the boys started a donut-throwing contest all around the garage. At that point my dad said, "Okay, that's it, we're done."

Another time my mother finally put her foot down with my dad spending so much time helping neighbors out whenever they had an electrical problem or their cars broke down and he would head on over, basically on call, fixing whatever it was—for free.

My mother asked him, "You do know that we have some things that need to be fixed here?"

My father got to work at our house. Harold Foodman, first and foremost, was and still is a devoted family man.

Although at times my dad traveled extensively for work—leaving my mom to manage the household, her own workload as a teacher, her continuing education in night classes, and caring for the three of us kids—he more than made up for it when he wasn't traveling. He helped us with homework in all of our subject matter, sometimes developing innovative techniques for mastering challenges—like an instance in the fourth grade when I impatiently attempted to speed up the time required to conquer my multiplication tables.

"Here, Melissa," he announced one evening after dinner, presenting me with a stack of homemade flash cards that he had designed and written out with prompts for multiplying all the numbers up to the twelves. That's another thing about Dad—in addition to his day job as an electrical engineer, he is a natural teacher, on top of being a professional-level craftsman and contractor who can do electrical work, plumbing, roofs, tiling, carpentry, and minor construction, along with being a highly skilled mechanic. Later on, whenever Warren and I had something in need of fixing at our house or with one of our cars, we'd call my father. My brothers did the same!

Dad sat with me for hours, holding up the flash cards, allowing me to visualize the answers, so that I could quickly activate my powers of memorization. Magic! As a result of my rapid mastery of fourth-grade math, I proceeded to use flash cards for many other subjects straight up through college and vet school.

By ninth grade, along with using flashcards I developed the organizational habit of charting my goals in small notebooks, often laying out my plans and listing the interim steps needed to accomplish them. My mother has always been a list maker, so when I joined the track team in tenth grade, it came naturally to create lists of workouts that would help me accomplish my two-mile time personal bests.

Becoming totally hooked on running and working out, I also wanted to run cross-country, starting in eleventh grade, but because the high school didn't have a girls' cross-country team, I had to join the boys' team. This gave me yet another goal. After my first year running with the boys' cross-country team, I was able to convince the school to start a girls' cross-country program for my senior year. Not only did I love running with the boys and then with the new girls' team, I really loved setting my sights, competing, and winning too.

My parents applauded the extra effort that I'd put in at home, running sprints around the one-third-mile loop that circled our neighborhood—over and over and over. The fact is that I wasn't a world-class athlete, but I knew how to grind, and that led to my doing very well at race time. The neighbors all thought I was a bit crazy.

Yet that's who my parents had enabled me to be. Perhaps that's why I knew at age six that I had to become an animal doctor one day. Not everyone's path in life is set at so young an age. But mine was. There are many wonderful vets who have the right skill sets and affinities for animals that eventually lead them to their chosen profession. There are others, like me, who don't choose so much as we feel chosen. We are just born that way—with an ingrained sense of responsibility that tells us we are here to understand, protect, and care for animals.

Whether we are hardwired with compassion or it develops over time, I think it varies. I do know that there are many of us who are just drawn to animals, especially the ones who are disabled, hurt, or traumatized. We can't bear to even learn about a dog that is hungry, injured, or in pain without feeling a strong urge to help in whatever way we can. Those are the lifelong feelings that drew me to care for animals, to become active in animal welfare, to tend to the needs of my own pets, and to absolutely, without fail, become a veterinarian.

The phenomenon that explains what draws some of us to the path that we follow is not something I've studied closely. All I know is that I've been this way from as far back as I can remember.

🐾

My goal to become a vet was the primary focus of my childhood and adolescence. My whole life revolved around getting into vet school, amplified further by the time I was in high school to do even more for animals. At that point, I had become well versed in concerns of animal welfare and exploitation. In elementary school and junior high, I had little tag sale fundraisers for the Humane Society of the United States (HSUS). From their newsletters, I learned about factory farming—where animals raised for commercial purposes were treated as nonsentient beings. Instead of living on grass, they were kept on cement, under crowded conditions that were abusive and horribly inhumane.

My revulsion rose to a boiling point in my tenth-grade Spanish class one day, when our teacher landed on the topic of menus and then launched into a stomach-turning description of how "stringy" duck meat could be. All I could think was, *If you don't like it, don't criticize the ducks. Just don't eat it!*

Prior to that class, I had been talking to a friend who was a vegetarian, and that did it for me. In the middle of Spanish class, I wrote my parents a two-page letter in my very small, neat handwriting, about all the reasons I was not going to be eating meat anymore. Up until then, my mom had been making me turkey sandwiches. I made sure to let her know that as a vegetarian, I didn't need her to buy turkey for me from then on.

My activism intensified from there. Soon afterward, I set up an appointment with one of the school's administrators, Mr. Richard

Follman, to protest the annual donkey basketball games. Though I had never been and I wasn't sure how many donkeys were brought into the basketball court, the basic idea was that basketball players on two teams would ride donkeys and shoot the basketball while sitting on these poor animals. True, these yearly events were well attended and raised money for the student government. But I found the idea of carting poor donkeys around in trucks and having them run around on a slippery gymnasium floor to be cruel and humiliating for the animals. Armed with HSUS literature, I walked in, stated my concerns and asked pointedly for the school to consider an alternative to the donkey games. He heard me out but made no promises. A short time later, Mr. Follman informed me that the donkey basketball games were being discontinued.

This was a powerful moment for me—my first big lobbying effort and a crash course in learning to advocate for something that I felt strongly about.

A short time later, I was sitting on a bench at the high school and was horrified to see three boys torturing an ant. An ant! They were bragging about pulling off its legs one by one and gloating about how tough they thought they were for causing it so much torment. Without one word, I walked over and stomped on the ant, performing my first act of humane euthanasia. "There," I said, "at least now he's not going to suffer anymore."

The most upsetting incident came during a run with the boys' cross-country team. Our coach had sent us on a run to the beach in Westport, where there was an inlet often frequented by ducks. Most of the boys had gotten well ahead of me on the run there. When I came down the road approaching the beach, there they all were standing near a split-rail fence, throwing rocks at ducks in the little inlet!

"What's wrong with you?" I shouted at them. They looked clueless. Holding back my tears, I blasted them. "I can't believe you're throwing rocks at ducks!"

I don't think any of them actually hit a duck, but I was so crushed and furious. How could anyone do something so cruel? What would possess anyone to consciously decide to scare or hurt an animal? And these were my good friends. I turned right around and raced back to school at blistering speed. Feeling bad, they all decided to return with me, but I'd gotten such a head start they couldn't catch me. When our prom rolled around at the end of the year, the food was taking a long time to be served. The big joke was that the chefs were out throwing rocks at the ducks they wanted to cook. Ugh. It was infuriating, but I think they all got my point. So much so, in fact, that in our graduating-class tradition of creating a will for departing seniors, in my high school yearbook I was bequeathed "the Animal Kingdom"—i.e., all living and extinct creatures of the world. Mr. Follman signed my yearbook, writing, *Melissa, I'll always remember your interest in animal welfare. I hope you continue to be concerned about moral issues.*

There was never any doubt about whether or not I would continue to be passionate about animal welfare issues. My only doubt—and the only thing I could think about for years—was my intense worry about getting into vet school. When I say "intense," I mean that it loomed over everything. Over the course of the summer months, throughout high school, I took nightly "what if" walks with my mother, during which I posed the question over and over: "What if I don't get into vet school?" Not kidding!

In her usual Arline Foodman upbeat way, my mother tried to wave off my concerns, but when that didn't relieve my worries she suggested I seek out advice from the vet schools themselves. Since there were no computers to send emails back then in the dark ages, my father's secretary typed and sent out letters to admissions officers at all eighteen US veterinary schools explaining my interest and requesting admissions policies and preferences. I got plenty of responses that made it very clear that coming from a state without a vet school was going to be quite the challenge— because state schools allotted the majority of their spots to in-state students.

Eventually, when I was a senior applying to college, I was given helpful advice from a neighbor's brother who had been on the vet school faculty at Purdue University in West Lafayette, Indiana. He recommended that I apply to Purdue for college, saying, "It can be helpful to attend an undergrad university that has a vet school on campus."

After I was accepted to Purdue's College of Agriculture, my mother and I thought it was best to see the school before making any final decisions. I had quite a few choices, but Purdue was high on my list. We flew out to Indiana to find that Purdue's campus was typical of a Midwestern Big Ten school. It was sprawling and well-manicured, every blade of green grass along every sidewalk trimmed evenly with the next. The terrain was perfectly flat, and the brick buildings were meticulously well maintained. At one end, there were large playing fields, and—perfect for me—there were dog-running areas for those lucky enough to have dogs while in college. On my tour, we were driven along roads lined with sororities and fraternities, as well as large dorms scattered about, and a huge student center that took up blocks in one corner of the campus. The football stadium, basketball arena, and field house were on the other side, making up an elaborate Big Ten sports complex.

Considering the advice given to me before my visit, I had already come to the conclusion that it was definitely best for me to attend an undergraduate school that was part of a university with a vet school. I planned to get a job at the vet school, where I could meet faculty while I was still in undergrad. Though I had no idea how to pursue that possibility, answers soon came from Dr. Gordon Coppoc, head of the physiology department at the vet school. My neighbor's brother had kindly arranged for my mom and me to meet with him so he could answer my long list of questions. We started off on the right track immediately when Dr. Coppoc welcomed us into the lobby of the veterinary school as if were old family friends. He gave us a personal tour of the vet school and reassured me that getting a job at the vet school while I was an undergraduate would not be difficult at all. He convinced me right then and there that Purdue was the place for me.

Before we left that day, Dr. Coppoc sent me to meet with the assistant dean of the College of Agriculture, who registered me for freshman courses. We stayed overnight at Purdue's Union Club Hotel, and I bought my first Purdue T-shirt at the bookstore across the street. With that, I was on board as a Boilermaker!

The nagging echo of *What if I don't get into vet school?* hovered over my undergraduate experience. Never forgetting my focus, I studied like my life depended on it—day and night, even during one-hour breaks between classes, so I could have the straight As that were necessary to get into vet school. Every night from seven to eleven p.m., I studied with my good friend Laura Genduso, who was my next-door neighbor for the first two years and then my roommate junior year. I broke the weekends up into seven sections: Friday evening, Saturday morning, afternoon, and evening, and Sunday morning, afternoon, and evening. I took two off and studied the rest. Though I socialized with friends from my dorm, and members of Alpha Phi Omega, the service fraternity I joined—having fun with the community blood drives we ran, our visits to nursing homes, and our Christmas caroling, among other activities—I was extremely disciplined about studying. I developed a very effective technique for imprinting lots of information on my memory after classes. In the Life Sciences building at night, I'd find an empty classroom and write my notes all over the blackboards in that room, filling up every bit of space on the boards until I'd committed all of that information to memory. This technique was a variation of my writing my notes over again in a notepad when I wasn't near a blackboard. By doing this after every class, I would retain the information and be that much more able to review and organize it later on. My small printing of notes on all the blackboards created works of art that I now wish I'd photographed for posterity.

In retrospect, I don't know why I couldn't banish my worries that straight As and all this hard work were not going to be enough to get myself into vet school. To offset those fears, I went above and beyond the requirements of my major. I worked briefly in a biochem lab during my freshman year. During my sophomore year, I worked at the Purdue dairy farm, which gave me the large animal experience needed for my vet school application. In those days, I didn't connect the controversial topic of removing baby calves from their mothers (commonly practiced at dairy farms) to animal cruelty—though I know it would not be a good job for me now. However, much of what I learned in that setting was eye-opening for a suburban student from Connecticut.

At the end of freshman year, my father came to pick me up to bring me home for the summer. On the way, he took a deep breath and said, "Melissa, I need to let you know that Pretzel died."

Bursting into tears that turned rapidly into sobs, I asked my father, "When?"

He looked very uncomfortable as he said, "Two months ago." My parents had decided not to tell me because they didn't want to traumatize me in the middle of my school year. Even though I wished they had told me when it happened, I understood their dilemma. I was very attached to Pretzel. She was my very first little dog, and they knew I couldn't imagine what it would be like without her there for me.

The loss caused me to cry most of the way home until my head hurt so badly from crying that I just became silent and sad. On that car ride, I felt the pain of losing my beloved Pretzel—my first major loss of a pet—which no doubt helped me to become a more understanding and compassionate veterinarian, especially for the families dealing with pet loss and grief.

Before I went back to Purdue for my second year of undergrad, instead of getting a dog of my own right away, I found a little schnauzer for my parents to adopt from PAWS (Pet Animal Welfare Society), a Norwalk-based animal rescue group. Living in a dorm, I knew that I had to refrain from adopting pets for myself.

During my junior year at Purdue, I finally got my job at the vet school. It was in the diabetes lab, where I was told that I would be put in charge of one of the lab dogs. The research project being conducted at the time was aimed at developing a computer-driven insulin pump with a glucose sensor that was to be embedded into the dogs, and eventually, a person's body. The goal of course was to more effectively regulate blood sugar for diabetics with a continuous insulin infusion rather than multiple injections per day.

Nothing on earth could have prepared me for the experience of falling in love with an animal as heroic as those who are forced to give of themselves to research that can improve and save the lives of people. There were a handful of dogs in this lab who had come from a Detroit shelter—which was legal at the time. I couldn't wait to meet "my" lab dog.

When the day arrived, I went with the professor in charge of the lab, down to the basement level of the vet school, where dog kennels lined a hallway. When she opened one of the kennel doors, I peered in to see two dogs, each in their own kennel run.

She pointed and said, "This is April. You'll be in charge of her."

When I looked closer to see where our director was pointing, I saw April, the most beautiful white collie mix, looking straight at me. She turned her head slightly at an angle and watched me as I approached. She had a longish nose and lovely soft ears tucked back with concern on either side of her face. Her eyes seemed to take in every inch of me—to make sure I was the one. Her person.

The second our eyes met, I knew that she was mine and I was hers forever. We locked in on each other and bonded in such a way that I imagined we had been together in a past life. Let's just say that this was not the scenario I imagined when I sought out a research job. Then again, looking back, it's pretty much what I should have expected of myself.

Our first meeting was one of the most memorable moments of my life. This beautiful dog who had been sentenced to life as a research animal living in a kennel, void of meaningful human interaction, was now in my care. When I think of the gift I was being given, I can't help but close my eyes and let myself have a good cry.

April was extraordinary, a once-in-a-million-lifetimes dog, an old soul and best friend. She was my heart dog. Inappropriately, I fell madly in love with her and dreaded the day that they would induce a lifetime of diabetes.

Our lab dogs were all kept in a small, clean room down the hall from the diabetes lab. When the dogs came into the study, we did a variety of baseline blood glucose testing. We knew that eventually one of our tasks would be to monitor the dog's status after having been given a toxic chemical that made them diabetic. We knew in advance that they could become ill, but with intensive treatment they would recover so that they could then participate in the second part of the research for the development of the glucose monitors.

At one point, I thought about sneaking her out at night. But, of course, I was trying to get into vet school, not arrested for kidnapping one of the valuable lab dogs there helping to find a new treatment for diabetes. I was an animal welfare advocate, but I'm not a rule breaker by nature and wasn't radical enough to walk out of the building with a dog that didn't belong to me.

The following spring I was given the official news that I'd been accepted into Purdue University College of Veterinary Medicine. April would continue to be my assigned lab dog, and, I was informed, if I wanted to adopt her, she would be available after being retired from the lab in a year or two.

Because I wasn't sure when I might be able to officially adopt April, I decided to adopt a beagle mix from the Norwalk dog pound the summer before starting vet school. Whitney was such a cute puppy but, as it turned out, not a good vet school dog at all. She had severe separation anxiety that led to chewing everything in her path when I couldn't be with her. That fall, sooner than I had expected, the option to adopt April was given to me. It took some time for me to rationalize and justify sending Whitney home to my parents, who literally would do anything for me, including taking in a puppy who would chew up doors, textbooks, calculators, and the front dash of their car. I felt really guilty, but she adjusted well, and as crazy as she was, my father, allergies and all, adored her. Meanwhile, I could not have been more thrilled to have April come live with me. The next year, I added a teeny ferret named Cindy, to make my little family complete.

Vet school was not easy. The class schedule was like going to work on a daily basis. We were in class and labs all day long. We studied all night. Weekends again provided only short spurts of relaxation. I did take time to run most days and I was usually joined by my beautiful, sweet, special April. I had to give her insulin shots twice a day, but I only lived two blocks from the vet school, so I had no trouble coming and going during lunch, and then we were close by to the vet school to go back and study at night.

Lasting friendships and a true spirit of a surrogate family developed between a small group of us who studied at the vet school every evening. April was always with me. There had previously been some problems with dogs barking and making messes, so there was an explicit rule against having dogs in the building. I had a choice to make. Leaving my dog at home in the evening was not an option, so I brought her with me despite the rules. My reasoning—which worked—was that she was originally at the vet school as a lab dog, which somehow gave her an exemption from that rule. The dean and assistant dean would always greet her first—"Hello, April!" "Good to see you, April!"—before saying hello to me. This pattern continued pretty much wherever I worked until I opened my house-call practice many years later.

Though I found vet school to be difficult, I had a nice routine, and I never lost my enthusiasm for the end goal of becoming a veterinarian. The classes were rigorous, and required full focus pretty much every minute of every day. The first two years were mostly academic classes with little hands-on experience. Then the fun began junior year, with clinical rotations in various specialties of small-animal surgery and medicine, food animal (what a horrible label), equine, clinical pathology, and ambulatory (going out to farms).

After graduation from vet school—one of the best days of my life—April journeyed with me to New York City (along with Cindy the ferret), where I did a rotating internship at the Animal Medical Center. It was a dream come true, living, studying, and working in New York City, at the busiest and most renowned animal hospital in the world. Adding to the intensity was a severe flare-up of seasonal allergies, exacerbated by recently discovered cat allergies—all while handling cats in clinics throughout the day. Overall, participating in such a comprehensive program was the perfect place for me to be following graduation. Each day was packed with cases, lectures, and experiences that were invaluable to me as a new grad no matter what path I would end up taking. Decades later, I still approach every patient I see with the same organized and thorough approach I learned during my internship.

At the Animal Medical Center, I arranged for April to come and go with me, and I did the same thing when I left New York to go to Philadelphia for my residency in small-animal internal medicine at the University of Pennsylvania School of Veterinary Medicine. This tolerance of my breaking the rules with my extra-special diabetic research dog was extended to her and to me, long before the emotional-support-animal designation was a thing. April was the ultimate emotional support animal, and I'm sure those who were in charge knew how important it was for me to have her with me. Most of the faculty in New York City and in Philadelphia knew and welcomed April everywhere we went.

While I was a resident at Penn, I was fortunate to work with a vet student named Charlie Duffy who happened to be one of the most diligent, hard-working members of our team. In one of those amazing, uncanny coincidences that happen in life, six years later, when Charlie and his wife, Janice, also a veterinarian, were starting their careers, the two wound up buying the Norwalk Veterinary Hospital—from Dr. Donald Hartrick, the same vet who had been the Foodman family's vet years before.

At one point, when I was looking for a hospital to serve as a base for my house-call practice, I reconnected with Dr. Charlie Duffy, my former student. Before I could even finish my question, he said, "Yes!" to an arrangement that made Norwalk Veterinary Hospital that very base. The dream that I had nurtured for my whole life while growing up had come full circle.

At some point, while standing in the treatment room examining a sick dog, Charlie and I began a running conversation about how much we loved our jobs.

No matter the daily concerns and challenges, I have always felt, every step along the way, that this was what I was meant to do. At every turn, I felt and still do feel lucky that taking care of animals is what I do for my living. More than once, Charlie has turned to me and asked, "Can you believe we get paid to do this?"

This is the way many of us veterinarians feel. Being a vet can be extremely stressful at times, yet it can also connect you to a network of people in your field who share the same joy and commitment to animals that you have. Charlie and Janice are more than colleagues; they've become family, along with their kids. In fact, whenever Warren makes the mistake of querying our three, "Who is the greatest dad in the world?" without hesitation they uniformly answer, "Charlie Duffy."

Always smiling and upbeat, Charlie regularly reminds the staff at NVH of his time spent at vet school as my student. "She's the teacher," he is fond of saying, a gracious acknowledgment.

Working in an arena that I'm passionate about has given me the ultimate prize. Even before opening my house-call practice, my job satisfaction rating was far above most people's I know. Never once have I regretted or questioned my path. Being a vet is my calling, my purpose. It's all I ever wanted to do.

April had been there with me from before starting vet school and along for the entire ride. Everyone who saw us knew how special she was, but they also knew how special she was to me. A friend from vet school had given me a photo of April and me during my second year. His note on the back of the picture said, *The happiness seen in your face along with the obvious love between you and your dog make you one of the most pleasant sights in the vet school*. I still have that picture sitting on my night table right next to my bed.

Chapter 3

PIGLET GETS HIS NAME

"Promise me you'll always remember: You're braver than you believe, and stronger than you seem, and smarter than you think."

—A. A. Milne, *Winnie-the-Pooh*

MARCH 4–5, 2017

Those first two days of the foster puppy's intrusion into our lives were so all-consuming that they became something of a blur when I later tried to remember the order of events.

To the best of my recollection, there was already an element of the unexpected during the time that I sat on the kitchen floor observing the six Shapiro dogs taking turns—more or less—introducing themselves to the very attentive tiny pink Baby Bart. Much to my relief and surprise, for that period of time he paused his anguished screams. So much so that I returned to my original assumption—*How much trouble can a one-pound puppy be?*

Famous last words.

Well, I didn't know that yet. Truly, I couldn't imagine how such a little fellow could become much of a problem at all. The horrible racket he'd put up earlier was understandable. He was in a state of extreme disorientation and distress. His anxiety would pass, I was certain. Besides, I again reminded myself, we were only going to foster Bart for three or four days or so. Maybe a week. No more than two weeks, *max*.

As our meet-and-greet proceeded in the kitchen, I felt encouraged. My own dogs were on their best behavior. Usually, whenever anyone rings or knocks at the door, or just comes in from outside, a barking cacophony ensues—often led by our black Lab mix Dean (named after Dean Martin by his Arkansas rescuers). But as this new little dog entered their lives, and as I observed them all crowded into the kitchen, no one made a peep. I had not expected that. It was as if they understood from the outset that I needed them all to be quiet and gentle.

There were lots of sets of ears twitching and noses wrinkling. Each of the six dogs appeared to be fascinated by the tiny pink boy, who was making little whimpery grunts. They were poking and gently sniffing at the new, unusual-looking puppy, who must have been quite the container of scents—considering he had been on a truck with dozens of other dogs traveling with him all the way from Georgia. The Shapiro dogs looked like journalists, waiting for Bart to explain himself and then glancing to me for input. *What* was he? *Who* was he? *Why* was he?

Dogs typically use their various senses—including their sight and their hearing—to identify and evaluate others who may be familiar or unfamiliar to them. Mainly, though, it is their powerful sense of smell that delivers the most information about what and who they are encountering. In this case, although the six dogs were aware of Baby Bart's appearance and could read his body language, as well as hear the small squeaks he was making, their focus was on exploring how he smelled. Ironically, he was assessing the others with only his nose.

It didn't take long for them to realize he was one of their own kind, and now that he was not a screaming Gila monster, he certainly must not have seemed like too much of an intrusion. Soon they all took a step back, still interested but not as impressed or wary.

Dean, our resident couch potato, the biggest and only male,

stood in the middle of our gathering and grumbled while the pink baby inched closer to him, literally sizing him up. Gina (the white Australian shepherd/border collie mix), who was a bit taller than Dean, and usually more aloof, gave an easy welcome to Bart, letting him sniff her even more closely. Without a long tail to wag (as it had presumably been docked by breeders), Gina observed Bart intently and gently brushed up close—enough to be cordial but not much more. Susie, the older gray scruffy terrier mix, in charge as usual, encouraged the other three smaller dogs to come close and follow her friendly lead. Shy Annie (the tan terrier mix) and playful Evie (the white poodle mix, who, like Gina, also had a very short docked tail) approached the tiny puppy but didn't go past quick sniffs before starting to look slightly concerned about how long he was planning to stay. It was only Zoey, the chocolate Chihuahua/Yorkie-Maltese mix and the littlest of the six-pack, who showed real curiosity and scampered up close, as if waiting for a sign from me that it was okay to engage.

Most of this first encounter was somewhat predictable. I had anticipated that the resident dogs would be curious about the new puppy, that they would greet him, and then they would retreat to their comfort zones on the couches and on dog beds in the living room.

Generally, when bringing a foster or adopted dog into a home with other dogs, most situations require days to weeks and sometimes months for new dogs to be fully accepted into the canine section of the household. Equally important is that most rescued dogs need a few weeks or longer to decompress before they can truly start to relax and settle into a new home. They require that the human and dog family members be patient and respectful during this adjustment period.

Watching the interactions in the kitchen, I was happy that everyone said their hellos and that they were able to leave the puppy without being terribly disgruntled. He was no threat to them, and I'm sure they could sense that he was a baby. They probably didn't realize he was deaf and blind, but I assumed they'd figure that out over the next couple of days.

Just as everyone appeared ready to wander off, a remarkable thing happened. Bart decided it was time to play. He did a twirl with a wiggle tagged onto it. A bit of an adorable show-off, he revealed a feistiness I had so far missed as he initiated puppy play—running around wildly even without being able to see. Zoey, ready to wrestle, came in for a gentle body bump as Bart bounced off her, skating and slipping on the floor before running into the wood gate that enclosed the kitchen. The surprise caused him to back up, spin around, and then feel and sniff his way over to where Dean was standing—where Bart managed to take cover in between Dean's legs.

Did I detect a mischievous challenge from Bart—as though he was telling Dean that his status as the only male dog in the pack was now in question? Dean looked down and the other dogs moved in, spurring Bart to weave in and out between all of their legs.

Carefully, I opened the gate and the five older Shapiro dogs flew into the living room, leaving Zoey in the kitchen with the tiny pink ball of energy, who was ready to match her playfulness. Bart, unrecognizable from the screaming rescue dog from earlier in the day, suddenly became so spunky, happy, and cute that I picked up my phone and started taking pictures and videos of this monumental meeting.

In and of itself, taking that video was not out of character for me. Over the years I have memorialized adorable moments with my three children, all of our dogs and birds, both fostered and adopted, and my patients of various species and breeds. The photos and videos are mostly for me—so that I can look back at those moments captured in time and remind myself how lucky I am to be a witness to so much cuteness. Of course, I would soon share this video of tiny Bart on my Facebook page—mostly because I knew everyone would be excited to see our new pink foster baby, but also the interest was an obvious solution for helping find him his forever home.

A feeling of immense relief and hope washed over me. This was the first time all day I'd been able to catch my breath, quiet the noise, set my concerns aside, and see the potential that was there. All over again, I became excited by the opportunity to learn from a special-needs dog while helping him learn and get him ready for his permanent family. Watching him and Zoey, I played the bits and pieces in my head of what I'd heard already from Gloria about the traumas and travels of the last month and a half for the deaf blind rescue boy. Some of the story had been spelled out in emails from Gloria:

> We responded to an ad on Craigslist needing to "get rid of dogs." The story we were given was this group of young folks—5–6—was living in a house with a few dogs. Over time, they multiplied and when the landlord found out they were evicted. Assume the place was trashed . . . When we called, they were living together in a tent with the dogs. My understanding was the dogs were kept in wire cages in the tent and let to run outside to potty.
>
> I tried to meet them at the Walton County Animal Shelter, but they apparently had been cited some time before and did not want to be anywhere near the place. We met them at a gas station near a Walmart parking lot. They drove a beat-up dark green jeep with the back loaded with the cages and the dogs that we were to be getting. There were three of them—two guys and a gal . . . They handed us the dogs that we got and that was it. They had already placed 12–15 dogs with other folks.
>
> They had a couple of females and a male that they wanted to keep and we tried to keep in contact to help them get the male neutered at least, but that lasted about a week. The rescue offered to pay for the neuter and vaccs but they never contacted us back.

Gloria had said that the reason she had reached out to me was that I had adopted Gina, also a double merle (dapple), from her six years earlier. She believed that with my network of special-needs dog rescuers, I would be a good resource for finding the right person for the profoundly disabled one-pound puppy. Bart's three littermates stayed in Georgia and went directly to their adoptive homes from there while their mother, Abigail, came in Gloria's transport RV—the same vehicle that brought Bart up to Connecticut. The part of his journey that most concerned me was the time period when he would have starved to death had Gloria not fed him with a bottle. Still, I was struck by the resilience he mustered to push his way back in with the litter to again be fed by Abigail.

The travel to a new place, even with the familiarity of Gloria, must have been terrifying. Yet, in spite of the fear he must have felt, in our little kitchen, I had watched him freely engage with our dogs.

After nearly an hour of introductions followed by wild play with ZoZo, most of the dog pack forgot about our foster puppy and wandered off to nap in their favorite spots. Dean had something of a grumbly attitude, almost as if he wanted to say, *Time for the pink dude to go.*

Bart, instead, was content to take a nice long nap, snuggled into my fleece jacket. Soon after that he started to get antsy and, sure enough, for no good reason, went right back to exercising his vocal cords again, making his unhappy screaming and grunting sounds.

It was then, in the late afternoon, when it was already getting dark, that I heard Warren's car turn up our driveway. My first thought was that he and Ellie had made fairly good time returning from Juilliard and probably hadn't stopped to eat, so they might be hungry. It was time to start feeding the dogs anyway, so I went back to the kitchen and tried unsuccessfully to figure out what the pink baby was so upset about now.

The minute the other dogs heard Warren and Ellie approaching the house, Dean, as usual, began to bark, kicking off a chorus from the rest, who ramped up fast into a typically loud, unnecessary ruckus. That's how we greeted my husband and my daughter as they walked in the door.

"Quiet down, everyone!" I said, but was ignored. Ellie came close to check out Bart, but after a few seconds of his screaming she changed her mind and hurried upstairs to put her violin away. Warren just grinned and reached for the howling pink baby, who went to him immediately, curled right up in his hands, and instantly went silent.

Relief!

As dinnertime approached, I had a new conflict to sort out. Before committing to taking on the foster baby—whom I'd weighed earlier at NVH to find he was all of one and a half pounds and who was complicating my schedule already—I'd planned to attend a five-hour Reiki healing workshop the following day in Fairfield, Connecticut. After spending the last several hours thinking about how Bart would do for the day without me, I couldn't see leaving him with Warren.

Mulling it over out loud, I finished feeding the dogs and then turned my focus to getting together some semblance of a meal that would appeal to him (a nonvegetarian), to me (a vegan), and to Ellie (vegan most of the time).

Before I decided whether or not to cancel the Reiki class, I told Warren that I probably shouldn't go and then asked him, "What do you think?"

Warren laughed. "You really want to know what I think?" he teased. "Or are you just stalling for time so you can still process your own answer?"

At that moment, I did want his input, but I was also hoping that we could prolong the banter so that he would continue to hold Bart and keep him quiet while I made us all something to eat. For the past hour, each time Warren had attempted to return the tiny boy to me or put him down in the little bed that I'd set up in the kitchen, Baby Bart would let out a siren of a scream until Warren gave in and pulled him back, close to his chest, petting and comforting him.

At a couple of different points, Ellie had run down the stairs to check on dinner and tell me about her day in NYC, but both times happened to have been when we were trying to give Warren a break from holding the foster pup, who had again let loose with his screeching. So each time, an annoyed Ellie turned around and headed back up to her quiet room.

"Where were we?" I asked.

"You wanted to know what I thought about whether you should cancel tomorrow."

"Well?"

"What are you thinking?"

"I could ask Monica. She met him today. If she is willing, that will solve the problem. If not, I'll cancel."

"I trust your judgment." I noticed he didn't offer to keep the puppy because he knew his own limitations, given the fact that we had already been given a taste of just how much trouble a one-plus-pound deaf blind puppy could be.

Neither one of us was ready to admit that my estimate of a couple of days or a week might have been overly optimistic.

The truth that we both could observe was that whoever was going to adopt the puppy would have to understand that this wasn't a beginner dog. Warren, as a dog person himself and someone with experience coparenting dogs with me, had insights I valued. We both knew that it didn't hurt that I was a vet and had a broader view of the whole dog, as well as the fact that I was a teacher of dogs and could gauge challenges. I rely on my own intuition and powers of observation, mixed with my veterinary training, years of experience practicing vet medicine and caring for animals in my own household, plus some basic common sense. Those are the skills that make it easier to gather information from nonhuman patients—leading to diagnoses and hopefully effective solutions.

My example to Warren was usually to remind him of one of our neighbors who had just gotten a new puppy and called me with an urgent situation. She worriedly reported, "The puppy is shaking and won't stop. She's sitting in the back of the crate and won't come out."

Sounded like a lot of brand-new puppies to me, but, out of concern that maybe something was wrong, I offered, "Let me come look at her."

When I arrived, I took the tiny puppy and cuddled her up for a while, and miraculously, she relaxed, the shaking stopped, and before long the sweet little pup wanted to play.

Our neighbor looked at me with astonishment as if I was a genius, and asked, "What did you do?"

At first, she didn't believe me when I said, "You have to hold her like you held your daughters when they were babies. This is your baby.

Just hold the puppy, comfort her, and let her know everything's going to be okay."

"That's all?"

That was it, I assured her.

Warren, a social worker and therapist by training, sometimes observes that my ability to treat dogs and animals in general is based on a holistic approach—involving not just the physical but also the emotional lives of patients. It's really an art, treating the whole animal, as well as the humans that care for them. Sometimes it's also a matter of stating the obvious.

One such time, Warren was with me when I paid a visit to a wildlife rehab center where I used to help with some of the permanently disabled non-releasable birds. I was dropping off an injured bird when my friend Dara Reid—who is the founding director of Wildlife in Crisis, in Weston, Connecticut—asked me to look at a young bird that had an issue with its wing. She was planning on bringing the injured bird to an avian vet but was wondering what I thought.

The thing is, I'm not an avian veterinary specialist. At the time, I hadn't cared for many birds in my home either. Nonetheless, I agreed to have a look.

The bird in question was a young grackle. They are very smart and often funny, although they can be very aggressive toward other, smaller songbirds. This was clearly serious. A wing injury like this would be a certain death sentence to a young fledgling who had just recently left the nest.

Looking at it, I could see the problem. I took the bird from her, palpated the wing, gave it a twist, and popped the luxated shoulder back in place. The anxious grackle gave out a sort of a sigh and immediately looked more comfortable. We all glanced at one another, sharing relieved yet slightly skeptical smiles because I'm not usually one to "do orthopedics" in birds. Even so, it did the trick.

Warren was enchanted. He loves to tell that story.

This was all context to say that though our foster project now appeared to be a taller order than we had anticipated, we were in no way second-guessing the decision to help this tiny, disabled puppy prepare for adoption and become a welcomed member of a forever family of his own. Warren had full faith in me, and he was willing to help. Confident that Bart would settle in soon, I had a game plan in mind and was sure we could make good progress in the next few days. Or so.

There was a lot to consider. Rescue dogs do need time to decompress, and foster parents need time to assess personality, lifestyle preferences, behavioral issues, and all sorts of other traits that help to determine the right match. A key to that, I knew, would be helping to provide an honest description of him and recommendations for care to be evaluated by prospective adopters.

These were topics Warren and I chatted about as he held the pink puppy while I set our big oval blond-wood country kitchen table, which took up most of our small dining area next to the kitchen. After calling, "Ellie, come and eat!" I took Baby Bart from Warren so he could go wash his hands.

This time, Bart only let out a couple of rasping barks, but he begrudgingly let me hold him and thankfully didn't start his screaming again.

At the announcement of it being time for gathering at the table, Zoey, in all her chocolate brown Chi/Yorkie-Maltese fluffy cuteness, cocked her head and came to wait at the foot of the chair on my right, where she had her own cushion. Evie, with her snowy white poodle mix coat and her expression of complete comprehension of my every word, took up her station at the foot of the chair on the left side of me. Zoey always sits on her chair during dinner. Evie would sit on the chair too, but only when Warren wasn't sitting at the table, because she considered his chair to be hers. Both seemed perplexed to see Bart in my arms, already in a seat of honor and not even a member of the family.

Looking down at the puppy, cradled at my waist in the crook of my elbow, I couldn't help being the teeniest bit smitten. No, not because he was so needy—although it's true, I do have a weakness for the littlest creatures in need of comfort or repair. But with this deaf blind seven-week-old pink baby, maybe I could have had a hint of a crush on him because of his giant-sized refusal to be ignored. He was adorable, annoying, and admirable.

I walked him around the living room, checking on the rest of the six-pack, making sure to remind everyone that the little guy was still our houseguest.

Susie, the gray terrier mix, got up from the spot she had chosen, of course, and came right over, sweetly stretching her front paws up toward my knees. With a head rub for her, I leaned down farther to let her sniff Bart. "Susan," I praised her, "you're being so nice to the foster puppy," and set him down next to her, observing how gentle and nurturing she was to the baby. He sniffed her and stepped back, tail up, like he was ready to pounce and play.

Susie's approach to our foster dog was the most mature of the bunch. We'd always imagined that she had taken care of her own puppies at some point before becoming a Shapiro—when she was already a young adult. Knowing that Bart had been rejected by his mother so early, I was touched to see Susie's maternal instincts kicking in.

Annie, our petite tan terrier mix, shyly hopped down from her comfy cushion on top of a dog crate, where she could usually be found, and came over tentatively. Gina, our white Aussie/border collie mix, whom I considered to be the activities director—given her organizational skills as a herding dog—vaulted off an armchair. Rarely do her hearing and vision deficits seem to bother her coordination except when she has to walk up stairs. At the bottom of the stairs, she hesitates and has to bound up three stairs at a time after she does a hesitant "getting ready" routine. Gina went over to gently sniff at the pink baby, and glanced around to see what everyone else was doing. Finally, Dean, the black Lab mix, roused himself from his usual spot on the couch and decided to amble over.

True to form, Dean began to grumble with laid-back growls, as in, *Hey, what's goin' on?* Everybody ignored him, thankfully, including Bart, who couldn't hear him anyway. With his nose and his tail going a mile a minute, though, he did seem to know he was the center of attention.

Settling them all down, I scooped the pink one up and returned to the kitchen, quickly washing my hands, and took my seat next to Evie, who had brazenly crawled up on a cushion and was sitting in a humanlike position with her paws on the table. Just then, Ellie quietly took her seat. Normally annoyed by misbehaving dogs, Ellie adores Evie and commented on how cute she looked—enough to encourage Zoey, who stood adorably to my right side, making little grunts to get my attention to pick her up and put her onto the cushion on the chair next to me.

In loving but stern dog-dad fashion, Warren admonished Evie, who hopped off her chair. Zoey, who was the best lapdog in the world and typically made herself comfortable in my lap when I was sitting down, pouted, looking at me and then at the pink puppy on my lap, the way that a sibling would, as in, *How come he gets to be in your lap and not me?* Rather than run off, ZoZo stayed on her cushion next to me, giving me quite the look, wondering what in the world I was doing with that intruder on my lap.

Somehow this set Bart off, and he began to whine, causing Ellie to wince. From the get-go, she was not a fan of the foster project. Later, when we talked about it, Ellie confessed that even before the deaf blind pink puppy's arrival, having six dogs was already too much.

"When we had only three dogs," she admitted, "that wasn't a problem."

Ellie was still okay at the end of middle school, when we added number four, sweet little cutie baby Annie (when Daniel was in tenth grade and Rachael was a senior in high school). But soon she started inviting friends over less and less. After there were five dogs, and then six, Ellie was embarrassed, even though her friends loved coming over to see the dogs. They didn't understand that she was now the only one of her siblings still living at home and watching the unfolding truth that, as she put it, "You kept replacing every kid that went off to college with two dogs."

She struggled with the reality that the six of these big dog personalities dominated our lives. Ellie loved them, without question, but the noise and commotion of so many of them was disruptive to her studies. I understood completely from having grown up with a brother who played the drums and from trying to study my freshman year at college in what turned out to be one of the noisiest dorms at Purdue.

Ellie's main concern about the growing canine population, she eventually explained, was about the toll it would take on me, especially, and on her dad. It was harder to travel with six dogs and not as easy to find people to come stay with all six of them. We couldn't go to restaurants and hotels without making arrangements for pet sitters, taking some dogs with us, or having to leave wherever we were going earlier than desirable. In the fall, Ellie was set to begin college at Princeton—and she was concerned that there would be no end to the madness.

My mother calls my younger daughter my "clone," which is not the case as she's very much her own person. But Ellie and I are a lot alike. We look alike, for sure. She has my same worker bee mentality, a similarly driven personality. Ellie is much more thoughtful in the way that she speaks and how she forms her points of view. She is very private and careful not to rock any boats. But she was genuinely concerned that I would wear myself out with another dog and wasn't shy about saying so.

Sitting in my lap at the kitchen table, Baby Bart must have had an uncanny sense of how to test the limits of everyone's patience and began to cry loudly.

"Oh my God," I sighed with great fatigue.

Ellie tried to put a positive spin on it. "He's just adjusting. But you know, you probably don't want him to be too adjusted . . . before he finds his forever home."

Warren reached over to pet the one-and-a-half-pound Chi/doxie and take him from me. I watched as the puppy wagged his tail and eagerly launched himself into his foster dad's arms.

Now, with dinner over, Warren returned Bart to me, cleared the table, and, as he did, wanted to return to an earlier, more serious discussion about our foster pup's name. He also wanted to bring Ellie into the debate. "As I was saying . . ." he said, taking charge.

Interrupting, I turned to Ellie. "What do you think?"

"I agree with Dad."

How did she know that the whole subject had come up when Warren mentioned he didn't like the pink puppy's name?

"Bart . . ." I cooed, looking down at him as I petted his silky pink forehead, and peered into his blinking, bluish, small eyes—one of which pointed downward and the other, which was smaller—and both of which bore the telltale signs of blindness caused by his double-dapple genetics. "Is that your name?" I asked out loud.

No response. Warren and Ellie raised their eyebrows in sync, telling me, without words, *Told ya.* The more I thought about it, the more I could see he wasn't much of a Bart. There was a tad of the mischievous bad boy Bart Simpson in him, but it was a stretch. Then there were other images of Barts that came to mind. Seemed like a better name for a big bruiser of a dog. Like a lumberjack who would wear plaid work shirts and steel-toed hiking boots. Actually, in his paperwork I noted that he had been named Bartimaeus.

In the rescue, foster, and adoption worlds, there are competing opinions about naming or renaming rescued animals. When pets are owner-surrendered, they have names and histories that many foster and adoptive families are wise to choose to keep. For pets who have been called by a name for a while, it can be confusing, in my view, to change a name to a new one that's unrecognizable. On the other hand, especially during instances when many animals have been rescued without known names, shelters and rescue organizations rightfully issue them new ones. In fact, names can be an enticement or a deterrent when it comes to getting adopted. Sometimes there's a reason behind the name selection; other times, rescuers assign names that follow an alphabetical order for that season, day, week, or month. When Gloria's rescue group received the eleven dogs (out of the thirty who were first identified in the hoarding situation), the letter *B* was obviously chosen for Bart and his littermates—Belinda, Blaze, and Barrett.

When families decide to adopt a rescue and rename him or her, most animal adoption activists agree that's a sign of inclusion and welcome. Most say that it's a good idea to change the name of a dog who comes from an abusive situation. This way the dog starts a new life with a new name. In the Bart, Barrett, Belinda, and Blaze case, they were so young that they didn't know their names, and three of them were deaf anyway.

All of this was at the heart of the discussion I'd been having with Warren for the last hour and a half. The original question came up not long after Warren and Ellie had walked in the door from New York. After holding the foster baby for a bit, Warren had sat down with him on the kitchen floor to take a good long look at him.

At that point, Warren immediately voiced his opinion. "Bart? We are not having a dog named Bart."

"Bartimaeus?" I offered. Warren gave me a look that said it all: *Really?* That was not going to fly. We all agreed, it was far too grandiose for such a tiny boy, even for a temporary foster puppy in our household. "Baby Bart?"

Warren had not been amused. Ellie had taken his side. That's when Warren glanced down at the apparently misnamed pup, who had begun to play on the floor next to him, and observed, "He's pink. He looks like a very tiny baby pig. His name should be Piglet."

Piglet? True, he was pink. He even had a little pink nose that looked like a baby piggy's snout. Actually, he happened to look a lot like Piglet from *Winnie-the-Pooh*, even though that clearly wasn't what inspired the name.

Back on the kitchen floor with the pink baby pig look-alike wiggling between us, we were back to decision-making time. Warren went further, insisting, "Piglet is the perfect name."

Before saying a word to seal the deal, I scanned the room, counting the six-pack, who were all in various postures of repose, and flashed quickly to their arrivals in the household and how each got their names. As I brought those stories to mind, I had to admit the name Piglet made sense for our foster puppy. What didn't make sense was the question I couldn't yet answer: *How* did *we get so far over the "two-dog MAX" rule?*

❧

When we rescued Susie, the gray terrier mix, the move that Warren had tried to stop until he met her, she was not a puppy and already knew the name that had been given to her by her rescuer.

Plus, she looked like a Susie—so Susie (sometimes Susan) she would remain.

When we adopted Gina, our Aussie/border collie mix with compromised hearing and vision, her name was listed as Gianna. We all sat and thought that wasn't her at all, but that she should have a G name—for continuity—which really didn't matter to her. Gina wasn't much of a stretch or change, though we also call her Jeannie. Our handsome black Lab mix, Dean Martin, was named by someone at the shelter where he was dropped off after being picked up walking down a country road in Arkansas with his dog friend, who was named Frank Sinatra. After three months of living in the dog shelter, Dean had gotten to know his name, and it fit him perfectly.

Gina had been with us for ten months and was still a work in progress when we heard about Dean. I was happy with my two dogs, Susie and Gina, and had no interest in adopting another dog. The critical factor when we broke the rule this time and went from two to three dogs had actually been Rachael. She had insisted on keeping Dean Martin. Her exact words: "I will do *anything* to keep this dog." From that moment on, he led the VIP welcome she was given whenever she came through the door, however long she had been away. The dogs would follow Rachael around as a pack, vying for her attention, somehow aware that she loved them all. On her visits home, they would crowd onto her bed in a heap and all snuggle together.

By March of 2012, we were good with dogs. We had three kids at home and, with Susie, Gina, and Dean, a loving threesome. We were firm that this was it, no more dogs for a while. But then, a few months later, I saw a picture on Facebook of an irresistibly sweet four-month-old puppy in the arms of the adorable two-year-old son of my rescuer friend Morgan. The puppy, named Dizzy, was a four-pound blond/tan terrier mix rescued from a kill shelter in Bakersfield, California, by Morgan's rescue, Pet Matchmaker.

Earlier, when we got Gina from Gloria's group, Colbert Veterinary Rescue Services, in Georgia, Warren had been talking about how much he wanted a tan terrier. But we couldn't find any that fit our household. Here she was! Ellie, throwing out her own desire to keep the dog count at three, thought Dizzy was adorable but that if she was our puppy, her name would have to be Annie. Ellie and I were in the car together, on our way to New York for her violin lesson, when Warren called to say, "It would make me so happy if you would get that tan terrier for me," and Ellie cheered him on, endorsing the idea completely. This was all Warren; if it had been up to me, I would not have gotten any more dogs, even that adorable little tan terrier. However, he had asked.

Ellie printed out Dizzy/Annie's Petfinder post picture, taped a tiny dog biscuit to the photo, and hung it on the fridge. Warren and I were practically in tears. Her affection for a puppy she'd never met was so sweet. We decided not to tell the kids that I was going to Los Angeles to pick up Annie, mainly because we were in a position to carry out a major surprise for them, which was a rare opportunity. Also, we were embarrassed to be adding dog number four, so we were keeping it quiet. We had to come up with an alternate explanation. Ellie may have guessed that we would adopt Annie but didn't question us. However, when Daniel asked where I was going, I mumbled something random like, "I have to go see Aunt Marilyn and Uncle Woody in Boca Raton."

"Oh?" he said. The look on his face was skeptical. He knew that was unlikely.

Deep down, I had a nagging voice that asked me, *Do you really need another dog?* Ironically, this was the question that I would put to prospective dog adopters to make sure they were ready for the commitment. But this was for Warren, after all, and Morgan reassured me that Dizzy/Annie was the sweetest dog I would ever meet.

We did know that when the tan terrier mix was pulled from the shelter by Pet Matchmaker Rescue a few weeks earlier, she had been very sick with pneumonia secondary to kennel cough (though supposedly she had recovered and was ready to fly home with me). In rescue situations where lots of dogs are kept together, various respiratory diseases and other viruses spread through the group, with puppies being the most vulnerable. Adoption plans can be upended at the last minute due to unpredictable circumstances—even with the most reputable groups. The reason is that puppies aren't immune until they have had their full series of puppy vaccines. It's important to be understanding and be aware that a change in plans can happen. In our case, once I got to California and was driven by my friend Lorraine Ring two hours to Morgan's to pick up Annie, I had concerns. When I took Annie in my arms, I noticed that her respiratory rate was very high. Even though she was active and energetic, clearly her pneumonia was not resolved. Fortunately, I had brought antibiotics with me and got her started right away.

By now, I was very worried about how safe it would be to fly with a dog who had severe pneumonia. Since she seemed to be responding to the antibiotics I gave her within two days, it appeared she was safe to travel. My next big obstacle was boarding the plane. I was a complete wreck going through security because I hadn't ever traveled with a dog, let alone one that wasn't perfectly healthy. My flight wound up being delayed for a couple of hours, which gave me too much time to ruminate over all the possible issues my new sick puppy could have while flying. By the time I got to the airport, I was so worked up I found myself nervously shuffling through papers to dig out my ticket and Annie's flying documents over and over—to the point that I thought airline security would think I was a terrorist. Then I had to take the puppy out of her bag, which really shouldn't have been the big deal I was making of it. I figured I looked like I was hiding something, but as it turned out, everyone in the TSA made a big fuss over my adorable tiny tan puppy, which helped me to relax as I boarded the plane.

Warren scooped us up at the airport, thrilled by how cute and sweet she was in person. When I told him about her health concerns, he said, "Melissa, I know you will do everything humanly possible to make sure she recovers." We were instantly in love with her. By the time we got home, our three kids were fast asleep and we had to wait until the morning to reveal the big surprise. Ellie was overjoyed. Rachael and Daniel were smitten too. Annie was her meant-to-be name, and we were her meant-to-be family. She was the most adorable precious shy angel dog, who made our lives better from the moment she arrived.

All three dogs loved her immediately. Next to the bigger dogs and even Susie, in the beginning Annie looked so small, we called her Tiny. As she grew toward her adult weight of twelve pounds, we would say, "Don't grow, Tiny, don't grow!" Like all of our dogs, Annie has a main job that she takes great pride in—getting the mail. It's a part of her regular routine that she gets to do without the rest of the dogs. When we say to her, "Job!" she comes to be picked up and carried out to get the mail.

On occasion, I've been asked why the other dogs don't get a turn getting to go get the mail. "Because," I explain, "this is not their job. This is Annie's job. They have their own jobs."

Annie can get a head of steam going and play rough, every now and then, but her main idiosyncrasy turned out to be an interesting preoccupation with small pieces of paper. Annie never did this in front of us. Whenever we'd return from having been out, we would walk in to find business cards and money shredded up all over the floor. We knew it was Annie because the other dogs didn't have the outrageous habit of visiting the top of the kitchen table in secret and because they weren't into paper! To prevent this ongoing paper demolition, we started scanning the kitchen table when we left the house to be sure there was nothing of value left for Annie the Shredder to shred.

Evie had been known to get in on the act and go up on the table too, only she was much more brazen and would do it in front of us. Once, Evie took a pen over to the couch to chew it open, leaving a large ink spot in the center of our cloth furniture. Small tip here: rubbing alcohol removes ink from upholstery.

Evie—whom we adopted at about seven months of age in November 2012—came with her name. The first I saw of her was on the same Facebook page for Pet Matchmaker where I found Annie. Evie had been dumped at the shelter in a box that had been taped up and labeled with her name on it. Usually, I change a name whenever a dog comes from a horrible past like that. In Evie's case, though she looked disheveled and worried, the name fit her, and I felt a strong connection to the puppy and her name.

"Oh, look." I showed Warren, joking because she looked nothing like Annie, "It's Annie's sister. We have to adopt her!" I couldn't get her face out of my mind. From joking I seriously insisted to Warren, "We should have Morgan send her to us. If it doesn't work out, she'll be easy to place." Little fluffy white nonshedding poodle-mix-type rescued dogs are very desirable.

Warren didn't bother trying to talk me out of it. "Just get her" was all he said, but I didn't dare bring it up again in case he changed his mind.

As before, I had to come up with a cover story when I went to JFK to pick Evie up. This time, my excuse was an appointment with a client's dog while Warren and Ellie went shopping. I'm not sure why it didn't occur to them that something was up, because I left the house before seven a.m. on a Saturday. I'll never forget how Evie—sometimes called Evita—looked at me when I picked her up at the airport after she had been in transit for twelve hours. Her expression said it all: *What a journey it's been—take me home!*

She bulleted out of the crate, wiggling and wagging her little stump of a tail. I cleaned the crate up but felt terrible putting her back in for the ride home from New York. But once I got her back to Westport and gave her a much-needed bath, her transformation began. With lots of love and what turned into a couple of years of dog-training classes, we eventually became quite the team.

When Warren and Ellie returned that first day from their shopping expedition, they hadn't even gotten out of the car when I went out to greet them at the top of the porch with our newly adopted fluffy white dog. When they stepped out of the car, I announced, "Look who's here."

"Oh, it's Evie!" Ellie said, recognizing her.

"No," Warren said, "that's one of Joanne Raus's dogs," mistaking her for Olivia, my client Joanne's dog.

"No, Ellie's right, this is Evie."

Warren gave me his *are you kidding me?* look. But here we were.

Why I went out of my way to get a fifth dog, I had no idea. The rational me knew it was a ridiculous thing to do, but the caretaker in me felt inexplicably connected from the second I saw her Facebook post. I could help this dog. That little white dog who looked so disheveled and in need in her picture had lured me right in. People say they need to meet the dog in order to know if it's a good match. It seems fair to say I'm not one of those people. I didn't need to meet

Annie or Evie or Zoey to know they would fit right in. I could have been wrong, but I paid attention to their descriptions and had an idea of what I was getting. I also knew that they were small, nonshedding, sweet dogs who would be very easy to find good homes for if they didn't fit in at our house. So if it really wasn't going to work, we would be able to move them on very quickly.

It didn't take long for Evie to trust and bond with me. We never looked back. I never knew her full story, but whoever threw her away had lost the most beautiful treasure of a loving, happy dog. In time, she became the ideal dog for veterinary demo workshops, especially for kids. She is a well-behaved, easy travel partner. Really, an all-around perfect dog.

The history of the name "Zoey" and the arrival of our sixth dog is probably worthy of professional analysis. Suffice to say for the moment, after five dogs, your powers of rationalization are so frayed by that point, you think, *What is* one *more?* How much work could an itty-bitty chocolate baby Chihuahua/Yorkie-Maltese mix be?

When we first saw pictures of the litter of six puppies rescued by a group in Arkansas, Warren wanted the tan puppy but I fell in love with the smallest all-brown girl—who had only a speck of white under her chin and on one of her back right toes. The others all had more pronounced white accents. I told Warren I was going to ask the rescuer, Belinda Minney, which one would be most likely to be the ultimate lapdog. She told me, "Noelle"—so named because it was right before Christmas—was the one I wanted, ha. So I reserved the chocolate puppy and told Warren, "You can rename her whatever you want."

The name he wanted was "Zoey"—which had been the name of his first, much-beloved dog. When I was pregnant with our first child, Warren and I had actually settled on the girl name "Zoey Rachael" before labor. We were happy with the name choice until there was a major drama at the hospital minutes after our first baby girl was born. Warren's mother—generally nonintrusive—came in to see me, literally five minutes after I had given birth to my first baby, and put on a hard sell that we name her "Rachael Alana," in honor of Warren's uncle Raymond who had recently passed away. I was in my most vulnerable of conditions—really. I had just been through eighteen hours of back labor, and at that point she could have named the baby Mud and I would have agreed.

So Zoey Rachael became Rachael Alana, which left the name Zoey open for another baby. When I was expecting our youngest and deciding on her name, Rachael had desperately wanted us to name her Pocahontas but settled for Ellie because her best friend in nursery school had a sister by that name. That meant the name Zoey was still available for our new little girl dog.

In my opinion, naming a dog after another dog who has passed away can cause the second dog to have to live up to unfair expectations. But Warren had waited for many years to grace a female family member with that name. So Noelle became Zoey—often called ZoZo. I was happy for Warren, as the Dog Dad to all of our six, that he had finally gotten his wish.

That extensive backstory was why I quickly agreed with Warren that Bart wasn't a great name for the pink puppy. For many reasons, I very much wanted Warren to feel good about the project.

I didn't dislike the name "Piglet." I was fine with it. But first, I had to think through the different parameters. I had so much respect for Gloria and her rescue group that I didn't want to offend them by changing the name. The real problem was that he was only going to stay with us briefly as a foster dog, so wouldn't it be presumptuous to change his name?

It didn't really matter, though. He couldn't hear us, after all. Finally, I said, "We could call him Piglet unofficially." The rescue group could list him as Piglet/Bart.

Warren began to clear the table and called over his shoulder, "I vote 'yes.'"

Ellie popped up from her seat in relief. On the way toward the stairs to return to urgent prep for an AP Physics test, Ellie added, "I think 'Piglet/Bart' will appeal to his new forever family."

Warren and I stared at the pink wide-awake baby in my hands. I asked him directly, as if he weren't deaf, "What do you think, Piglet?"

Like clockwork, he started to scream—which was as good a "yes" as I was going to get.

MARCH 5, 2017
ON THE ROAD TO THE REIKI WORKSHOP
IN FAIR⁵ELD, CONNECTICUT

The Sunday highway traffic on my early morning drive to Fairfield for a long-planned Reiki workshop on Piglet's second day as our foster dog was unusually sparse. Inside the car, without any of the dogs accompanying me, I decided against putting on any music. Instead, I chose to soak up the silence and get myself into a pre-mindful state—an oxymoron when you consider how my brain was going a mile a minute about whether or not it was a good idea to be going to this Reiki healing workshop in the first place.

The night before had been nearly sleepless. Most of it had been spent on the couch downstairs with the pink tiny one asleep in my arms.

As we were to learn increasingly, Piglet is an unusually engaged dog who connects to his environment and the people in it with his whole being. He gets to "know" his space in a most practical, survivalist, intelligent way. In seven weeks of a life filled with passages of terror, he had already managed to cultivate his extrasensory-powered ability to "see" with his nose and maneuver with his tactile facilities—both giving him his own inner GPS system. I'd watched him on day one, without hearing or sight, begin to map his surroundings and connect details to the distinct smells of the different inhabitants—remembering all of that in his brilliantly compartmentalized brain for the next time. The amount of work this entailed must have been exhausting, yet every time I tried to get Piglet settled in our bedroom in either the little cocoon bed or his crate (clearly his mortal enemy), he'd go ballistic crying.

Not knowing what to do, I spent the first night (as I would most of the second night) holding Piglet as I sat on the couch, trying to strategize how to get him to sleep outside of our bed. No solutions were imminent. One of the big challenges of fostering is to make sure that your foster pet doesn't develop habits that will make him or her difficult for the new family. Many people don't want dogs sleeping in their beds, especially tiny puppies. I was also worried that he'd wedge himself under me, or fall off the bed, or that either Warren or I would roll over and crush him.

In the meantime, I'd decided not to back out of the Reiki workshop I'd planned and prepaid to attend that Sunday from ten to three. Up until this time, I'd been taking a gentle yoga class at Yoga for Everyone in Fairfield with instructor Joy Levine Abrams—who had a real talent for bringing her students to a new level of awareness and relaxation. When the studio offered the Reiki course, I was eager to attend and curious to learn how it worked, mostly for personal reasons, but also for possible uses in helping some of my older arthritic dog patients.

Hoping to be able to go, when I called Monica—my friend and colleague, and the vet tech who had already bonded with the pink foster baby—I wasn't sure how she would respond to a last-minute request for babysitting a puppy who needed so much attention. "I hate to impose . . ." I had begun on the phone call to her.

Before I could complete my request, Monica—who is from Spain—burst forth in a musical rush of excitement, telling me, "Piglet! I love the name. So much better than Bart! Would I mind? No, you would never impose. I would love it! Bring him!" She called to her husband, Armando, her daughter, Amanda, and son, Manuel, telling them, "Dr. Shapiro is going to let us babysit the pink puppy I told you about!" Back to me, she added, "We can't wait. Don't worry. I got you, girlfriend."

Bright and early, I roused Piglet—who had slept fine even if I hadn't—and got him ready. I packed up everything under the sun—food, toys, pee pads, little sweaters, blankets, his harness and leash, his little crate, and lots of treats. This was ten times worse than sending my kids to camp. I was a nervous wreck. Piglet was teeny. At the same time, the novelty of the situation made me a little bit happy, knowing how much I would learn from all sources of information about how to connect with this teeny little creature.

When we arrived at Monica's, he immediately began to wag his tail with exuberance and recognition. She took him in her arms and started kissing him, murmuring sweet nothings that were part Spanish and fragments of lots of other languages.

"He remembers you from yesterday." I smiled, relaxing slightly.

We realized he was smelling her breath. "You know what it is?" she noted, with an added insight. "The cilantro!" At that, Piglet slid down and made his way under her sweater to the comfort zone he recognized from the day before. This was one of many ways that Monica had learned to calm scared little creatures who liked being warmed by her body and where they could hear her heartbeat. "He'll be fine!" she called after me as I left, feeling like the parent of a child who has been dropped off at school and doesn't give a second thought to Mom or Dad.

Back in the car and on the road, I was both grateful to Monica—knowing what taking responsibility for such a special little guy meant—but also beginning to feel conflicted about the reality of how fast he would find a home once his adorable picture was posted on Petfinder. *The adoptive home had to be just right,* I thought, already starting to feel myself becoming protective and concerned about every aspect of Piglet's future.

In a way that was somewhat awkward, I could see myself becoming disproportionately concerned as I left Piglet, considering that I barely knew him. Logically, I knew all would be well with him in Monica's care. He was already in love with her, and she is one of the most reliable friends I have.

In hindsight, I should have realized that my discomfort at being separated from Piglet/Bart was a sign. I had fostered enough dogs and birds to know that this one was already panning out to be a much different experience. My attempts at keeping an emotional distance—so important for fostering dogs—were already not working.

With that small, mindful lecture to myself, I drove on to my workshop, confident that Monica would handle anything that came up. Monica is one of the funniest people I know. She is a rock star at the hospital—sincere, caring, with high energy for doing whatever needs to get done in any situation. She is smart, friendly, and has a special touch with all animals. She is always taking care of an orphaned or injured puppy, wild baby bird, chicken (she has chickens), or even a turtle. One of her three dogs was a purebred puppy who had been brought in to the vet hospital to be euthanized because she had congenital front leg deformities. The puppy had been born without elbow joints and had to move either on straight legs like stilts or by crawling. Monica stepped in immediately with an offer to adopt the puppy and provide whatever accommodations were necessary to assure that the little one had a good quality of life. To Monica, her new puppy was an amazing, adaptive creature who learned to hop instead of walking in pain.

Monica said she'd felt deeply that her adopted special-needs puppy just needed a chance—the name she ultimately gave her. Her philosophy was always that every creature deserves a chance. After a few months, Chance was out of the woods, and thriving! Everyone in Monica's circle adored Chance, including her family from Spain—which was where Chance eventually went to live. "That traitor," Monica joked, happy that her world-traveling dog could bring her mother and aunt such happiness.

Although the Reiki workshop was calming and meditative, I found my mind wandering to wondering how the tiny pink puppy was faring. By the end of the five hours, I was anxious to get back to my foster project, and I hurried back to Monica's. When I picked him up, saying, "Well, hello, Piglet," and bringing him in for a snuggle, I noticed there wasn't much of a tail wag.

"So much for being excited to see me." I laughed. He honestly couldn't have cared less about me showing up for him.

This would soon become a pattern. Piglet would dance in circles for others but never for me on those occasions when I would come home from being out. There has never been a doubt about whether or not he loves me; our bond is evident—but I've made peace with the knowledge that his tail wags were reserved for others. Maybe I took on the role of mother/teacher, and not a playmate. The funny, poignant part of it was that over the next couple of weeks we became closer and more connected by the day. Maybe there is something in our wiring as humans and animals that tells us one day we will need to separate from our moms and be okay in the world without them, and Piglet was just getting started early.

At any rate, the day had been a total success. I was happy and relieved to hear all about how he'd just hung out, bundled up under Monica's shirt with his head sticking out, and how his nose never stopped as she cooked and cleaned. He had "watched" television with them, sitting on Armando's lap, and played on the floor with her kids. They spoiled him with treats, catering to Piglet's every whim, supervising him as he played with their two dogs, Rosa and Linda.

The big outing was a trip to the Stop & Shop food store. Monica couldn't leave him at home or in the car, so she tucked him in her shirt to hang out while she shopped. Only his little pink face was showing, which drew quite a bit of attention and double takes from unsuspecting passersby.

When Monica walked us to the car, Piglet had an expression on his face that looked as close to a smile as I had seen on him. "Thank you, Dr. Shapiro," she said in her formal Spanish way, even though she also calls me Melissa. "We had a wonderful day! We'll never forget it."

Without saying so, we both knew a day like this one might not come again. Soon Piglet would find a family, not unlike hers, that would be his forever home. "No, please, Monica," I told her, "my thanks are to you and your family. Seeing him bond and engage with everyone has been a true relief."

Why I expected anything different, I don't know. Piglet was a dog who happened to be deaf and blind. That in no way would keep him from developing close relationships with people and other dogs. This little guy was capable of everything any other dog was. It was an important reminder to me that with my background and interest in dogs with special needs, a priority of fostering was to give him a chance to find his best life. Keeping that in mind would help us prepare to let him go.

When we arrived home from Monica's, he sniffed around and sorted out who was where, checking in with the other dogs and, of course, his foster dad, who got an enthusiastic tail-wagging greeting. Piglet seemed content, after a day spent with Monica and her family. At least, that's how it seemed for a minute, before he launched back into his screaming self.

After that, Warren and I were pretty clear that I would have to focus on getting him out of here ASAP, to his forever home, which was not ours!

During the next week, I wasted no time in starting to teach Piglet tap signals—which began one evening after I put the pink puppy's little bowl down for him in his eating crate.

He was extremely food-motivated, diving ravenously into every meal, which set us up with the opportunity to start to communicate using a process of teaching tap signals that is much like clicker training, without the click.

My own tutorial for using tap signals had come from my dog trainer friend Allison Holloway, from Columbus, Ohio, who specializes in teaching dogs who are blind, deaf, or both. There really is no difference in the fundamentals used for teaching dogs who don't have special needs—except that the voice or the hand signal is replaced with a tap. The tricks and the treats are the same. The biggest challenge with taps for Piglet was that he was so small there were limited places to tap!

In my first attempt, I lured his nose up into the air with a tiny treat, which in turn caused his little butt to plunk down, putting him into a sitting position. I gave him the treat as he sat, and he quickly realized I was rewarding him for the sit. After he was sitting reliably, instead of saying the word "sit," I gave him a gentle tap on his lower back as he was moving into the sitting position, getting his treat as he completed his "sit." It only took a few times for him to put things together—the tap meant "sit," and then a treat was coming.

With that tap on his back, just above his tail, I'd say, "Piglet, sit" (even though he couldn't hear), as he'd sit back on his haunches, understanding completely what I was asking.

When the cookie was accompanied by an approving pat from me, he clearly knew that we had just connected in a new and delicious way. Flash forward a few days—his real excitement over learning to sit came when Warren practiced with him. After a perfect sit followed by a cookie from his foster dad, Piglet broke out into an exuberant celebration, with boisterous tail wagging and squeals of delight.

That's how Warren, right then and there during that first week, got his name and title as Piglet's Favorite Dad. He was clearly the deaf blind pink puppy's favorite person and his only dad in the picture for the time being. Warren was crowned Favorite Dad and known far and wide as such from then on.

Chapter 4

FAVORITE DAD

"I want you to know, no matter what happens, you will always be my first wife."
—Warren Shapiro, lovingly spoken to me just after
we exchanged wedding vows

From the start, the pink boy had connected to Warren so definitively it was no mere accident—whether it was greeting his foster dad with the most adorable tail-wagging wiggle dance, running around and through Warren's legs out in our yard, or snuggling into his warm winter vest for a good nap.

Warren—who made a career switch from social work to biotech pharmaceutical sales when we both realized that we had three kids to put through college—had grown up without pets in the household. Warren's mother, Ruth, a warm, deeply compassionate person and a Holocaust survivor, who wanted her four kids to have whatever would make their lives happier, couldn't convince Warren's father to even consider having a dog. A towering and challenging personality, his dad was an Ivy League–educated mathematician, a contemporary of both John Nash (*A Beautiful Mind*) and Einstein at Princeton, and a celebrated academic in his own right. He didn't care for dogs, and that was the rule: NO DOGS. In Warren's house—when he was growing up—rules made by his dad were NEVER broken! In our house that was not nearly the case.

This may well have fueled Warren's lifelong fascination with making "rules" that were not rigid and sometimes limiting, but rather enabled growth and enrichment. He also developed a disarming, hilarious, and sometimes really inappropriate sense of humor that served him well professionally and socially.

"When I left home," he recounted to me when we first met, "it was no longer my life according to my dad's rules, so I took the lead in the *Warren Shapiro Show*, starring Warren Shapiro." Of course, that changed, according to Warren, when the two of us got together and I became the star in the *Warren Shapiro Show* and the credits then read "Starring MELISSA SHAPIRO, with Warren Shapiro."

As soon as Warren graduated from college, he got his first dog— the first Zoey—whom he shared with his then-girlfriend, Sandee. Zoey, in Warren's eyes, was a perfect dog—a medium-sized scruffy black-and-gray mutt from the Detroit dog pound, totally street smart, who followed him everywhere without needing a leash. She immediately transformed him into a dog person. Soon after her came Jamie, a light tannish, cream-colored female wheaten terrier mix.

In Warren's mind, being a two-dog household was ideal. Zoey and Jamie kept each other company when Warren and Sandee were out at work. Once Jamie grew out of her puppy stage, she, like Zoey, was attentive and well-behaved. When Warren and Sandee broke up, they agreed to each take a dog. Warren had the hardest time deciding, so Sandee offered, "Why don't you take Zoey and I'll keep Jamie?"

Two years later, when Warren lost Zoey to cancer, a devastating heartbreak, Sandee called him and said, "Why don't you take Jamie? You need her more than I do." Sandee's generosity was a complete selfless act of kindness. She loved Jamie as much as Warren did but couldn't imagine him without a dog.

When I met Warren, he was as attached to Jamie as I was to April. Jamie went to work with him at the nonprofit family services agency in Greenwich where Warren was employed when he moved to Connecticut in 1989. When he later took a position as director of admissions at a nearby nursing home, Jamie could roam the halls on her own—making friends with the residents and welcoming newcomers with her calming presence and always-wagging tail.

Even though Warren's history with pets started later than mine, by the time we started dating one of our strongest initial bonds was that we were both absolutely devoted to our dogs. Whenever we're asked how Warren and I first met, I gladly defer to him to answer—with some interjections from me. For obvious reasons, we have very different backstories that led each of us, separately, on the evening of Friday, June twenty-second, 1990, to the bike racks outside the Darien, Connecticut, train station, the starting point for the Sound Cyclists Bicycle Club's weekly Friday-night ride.

At that point, Warren was not an experienced, hard-core cyclist as I already was—even though he was naturally athletic and pretty competitive. In high school, he'd been an avid, serious basketball player. Once he was in college, however, he didn't have much time for sports, so he started running for exercise—in addition to pickup games of basketball now and then. Whenever he went home to New Hyde Park, Long Island, he had a particular route that he'd run from his parents' house all the way to the high school, around the track, and back home again—a good four miles or so. Warren has told me, "I ran all the time but didn't really like running, so I used to daydream to keep going."

Turns out that as he ran, Warren frequently imagined that along the way, as he was running through the neighborhood and around and around that track, somewhere, somehow, there was a very nice girl running around a track whom he would meet someday and that "She would be perfect for me."

That is his version of Genesis, the "in the beginning" part of how he saw something of a divine plan in our initial encounter. Good timing—or, you could say, a blunder of timing—must have been part of the divine plan too.

When he started work at the family service agency in Greenwich, he was single. In the days before the Internet and dating apps, the main way that people socialized and connected was the old-fashioned blind-date setup. Apparently, a friend he knew from his work thought the perfect girl for him was a member of the Sound Cyclists Bicycle Club and that the best way for the two to meet would be for him to go on their regular Friday-night ride and join the rest of the group for the usual dinner afterward. That way, if things didn't work out, there was no pressure, and they would still have a good time. Their mutual friends made the introduction, and the fate of Warren's love life was all but sealed.

By this period, I was already a graduate of Purdue University College of Veterinary Medicine and had completed a rotating internship at the Animal Medical Center in New York City, as well as a residency that followed in small-animal internal medicine at the University of Pennsylvania School of Veterinary Medicine in Philadelphia. Coming almost full circle, by the end of 1989 I had moved back to Connecticut with my beloved April and my tiny ferret, Cindy, for a job at Davis Animal Hospital in Stamford. Close to Darien, Westport, and Norwalk to the north, and Greenwich to the south, Stamford was a convenient location. My apartment was close to work, the shopping mall, and many great public spaces, including the Stamford Nature Center, and the Cove—the town beach with a beautiful park that's situated on a scenic stretch of the shore along the northern side of the Long Island Sound.

My parents were, of course, delighted for me to be close to home again now that I was moving ahead with my professional calling. In their loving, generous, enabling fashion, my mother and father were especially eager to help improve my love life. Ever since my high school days and my first serious boyfriend, they had happily cheered the news whenever I told them that I was going on a date. Now that I was back in the vicinity of my home turf, they started to drop frequent hints that maybe I should do a better job of actively looking to meet someone. Whenever I stopped by, always with April attentively at my side, my parents would greet us both and usher us inside, offering a cold drink, as they'd ask, "Have you eaten?" By the time I'd leave, I would have not only had a snack but I'd be sent home with full meals in plastic containers, and supplies for my apartment—toilet paper and paper towels.

On one particular visit, I can recall complimenting my mother on a new outfit she was wearing—"Nice shirt, Mom!"—and her immediately responding, "You want it?"

Laughing at this sweet, funny, and familiar response, I told her, "No, Mom, it looks good on you!" Besides, I added, I had just gone clothes shopping for myself. After prodding from her and from Dad to hear what I'd bought, I described some of the slacks and tops I'd purchased for work and the latest in workout items that I wore on my longer bike rides.

The minute I reported my purchases, I regretted it. "No dresses?" my mother asked. For most of my teen years she begged me to wear more dresses. In my professional life she was even more adamant and wondered why I didn't wear a touch of makeup. "You know, a little lipstick?" It's not that I disliked dresses, it's just that as a vet, we spend a lot of time kneeling and talking to animals at their level, and makeup wasn't in my repertoire. Not to mention, I'm allergic to even the hypoallergenic products! When I told them about my new bike clothes, I braced myself for comments about the amount of time I spent riding my bicycle.

Even though I had continued to run throughout college, by my junior year at Purdue I'd become a devoted bicyclist. As a member of the Wabash River Cycle Club of Lafayette, Indiana, I looked forward to going for long rides with the club on weekends—all of us out for hours, traveling on picturesque county roads that wound through fields of corn and soybean crops. As summer progressed, I loved observing how the cornstalks grew higher and higher by the week, so that by the end of the summer it was like riding through a tunnel with cornstalks planted right to the edge of each side of the road. The rural Midwestern scenery looked like a scene from a movie. On a hot summer day without a cloud in the blue sky, I threw myself into the joy, freedom, and challenge of the ride.

So it was only natural for me to quickly join the Sound Cyclists Bicycle Club as soon as I moved back to Connecticut. Most of the members were serious if not seasoned athletes, and many of the rides were long and tough. Throughout the winter of 1989/1990, I was out on freezing-cold weekends racing up and down hills, clocking countless miles, and getting into the most amazing shape of my life.

"You know," my mother mentioned, as soon as I described the new bike shorts I'd bought, "instead of all the bike riding, why don't you attend some organized social events for singles?"

My father added, "That's not a bad idea. You know the ones that go to some of the nice bars?"

Mom piped up again, "Or get your girlfriends together and go do some aerobics classes."

This was not the first time they had made suggestions along the same lines.

For a minute I tried to rationalize going to a nice upscale bar to meet prospective dates, but then I asked my parents, "Can you see me in a bar? Standing there with a glass of water, talking about dogs? You know I don't drink, and I can't be around cigarette smoke."

My parents carefully noted that they didn't see the bike club as a way to meet a potential boyfriend. To them, bike riding was not really social enough. My mom, who only meant well, suggested that the problem with the bike clubs was that the guys were "kind of odd." How she came up with that, I have no idea, because the male cyclists I knew were generally really nice and exceptional athletes. It's not like I was one of those cool types. I couldn't resist saying, "I have my own odd side, and I am perfectly capable of meeting the right person at the right time."

Two weeks later, after a ride, I had my first sighting of one Warren Shapiro. Tall and good-looking, he strolled over confidently—despite his lime-green short shorts, Converse sneakers, and a mountain bike with nubby tires that was a good thirty pounds heavier than almost every other lightweight bicycle ridden by the well over sixty riders who were out that June evening. Here's how Warren tells that story:

Late that afternoon, I went home and settled my dog, Jamie, in at my apartment (she had been with me all day at work) and hustled out to the railroad station in Darien for my first Sound Cyclists bike ride. A twenty-one-mile-long course, the ride had a short break at mile twelve or so. But it was mostly a sprint. Neither I, nor my bike, were built for speed. Still,

I wasn't concerned, even when I showed up and saw a lot of folks all decked out in top-of-the-line biking apparel, and seemingly everyone had a fancy, lightweight, built-for-speed road bike. The gathering was quite hectic before the ride, and I could not find the girl who was supposed to be my blind date. My friends had described her in a way that made me think of the runner who was going to be the perfect girl for me. Certain that we'd meet afterward, I was confident that this ride would go well because I was pretty fit and a decent athlete. Nothing could be further from the truth. Out of nearly five dozen riders, men and women of all sizes, shapes, and ages, I came in dead last. I thought I was going to die! The lesson I learned that evening was that cycling isn't just about fitness; it's also about your skills as a cyclist and your equipment. I had a very heavy bike and no skills.

After finishing the ride, I rolled into the parking lot of the railroad station, ready to go find my date, and saw this very pretty girl leaning up against the back of a car. She was next to a guy who was all decked out in oddly colorful, trendy bike attire. She looked fresh as a daisy and really spectacular in her formfitting Lycra bike outfit. I remember thinking, *Why is it that all the great girls end up with guys like this?* I'm sure I was quite the sight in my neon green short shorts, with my totally out-of-place mountain bike, looking like I was on the verge of collapse! Nonetheless I rode over, tried to fake some dignity and confidence, and introduced myself. We chatted. She was very nice, and I found out that she was just friends with that guy and not "with" him. Everyone went out to dinner after the ride, and when I asked how to get there, she offered for me to follow her to the restaurant in my car. I did eventually find the blind-date girl who was supposed to meet me. She was nice but, ironically, she had to go home to walk her dog, so she wasn't able to go to dinner!

I followed that first girl, Melissa, to the restaurant and did my best to be amusing. She also told me she was a vet and gave me her card. I wasn't sure if she was looking to get me as a customer or what, but I was just happy to have her phone number. I asked her if we could go for a bike ride sometime with the club. She said sure.

Despite the fact that I was thirty-four years old at the time and I had dated an average number of women prior (more than one, less than fifty), I remember calling my sister that night and telling her, "I just met the girl I'm going to marry."

Two days later, at around three p.m. on Sunday afternoon, I heard from Warren Shapiro, who greeted me warmly, asking which rides I was going on that weekend—which I still think is such a bad icebreaker. The weekend was almost over, and I had already gone on a forty-mile ride both Saturday and Sunday mornings. Sitting in my apartment in Stamford, I glanced over at April with almost a shrug—as if to ask her what she thought about a guy who calls up late on a Sunday to ask about weekend bike rides that had already happened.

Nonetheless, I said yes to going for a dinner date a couple of nights later. He scored some points when he suggested we both bring our dogs to the Cove in Stamford—the beach area that has very nice walking paths. We talked, walked with the dogs, ate some Chinese food we'd picked up on the way to the beach, and sat on a stone wall looking out at the Long Island Sound.

At one point, I confessed to having a wicked stomachache, and Warren was very reassuring and comforting. He made me laugh a lot, but he also laughed even harder at my quips. We hit it off with each other's dogs—a major test, though April was somewhat aloof with Jamie.

On that first date, as we chatted about a variety of subjects, we stumbled onto a series of coincidences that added even more luster to the growing sparkle of our connection. Talking about our families, Warren mentioned that his father's first name was Harold, that he had been educated at an Ivy League college, and was born in the Bronx.

"*My* father's name is Harold, he went to an Ivy League College, and was born in the Bronx."

The next coincidence we discovered was that not only did we both have fathers named Harold but we both had brothers named Marc—and both spelled their names with a *C* (not a *K*) and both were lawyers. We thought all this was rather comical and a good sign.

Between a love for dogs and animals in general, along with classical music concerts, and, yes, biking, we had a busy, wonderful courtship. Warren, competitor and athlete that he is, soon rode at the front of the pack, giving me a run for my money. We went for long rides every weekend and sometimes during the week.

Shortly after we started to see each other, I invited Warren to come over to meet my parents so he could see for himself what he was getting himself into. I'm not sure what I told him directly other than that my mother would be delighted that I had a boyfriend.

Well, not only was she thrilled to meet Warren, but also she immediately changed her stance on bike riding and became a devoted fan of the Sound Cyclists Bicycle Club. She was soon touting its virtues and recommending that her friends' kids join like I had.

After several months of spending all our free time together, we were hanging out at my place one night when Warren said, "I've been thinking that we probably should get married." He waited for my response. Had he just proposed?

"You're right," I agreed.

Warren swooped in for a kiss with our dogs as witnesses. "Are you happy?" he asked.

"Yes, I am," I said, and I was.

In that romantic state, I clarified, "I am happy, but my mother is going to be REALLY happy."

And she was. Even though we weren't at all into the hoopla of a wedding, my mother was so over the moon, we agreed to let her plan a more traditional celebration, which she'd wanted to do for years. She dragged me to Brooklyn to find the very best bridal gown, when I would have been fine with a choice off the rack, and to an expensive florist who was aghast at the simple flowers I requested.

Weddings tend to fill me with dread. I didn't even want to go to my own. Some of the traditions that go along with weddings are even worse—like wedding showers. I understand why others are so into these kinds of parties, but they're just not for me.

"Mom," I said, "under no circumstances are you to make me a bridal shower."

She agreed without argument at the time but somehow got caught up going all out with planning and decided instead to make the shower a surprise—inviting many guests who traveled for miles to attend. Warren had to spill the beans because he couldn't figure out how to keep it a secret and tell me enough lies to get me there. I showed up and acted surprised and tickled, knowing that my mom couldn't help herself. The gathering was actually fun—although I ended up returning most of the Victoria's Secret-themed gifts that I received.

Our one request was that Warren and I wanted our dogs, April and Jamie, to be in the wedding. We set the date for a few days shy of a year after we met. As it got closer to the date, the rabbi couldn't okay having dogs inside the temple, so we settled with having them in the wedding photos that were taken outside before the ceremony. Thankfully, we took the photos then, as there was a huge thunderstorm that struck afterward. When we gathered the wedding party outside for the photos, it was one hundred degrees and rising. Everybody was sweating, the dogs were panting, eager to go home, and I was wishing I'd gone with my gut, had a small outdoor gathering at a beach or park, and had our dogs there. But ultimately, I'm glad my mother got to plan the beautiful wedding that mattered so much to her. The lesson was a valuable one in other respects—that while I'm not always of a mainstream mind, I am comfortable enough participating in the mainstream.

We planned an adventurous biking honeymoon that took us to the San Juan Islands of Washington State and almost ended the marriage that had barely begun. This was a tour that included excellent lodging, food, and daily rides that varied in levels of difficulty. By that time, we were both serious cyclists, so we shipped out our own bikes—only to discover in our hotel room that they had arrived broken down into more pieces than we could begin to easily reassemble. Warren, propped up in the bed with pillows like a king, was screaming at the top of his lungs that a screw was missing and "We're leaving! That's it!"

Warren's family members do not fix things that are broken. They have other skills, but figuring out instructions that involve construction or engineering are not in their repertoire. Luckily, my father had taught me to see the big picture, stay calm, and take one step at a time. He had also shown me how to do those kinds of fix-it things. So I put both bikes together, even though I was thinking, *My Prince Charming is ruining our honeymoon!* Recalling this scene years later, Warren, mortified, swore that if he had been me, he would have left him right there!

As soon as I got the bikes built and ready to roll, everything was fine. We had an amazing time, and rode up the switchback road to the top of Mount Constitution, one of the toughest road bike climbs in the country. We could not have been more perfect for each other, and I agreed with him from then on that the day we met was the luckiest day of both of our lives.

🐾

Lots of people say that there's nothing like coparenting pets to let you know how you and your partner will be at parenting actual children. In our case, I know that we benefitted from having time together to learn how to be a team. Warren and I were great at balancing each other out. When I was serious and focused, Warren worked hard to be supportive but also kept things light. When he became impatient and frustrated, I knew how to step in and break the problem into solvable smaller parts. He is a big-picture person, and I am too, but I also like to get down to the nuts and bolts. We both knew from the start how to pick and choose our battles, and we both recognized that love means participating in each other's passions. The nicest thing for me was that we were similarly invested in each of our dogs, April and Jamie.

During the three years before we had kids, we wasted no time pushing ahead with our respective careers and, at least in my case, daring to go against the traditional grain.

Early on in my veterinary career, building my own house-call practice was the furthest thing from my mind. I was planning to be a specialist, and I was going to work in a referral hospital with the latest high-tech equipment and support staff. Little did I know, my extensive postgraduate training was preparing me for a wild ride as a "specialist," but not a mainstream specialist that would be certified by a battery of tests and other requirements.

Around the time when Warren and I had first started dating, I realized that my original plan—to become an internal medicine specialist, for which I had done all the required training—wasn't going in that direction. Instead, I ended up working in a large multidoctor general practice. Though I was able to offer high-level care to my patients—thanks to all the latest in-house technology—the demands of seeing numerous animals per hour in fifteen-minute appointment blocks made the working environment into something of a rat race. No offense to rats! After a year or so, following a denied request for a raise, I understood there were disagreements about my worth to the practice, and I realized it was time to move on.

The concept of veterinary house calls was not trending at the time. However, as I'd already been doing some house calls for friends on the side, the idea wasn't completely out of the blue. There was only one vet doing house calls in our whole county, but I found his practice model to be very much what I was looking for. As I chatted about it with Warren, I admitted, "I like the idea of being out on my own. Plus I'd be able to take the dogs with me every day."

Warren echoed, "Knowing you, you'll feel good about having flexibility in your schedule, and the extra time that you can enjoy spending with your clients and patients. No more fifteen-minute appointments! And you'll be your own boss."

Was that radical? No. My dad had built his business after years of working for big institutions and corporations. So could I.

I slid into it slowly and gradually, with two part-time jobs that replaced the salary I had left in my full-time job. During my launch period, I advertised and began to build the Visiting Veterinary Service. The name was eventually shortened to Visiting Vet Service. Within six months I had accumulated a healthy client base that allowed me to quit both part-time jobs. House calls appealed to people in all walks of life, and I understood that in the beginning, to be successful, I needed to make myself available for appointments wherever and whenever. I would drive around house to house in a white VW Jetta filled with veterinary supplies. There were no in-house blood analyzers, no vet techs or receptionists, no X-ray or ultrasound, no computers, and certainly NO cell phones. But I had years of clinical experience, and a carefully crafted veterinary supply box, which enabled me to do a thorough in-home physical exam and assessment of most dog and cat medical situations. I also carried a wide variety of medications, which I was able to dispense as needed. I made an arrangement with a local vet hospital that enabled me to provide full-service veterinary care to all of my patients.

Warren would come with me to appointments on occasion, but mostly, I hit the road in my white VW Jetta with April and sometimes Jamie, the two sprawled out on the back seat. I set a rule that I would only buy the next-level-up equipment when I had built the practice up enough to cover the costs. So I drove that old car, packed with files and equipment in the trunk and on the back-seat floor for a year or so until I finally rewarded myself with a brand-new Dodge Caravan with one sliding side door! It was silver gray with maroon interior, and it didn't even have power windows or locks. We took the first back seat out so the dogs would have a full hangout area that was covered with blankets and dog beds. My equipment stayed in the back behind the second seat, along with a metal barrier to keep the dogs safe—probably not terribly safe at all, but that was what was available at the time. We traveled all over the county, seeing up to ten appointments a day.

Barely in practice for two years, I was shocked one day when I received a phone call inquiry from a *New York Times* journalist wanting to do a story about my work as a house-call veterinarian. I was thrilled! Not so much because of the prestige that went along with a feature story in the *New York Times* (extremely exciting, though!) but because this was an opportunity to share my experiences taking care of animals in a context that would be seen by a range of readers, including potential clients, animal advocates, and veterinarians.

My house-call practice allowed me to practice medicine much more intimately than most vets could in a brick-and-mortar hospital. Being in the home environment with my patients and clients, I was able to take my time to offer the custom care I was passionate about. The physical act of doing house calls was a step away from the norm, but the care I was able to offer was new and well received.

When I first started my house-call practice, there wasn't much discussion about the concerns of senior and disabled special-needs pets, but through natural selection, my client base gravitated toward those with pets who were difficult to move, and who were nearing the end of their lives. It quickly became obvious that house calls were particularly suited to senior and special-needs pets, which happened to be my favorite patient population (not that I didn't enjoy caring for puppies and kittens!).

The journalist, Andrew Malcolm, joined me for a day of calls that included a variety of pets with a range of issues, as well as a nice sampling of clients. My clients were all very excited to be included in this very special *New York Times* adventure.

The feature ran in May 1992 with the headline "Important Patients Get House Calls," and began with a visit to Coco, a Lhasa apso, who needed an injection and tried to bite me in the process. The story continued with the chiding of "Marilyn Diamondstone, who belongs to the dog," and my quip that "by my second visit, some of my patients don't like me." The story referred to me as Dr. Foodman, because I hadn't changed my last name right away after getting married, and went on to explain the context for my comment:

> Dr. Foodman is known for her visits to pets across
> southern Fairfield County. House calls for humans
> went out of fashion years ago when doctors decided
> it wasn't worth the effort. However, we're talking pets
> here. Americans have four times as many cats and
> dogs as Canada has people. Americans buy more food
> for their cats than for their babies. Americans like
> house calls for their pets. . . . Enter the 31-year-old
> Dr. Foodman, one of the rapidly growing number of

women among the more than 60,000 veterinarians tending America's creature companions. Whether in crowded urban areas where pet-friendly transportation is sparse or less-crowded suburban environments where the question of convenience rules all, house calls are hot now.

For every animal story he told, he gave context to their experience. He made sure to mention that the reason Coco had been nervous was that there were renovations going on in the house while I was giving her the shot. The writer also addressed another important aspect of my house calls—compassionate care of my elderly clients who rely on their pets in the most heartwarming ways. It went on:

> For some elderly owners, the vet's visit is a social highlight, providing opportunities for conversations that often last longer than the actual exam. During one call Dr. Foodman found herself making a quick grocery trip for an infirm (human) customer. . . . A favorite stop is the Ellig residence . . . where Kent lives. Kent is a slow-moving, doe-eyed 12-year-old collie with arthritis. "She treats Kent like he's the only dog in the world," said Marie Ellig, who has only one dog in the world. "And I could never lift him in the car myself."

Our "two-dog MAX" rule firmly in place at the time, the family and I got plugs—Warren, of course, and April, described as a "diabetic dog rescued from a medical lab," and Jamie, "a wheaton [*sic*] terrier and sock fetishist." Hilariously, the article touched on how Warren and I had met and gone on a first date together with our dogs but then suggested the real story would have to be told one day in a magazine called *People and Canine Confessions*.

Warren and I laughed when we read that made-up name, naturally, never for a moment guessing the *People* magazine part would come true one day in the distant future. Beyond what the article did for my practice—which was a big deal—some of the most attention I got came from this quote:

> "If you like animals," notes Dr. Foodman, a Purdue graduate, "go work in a zoo. If you like people, then be a vet. People take care of the animals. People love them. People make the decisions. And you see them at the best of times, and the worst."

I probably would have stated that a little bit differently now, but my point was that vets need to be people-oriented and know that they are ultimately treating the humans in the exam room as much if not more than the nonhumans. Most vets who congratulated me about the article liked that quote and felt it was worthy of repeating. In fact, the medical director at the Animal Medical Center used my quote in client relations discussions with their intern classes. All in all, I was given a lot of "likes" in a pre–social media context.

As time went on, I learned that there were definite negatives to the house-call line of work. It doesn't happen often, but I remember each of those instances when I arrived at an appointment to find a frantic client, cat-less, in the driveway, saying over and over, "He always shows up at five!" or "She was just in the house" as I watched the cat or dog racing off to another part of the planet.

Sometimes my house-call patients would recognize my car and take off. One of my clients had a very friendly dog named Clinton who was always excited to greet cars as they came up their driveway. Unless it was mine. It took a second for him to realize it was me before he'd run around to the back door and into the house. He must have thought that I'd turn around and leave, but in fact, he made it much easier for all of us. Thankfully, most of my patients would eagerly greet me when I arrived.

I have explored cellars, crawled around in dust under beds, and searched more cluttered closets and laundry rooms looking for cats than I care to recall. One calico cat named Autumn blended completely into the stone cellar wall. I happened to notice her beautiful orange owl-like eyes staring at me as I moved past her. Her sister cat, Mischief, didn't appear until hours after I had left the house.

There were also days when I would have to deal with inconsiderate, unrealistic clients who'd leave their nanny in charge of their aggressive dogs without a word of warning. Or cases where the client misjudged the severity of the medical condition and thought that because they had to be at work, a house call was appropriate for their dog who in fact needed urgent surgery or critical in-hospital care. Sadly, I have arrived at houses where I've been alone with animals for their last breaths. Fortunately, most of the time I would get a good idea of what was going on before agreeing to a house call, so such situations were not a regular occurrence.

🐾

On October 11, 1993, a short time before Warren and I learned that we were expecting our first child, I found myself having to make the crushing decision to let my beautiful April leave peacefully. She had been deteriorating due to end-stage liver failure, which I had been treating palliatively for quite a while. I chose to put her to sleep myself, in my van, one of her most favorite places of all. Warren was there with me as we both said goodbye to my beloved, sweet, special friend.

I had plenty of warning, but making that last final decision was very difficult. Some might think it would be a little bit easier for a veterinarian, but when I'm dealing with my own pets, I go through the same agonizing debates, conversations, and rationalizations as my clients do. April had been a dog with a calling, a higher purpose, and, because I was able to manage her diabetes successfully, she lived to a ripe old age of seventeen. She was with me through one of the most transitional chapters of my life. She prepared me for the many dogs, birds, and human children who followed her. Looking back, there's no question that caring for April's medical needs set me on a path of passion for those with disabilities and special needs, all eventually leading up to the foster project of Piglet, the deaf blind pink puppy.

Soon after we lost April, Jamie started showing signs of heart failure, which was confirmed with an echocardiogram. We treated her with various heart meds, and she did well for a few months. But in June 1994, when I was five months pregnant, Jamie started to deteriorate during the week before we had to go out of town to attend our nephew's bar mitzvah. We couldn't leave her at home so we brought Jamie with us. Our plan was to leave her at Warren's brother's house while we attended the service and party. As we were getting ready to leave for the synagogue, we called Jamie over to tell her we'd be back in a few hours. As she approached us, she collapsed at our feet, in full cardiac arrest.

Warren and I were heartbroken. We attended the service and the party but were devastated and looked shellshocked by all accounts. We avoided sitting together to keep ourselves from sobbing excessively and everyone thought we were having a fight. We didn't say anything because we didn't want to ruin the festive mood for anyone else.

Losing April and Jamie, the two dogs that were there for our first years together, made it feel that a large shared volume of dog history had been completed and a new one prepared itself to be written—now with the added dimension of human children to grow up as the center of our lives.

We took so much joy from just looking at our three blue-eyed, rosy-cheeked cherubs—who arrived in a matter of less than five years—that it took the edge off the sleepless nights. Actually, Warren managed to sleep through most of the crying and nursing through the nights. He was a wonderful, hands-on dad during his waking hours, however, and was always amazing with calming our babies, as was his entire family. Shapiros love to hold babies. Warren's dad, Poppy, would sit for hours holding our newborns, and his mom, Ruth (Oma once we had kids), gave me all the instruction I'd need for bathing, feeding, and diapering her grandbabies. Warren would always be the one to volunteer to calm other people's crying babies, too, whenever we were visiting with relatives and friends.

Warren and I learned quickly that though we had almost seamlessly coparented dogs together, there was still lots to learn about parenting children.

I felt fortunate to have a job that provided variant, warm interactions, and lots of dogs and cats to get to care for over their lifetimes. When my children were very young, I had a full-time babysitter at home while I was working, but the kids would occasionally join me and the two dogs that we had gotten after April and Jamie—Wendy the whippet and Lucy the border collie—on house-call visits.

When our son, Daniel, was turning six years old, I remember the pace of our lives turning from a healthy trot into a constant sprint. My schedule was my own to make, but there were rare occasions when I had no choice but to say no (to my kids). On the day when Daniel's first-grade class was going to be celebrating his birthday, I'd promised to bring in cupcakes. When I arrived, we gathered around to sing "Happy Birthday," and he blew out the candle on his cupcake. All the kids called out, "What did you wish for?" "What is your wish?" Daniel wouldn't tell them. Instead, he waved me over close to him so he could whisper in my ear.

I leaned in and he said, "I want you to be home."

A shock ran through me. It was a stunning comment from a six-year-old. I paid attention to that six-year-old birthday wish. On my way home from the elementary school, I changed my approach to my work-life balance. In that moment, I transitioned from fitting my kids' schedules into my work life to fitting my work life around my kids' needs. It didn't always work. There were times when I had to make compromises. But it was a liberating pronouncement to myself, above all. My boundaries had been reset.

Those boundaries were also ones Warren and I discussed often, making sure that we helped each other from going overboard and doing crazy things like thinking a tiny one-and-a-half-pound pink puppy wasn't going to disrupt our lives. That assumption had gone out the window immediately. I don't think Warren had expected for Piglet to bond with him so deeply and so soon.

I'll never forget what happened when Warren had to go out of town for a few days about a week after Piglet's arrival. Overall, Favorite Dad's absence seemed to unsettle our foster child. Yet I didn't expect to witness something that stopped me in my tracks as I was getting dressed for the day. Piglet was wandering and sniffing around on the floor in our bedroom when suddenly he bumped into a large object by the dresser that caused him to twirl once around with excitement.

"What is it, Piglet?" I asked, not noticing anything that should have startled him—as if he could hear me! When I went to him, I realized that he had come across Warren's sneakers, which were sitting by the dresser. He had immediately begun to dance around, wagging his tail, and biting the sneakers with pure and unadulterated joy. Piglet had made the connection that these were his Favorite Dad's sneakers, and fully expected that his Favorite Dad was standing in them.

"Piggy," I said, "your dad isn't here now but he'll be coming home soon!" trying to console him as I broke the news that his foster dad wasn't actually attached to his shoes.

No, Piglet couldn't hear me, although this was where his sixth sense started to make itself known. Maybe it was the way the air came from my mouth or the changes in my touch that portrayed feelings of disappointment on his behalf. Whatever it was, I could see Piglet go from joy to utter disappointment as soon as he realized he had found only sneakers, not Warren himself.

Their reunion upon Warren's return the next evening was historic. When Warren's car pulled up the driveway and he approached the front door, Dean started the barking fest and the rest of the dogs joined in a loud chorus, all of them hurrying to door, like he was returning from a perilous journey and they'd wondered if they'd ever see him again. Piglity somehow picked up on the excitement and began to bark his head off too. When Warren walked through the door and all the dogs started crowding around him, wagging their tails, I had to hold Piglet back to keep him from being trampled by the other dogs as he tried to get to his Favorite Dad. No doubt he could smell him.

With a grin, Warren made his way over to me and took Baby Piglet from my arms. The tiny pink boy instantly sniffed Warren's mouth to be sure it was in fact his Favorite Dad, then burrowed close to Warren's chest, scooched right under his winter vest, nestled in, and completely relaxed. Warren plopped down on the couch and just held Piglet tight.

An hour later, somehow, the puppy had managed to poke his pink little nose out of the sleeve hole of the vest on Warren's left side. Favorite Dad was home. It was beyond adorable and a moment of sweetness that I thought maybe I'd never catch again. Watching Piglet relax in Warren's arms was truly one of the sweetest gestures I had ever seen from a dog.

Chapter 5

FOSTER PUPPY

One day a plow horse was brought to him; and the poor thing was terribly glad to find a man who could talk in horse-language.

"You know, Doctor," said the horse, "that vet over the hill knows nothing at all. He has been treating me six weeks now—for spavins. What I need is SPECTACLES. I am going blind in one eye. There's no reason why horses shouldn't wear glasses, the same as people." . . .

"Of course—of course," said the Doctor. "I'll get you some at once."

—Excerpt from "Animal Language,"
in *The Story of Dr. Dolittle*, by Hugh Lofting, 1920

MARCH–APRIL 2017

The importance of creating familiar routines for life can't be overstated—whether it's for your dogs, your birds, your kids, or you. On day three of Piglet's stay with us, with a plan of action in mind (and some guidance from colleagues who had expertise in training deaf and blind dogs), I sent a text to Dr. Gloria Andrews that I'd begun the process of helping them search for the right adoptive placement for Piglet by posting my first photos and videos of him to my own Facebook page. A friend, Ann Jordan, who is the founder and director of Connecticut Dachshund Rescue and a no-anesthesia dental hygienist for pets, called me and suggested, "You might want to contact Corinne Zoscak at Sophia's Grace Foundation. I'm sure she'd help spread the word." Ann went on to say that this was a well-run dachshund rescue group with a wide reach in Pennsylvania and surrounding states. When I followed up with Corinne, she kindly posted Piglet/Bart's story and photo on her page.

Over the next hours, I was astounded to see that one post drawing hundreds of responses. There were risks associated with putting the word out far and wide. Still, that was how we were going to find the right home. Without question, I had faith that all care would be taken to make sure our foster boy would be placed in the best possible setting, where he would be safe and understood. This same thoughtful effort led to the placements of Piglet's three littermates.

A few weeks in, instead of continuing to post on my personal Facebook page, at the request of friends who wanted to have a reliable place to come view pics and videos of my foster boy, I created a new page devoted just to him—which I called "Piglet, the deaf blind pink puppy." Soon I sent notes to other rescue groups asking them to cross post my posts with a focus on finding Piglet's forever home. Gloria and her sister started to field all kinds of queries and then applications.

The thought of sending him off in the same condition in which he'd arrived was worrisome. Placing him too soon would give him the feeling of being tossed around like a hot potato. That's why one of the main goals of fostering was to get him settled into a routine that he could integrate into his new life once adopted. After nights one and two of his stay with us, I knew that the first order of business was creating a reliable bedtime routine that he could take with him to his forever family's home and, at the same time, allow me to get a decent night's sleep and be functional the next morning.

After those two exhausting nights of trying to fall asleep while sitting up on the couch holding Piglet, I reconsidered my well-kept rule that puppies should sleep in their crates. The rule exists for a couple of reasons, mainly to avoid having baby dogs pee and poop in the bed. Crate training works because puppies are less likely to soil a small area where they sleep, which is especially useful at night. There is a safety factor to be considered too—because when you're asleep you can't watch them to make sure they don't chew on electrical cords or get into any number of other dangerous situations. A protective crate, covered by a blanket (except for the opening) can be cozy and den-like, a comforting place of refuge for young dogs and even older ones.

We were usually strict about crating dogs, but of course every rule has an exception. For me, the first time I broke my own rule was when we brought Zoey home.

There is no amount of rationalizing or explaining the craziness on our part that led to our bringing home a sixth dog, but one bit of history should be mentioned. Some months earlier, we had success-fully fostered Daisy, a darling tiny Chihuahua whom we continued to regret sending off when our foster term was over.

Though we were in no hurry, this was when Warren and I had both seen a listing for six tiny Chihuahua mixes in Arkansas and were both sorely tempted, though separately, because we wouldn't admit to each other that we would even consider adding a sixth dog. This litter of puppies had been born in a home in Arkansas where people didn't regularly spay or neuter their dogs. Some of these set-tings have revealed attempts at being backyard/home breeders—that is, small-scale unqualified breeders with commercial intent who also experiment with mixing breeds to see how cute the litters turn out. This is somewhat different from the hoarding situations that "acci-dentally" produce crossbred dogs who may be genetically prone to birth defects and severe disabilities, but neither is good. The Arkan-sas home may not have been such a so-called backyard breeding operation, but we did know that puppies in the listing had been born from the mating of a Chihuahua dad and a Yorkie-Maltese mom.

When I heard the name given to the mom's breed mix—"morkie"—my stomach churned. The notion of "designer breeds" is a relatively new method of exploiting dogs. There is a market for the adorable, usually fluffy, mixes. But while there are some designer dog breeders that do appropriate health testing on their breeding stock, there are large numbers of irresponsible backyard breeders and puppy mills who commonly have no concern for medical histories or ongoing veterinary care. They maintain beautiful websites with pictures of adorable puppies, and some sell directly to pet stores. They come across as reputable and caring but, in fact, they should be avoided.

When the Arkansas puppies were all of five weeks old, the people who had them chose to give them away for free on Craigslist. A group in the area, Allie's Hope Animal Rescue, saw the listing and contacted the people. They were able to pick up the puppies and get the adult dogs spayed and neutered—a standard requirement of most rescue groups that take in dogs from backyard, in-home breeders as well as hoarding situations.

We first heard about the puppies and saw the pictures of them through my wonderful rescue friend Holly Chasin, whose Connecticut-based dog rescue organization is the Little Pink Shelter. Holly works with a number of rescuers in Arkansas to bring adoptable dogs to their forever homes in Connecticut. We actually met as fellow moms—when our sons attended the same nursery school. Soon afterward, Holly's dogs and cats became my patients, and I started to learn more about her rescue work. Exemplary in many ways, Holly's approach is to take the extra time and effort to describe her adoptable dogs as accurately and reliably as possible. Holly did so by partnering with reliable rescuers in Arkansas who took great care of their rescued dogs and were helpful in providing those very accurate descriptions of what the dogs were like so that Holly could then give them reliable write-ups for their online adoption pages. For years I helped her rescue out whenever some of the foster dogs needed additional veterinary care such as health certificates, routine vaccines and other checkups, and occasionally unforeseen medical issues.

Warren and I, separately smitten by the photos Holly posted, were enchanted by her thoughtful descriptions. It all came out in a confession to each other one night. Warren admitted with a sigh, "I love the tan puppy. That's the one we have to have."

"Oh, that baby's so cute, but have you seen the solid brown one?" I was in love with that tiny piece of chocolate.

Now we had a problem that might be the solution to our dog addiction. We could have argued and just decided against adopting a sixth dog. Instead, when I spoke to the woman who was fostering the puppies in Arkansas and learned that Noelle (soon to become Zoey) was the most people-oriented and the most affectionate lapdog, I was given my get-out-of-jail-free card—the fact that I didn't have a lapdog and really, really had always wanted one.

We had to figure out how to get her up to Westport ASAP. I was worried that the longer she stayed in the South with other dogs, the more likely it was that she would get sick. Noelle/Zoey was very young and very tiny, and not yet fully vaccinated. Transporting young puppies long distances in crowded vans leaves them vulnerable to many dangerous dog viruses. Most do fine, but of course, I was worried about my tiny gal, whom I hadn't even met.

After exhausting all possibilities to have her flown here, or going down to pick her up myself, I decided to have her come up on the usual transport van. Warren and I didn't tell anyone outside of the family that we were getting a sixth dog. We just couldn't bear to hear about how crazy we were. But we were unified in our excitement at bringing home the pint-sized three-pound chocolate puppy.

When we went to pick her up at the transport drop-off, Zoey was in a small crate on the top row with her sister who looked exactly like her. The driver opened the crate and took both puppies out, and along with their information envelopes, handed one to me and one to another woman, who was as excited as I was. We both hugged our new chocolate-chip puppies, took a few pics together, and rushed off to take our babies home.

Warren and I couldn't get over how right our decision had been. Zoey was wearing a heart-melting little black-and-hot-pink coat—and settled right into my arms with what sounded almost like a purr. We brought her inside and the five Shapiro dogs gave her a sniffing over and welcomed their new sister puppy home.

It was already late when I tried to get her to go to sleep in a crate.

That was the plan—to get her used to sleeping in it from day one. She cried every time I put her in. I ended up sleeping downstairs with her, in and out of the crate, and on my lap mostly. When Warren came down in the morning, he saw a worried look on my face.

"What's wrong?" he asked.

"She's not well," I announced, concerned about her weak and dazed state, then took her to NVH, sent out some lab work, and started treating symptomatically. After two days with no improvement, I had her admitted to the emergency vet hospital. We thought we were going to lose her, but after a week she began to improve and, thankfully, with very intensive care, made a full recovery.

When Zoey came home, we were back to square one as far as where she would sleep. After outgrowing her puppyhood, Annie had graduated from the crate to sleeping in our bed, curled up next to Warren. But we had maintained a strict policy that all puppies slept in a crate. The logic for breaking the "no puppies in bed" rule was, as I explained to Warren, "She is all of three pounds and part Chihuahua. She's like most tiny lapdogs. They get cold and crave their people."

Warren asked rhetorically whether it was possible that some people had their Chihuahuas sleep in crates and dog beds. He had a point. Giving it one more try, I put a space heater next to the crate but that didn't end her little plaintive doggy cries to come bring her into our bed. Warren slept through that while I was up all night with her.

The next night Warren was out of town on a business trip and I gave in. That first time I brought her to bed, she tucked in under the covers with me. There was no moving around, and no accidents. I got a full night's sleep and had no intention of turning back to the crate debate. It was over. Zoey was a bed dog!

In theory, Zoey was supposed to be Warren's dog; he'd encouraged me to find a dog like Daisy who we'd only fostered, and he'd named her Zoey, of course. In practice, however, though Zoey loves her dad, she's a momma's girl—and really the first real lapdog to stake out that claim in my life. Once she's committed to a lap, she gets very attached. She is also the most enthusiastic eater I've ever met. She loves her meals, and loves her treats, especially the bedtime snack party that all the dogs get to enjoy. She also knows who doles out the most treats and who serves most of the meals. She is extremely expressive, deeply sensitive, and very feisty. She did not get the *you are so tiny in size, so have a small personality* memo.

Piglet may well have benefitted from the Zoey rule-bending, as hard as I tried to avoid doing it again. Whatever I tried, I could feel my resistance slipping during those first two nights of sleeping on the couch and trying to figure out how to get baby P to sleep in a crate so I could get in my bed *with* Zoey. There was only one thing to do. On night three, Piggy joined Zoey and Annie in the nighttime snuggle fest. He slept straight through the night. No fuss, no muss. Other than a little bit of worrying about him falling off the bed, which did not happen, I was finally able to catch up on my sleep. Given the fact that I am a light sleeper anyway, I kept pretty good track of him throughout the night. Piglet learned very quickly that he was a bed dog.

From the start, we developed something of a bedtime routine that became even more elaborate in days to come. So as not to wake Warren, once I quietly settle the five other dogs into their respective spots for the night—with a last kiss on the top of Evie's head as she curls up on a fleece blanket covering our expensive bedroom chair from Pottery Barn—I secure Zoey and Piglet under each of my arms, and then take a huge steplike leap into bed. Both of the tiny dogs immediately scoot under the blanket, curling up into little tucked-in balls while I get comfortable, and then Zoey always goes to my left side to sleep as Piglet places himself right on top of me.

It was amazing that our foster boy knew how to conform to a sleeping human as a one-and-a-half-pound little thing. The evidence reinforced my understanding of how much love and bonding he needed at the start. This would lay the foundation for my insistence that anyone who adopted Piglet would have to agree in advance that he would be sleeping in bed with them.

Initially, Warren was not as delighted as I was with my solution to the problem of Piglet's sleep training, but he accepted it as a measure of last resort. He knew that I couldn't function being up all night much longer and that the best thing to do was what I did. Besides, as we kept reminding ourselves, this wasn't going to be forever. It's true that my original estimate of a few days of fostering soon proved to be overly optimistic.

Warren accepted the news stoically when I told him, "It's probably going to be more like two weeks." His smile indicated that he had known this was coming.

It's not that I questioned my ability to help Piglet/Bart gain life skills he would need for adapting to a forever home. It's just that it was going to take more work than I'd first imagined. His disabilities aside, Piggy was really young. From what was known about the hoarding situation at the time of his birth, he was supposedly eight weeks old when he arrived in Connecticut. My hunch was that he was more like six weeks or younger. In fact, in that first week, when I took Piglet with me to Norwalk Veterinary Hospital a second time, one of the vet techs, Gina, made a comment to that effect. "He looks half-baked," she observed, half-joking, half-not.

Maybe she was onto something. We knew he was double dapple, and that told us his disabilities had been caused by genetics. But it was possible that due to his being a double dapple some of this development was delayed. That being said, much of his puppy behavior was age appropriate. Plus his mapping and adapting skills indicated a high level of intelligence.

It had amazed me that the second time Piglity and I visited the hospital, as soon as I took him from the car, he sat up at attention in my arms as I carried him up the path in the same direction we'd gone the first day. At home, I noticed after just a few days that he would avoid running into the gate in the kitchen. He had already mapped his way around the dining area, where the table was. In those moments, I would hover next to him, letting him go off on his own exploration, but making sure he stayed safe. On a daily basis, I'd marvel at how compartmentalized and brilliant his brain had to be to navigate the room as well as he did.

Our refrain of asking, *How much trouble could a little teeny deaf blind pink puppy be?* seemed to come from yesteryear. Warren's magic touch at getting Piglity to quiet down was not all powerful all the time. Piglet might be completely buoyant being in his Favorite Dad's arms for a while. But then he'd often end up having a screaming episode for one unknown reason or another. It was hard to read what he was upset about or needed. When Warren wasn't at work and I needed to run an errand or attend a vet meeting without him, I'd leave Piglet at home. Sometimes they'd be fine. Other times I'd get an urgent text or call about how to handle something with Piglet that appeared to be a crisis. Though I was very keyed in to his doggy schedule of needs and could often advise what to do, there were instances when the screaming continued endlessly until it reached a peak and I'd be texted or called to come home.

Although we were subject to a mix of emotions that tore at Warren and me, our six-pack of dogs steadied us. They seemed to figure out right away that the pink puppy was different and needed extra care. They were sensitive to his carryings-on, and learned to play with the tiny deaf blind dog in the most inclusive way. Had we taken for granted how impressive they were? If, in fact, we had, Warren and I tried harder than ever to acknowledge how each tried to calm the screaming baby down. Susie was the best, almost like a canine nanny who knew how to engage Piglet when he was out of control.

She would cheerfully approach him and then curl up at his side, which seemed to be most comforting. Susie initially volunteered for the job of surrogate mom, and after a while we were begging her to go babysit so we could have a break from the screaming and from having to hold him ourselves when we were trying to cook, write, and do other things that required more than one hand.

My drives to and from work appointments were, frankly, torturous. Piglet could scream for an hour at a time in the car. I'd drive along while holding a chewy stick for him from outside the crate. Not a safe way to drive!

The chaos the tiny boy brought into the household is hard to describe. Time has clouded our memory of the specifics of the deep anguish we all felt during the first few weeks, Piglet included. But we all remember the experience as stressful and agitating. Maybe if I hadn't been so determined for my part to end very quickly, I might have recorded more of it. We all felt compassion for Piglet. It was very upsetting to witness his ongoing distress.

As we searched for an adoptive home, I realized that all these irresistible pictures and videos of our pink foster puppy were only telling one side of the story. The other side wasn't so cute. If he was frustrated, scared, bored, alone, or, it seemed, not the absolute center of attention, he would turn into a little howling Gila monster that made Ellie literally cover her ears and run from the room, reminding me over her shoulder, as if I'd really forgotten, "Find him his forever home, Mom!"

The problem with the inquiries coming in was that I could see they were mostly all underestimating the amount of work it would be to bring the adorable pink puppy into their lives. His disabilities were profound and, at least for the time being, he required constant care and supervision. Some of the applicants who contacted me had experience caring for blind dogs or deaf dogs, and that was encouraging— but none of them seemed to grasp the extent of accommodations this deaf and blind puppy needed.

One of the first serious inquiries was from a lovely woman who had experience with dachshunds, including senior dogs who actually had lost both their sight and their hearing over time. She was sincere in her interest, but the more we communicated, the more I realized she wasn't prepared to handle a Chi/doxie, high-octane, demanding deaf and blind puppy who would unsettle the calm she had established with her older special-needs dogs. She agreed and soon after adopted another special-needs senior dog.

Another woman and her husband sounded promising at first, and I was ready to pack Piglet/Bart in the car and drive him a few hours to meet this couple. That plan was derailed when they clarified that they would need to put the little guy in an all-day doggy day care. As diplomatically as possible, I advised the couple that the rescue agency had said no.

Every night as I settled everyone into their beds, I ran through the concerns with Warren about what I thought we needed to find in the right adopters. Warren listened patiently, reassuring me we'd find the right applicant, that it was early still.

"He is not a beginner dog, you know."

Warren nodded, agreeing.

Throughout my veterinary career, I'd seen thousands of puppies enter homes, many of them perfect matches for beginner dog families. "But," I pointed out, "some dogs are so complicated only the most experienced dog people would dare to take on the challenge."

At that, Warren raised an eyebrow, sending me his *Hmmm, what are you trying to say?* glance. I paused to gather my words.

"You and I aren't the only dog people with the experience, time, and energy for a puppy like Piglet. We just have to find a situation like ours."

Warren reminded me, "We're not making this decision alone." Gloria and her sister Carolyn were really in charge of the adoption decisions. We had input to offer, but Piglity wasn't our dog.

My solution was to do a better job communicating those needs based on what we were finding out through our experiences as foster parents. This would allow us to make sure to place Piglet in a home where he could adjust optimally, and be given the time commitment and care he deserved.

"The big problem," as I must have said to Warren a few times, "is that his sensitivity and intensity alone make him a potentially poor candidate for most households."

Irrationally, at times, when we were having these nighttime conversations, I imagined Piglet following everything we were saying. Occasionally, if Warren hadn't gone to sleep before I got into bed, he would take Piglet and Zoey so I could brush my teeth hands-free. The sweet puppy contentment that I observed whenever Piglet was snuggled in with his Favorite Dad was always remarkable. He also knew—however he figured it out—that he was expected to sleep with me. With very little prompting, as soon as he sensed that I was in bed, Piglet quietly got up and slowly made his way over the blankets, and sometimes past Zoey, to me.

I'd hold the blanket up and, having mapped it once, he would go right under, really as if he could see the whole thing.

"How does he know?" I constantly asked Warren, praising our foster boy's mastery not only of our bed but our whole house.

"He's just a prodigy," Warren answered one night, as if we were talking about one of our own kids.

In the mornings, if I wasn't in a hurry to get out of bed—and if

ZoZo wasn't there with her raised eyebrows and cocked head, tugging at me to get up and get breakfast going—Piggy would pit-a-pat in the bed over to his foster dad to say a very happy good morning. That involved some serious tail wagging, more snuggling, and gleeful groaning.

Those mornings were rare, as I'd chosen to rouse myself at six thirty every weekday to pack Ellie's lunch for her, which I did until she graduated from high school. It was a big help to her, and I was subconsciously doing my last bit of morning mothering before our impending empty nest.

On one such early start to the day, going into our second week with our foster baby, I sat down to check in with Gloria with a text to ask about the progress of Piglet/Bart's littermates. I confided to her that we probably needed another couple of weeks to really get him ready to go and that it wasn't going to be easy. In hindsight, I now see that two compelling and somewhat contradictory goals were in force—the intention to find him the right home and preparing ourselves to say goodbye. I told Gloria:

As you can see from the Facebook posts, he's doing very well. He still has his moments of panic, crying, and then becoming hysterical. But they aren't as frequent as a week ago. He still loves to be held, of course, but he's able to play, run around and finally, he's starting to chew on toys and bones. He's a very smart puppy. I have no idea how I will part with him. For now, we have quite a few things to accomplish over the next couple of weeks. Then, we'll have a better idea of his limitations so we can characterize what he'll need in the long run. He still can't deal with the crate but I'm hoping that once he figures out that he's going someplace good when he goes into a crate in the car, it will be easier for him. He's only 9 weeks old so he's pretty much acting his age. I hope the others are doing well. Did you find fosters for them? I'm sure that having the little Piglet in a home has made a huge difference in his long-term outcome.

The key to that long-term well-being, I believed then and later, was the amount of time that Warren and I both spent holding Piglet—so crucial for every puppy's overall bonding with humans and especially for a traumatized baby dog without the ability to see or hear. In this respect, we were lucky to be fostering him before he was much older and already moving out of the bonding phase.

It helped to remind myself that Piglet's anxiety stemmed from his inability to communicate what he wanted and needed. He still didn't fully understand we were here to be a constant for him in his daily routine. Tap signals continued to offer us a way to connect and communicate, which increasingly helped to reassure him and soon changed his whole demeanor.

After learning the tap for "sit" right away, he quickly grasped that taps were a form of communication. Once that idea clicked, we were able to add more and more taps to Piglet's "vocabulary." We went from "sit" to "OK" (a tap on his sternum) and then began working on "wait" (his version of "stay"). In addition to taps, I eventually added the use of breath—even blowing at him to signal "come." When I whispered into the side of his cheek, telling him to calm down, be a nice boy, he didn't hear or understand those words per se, but my breath and the vibration of my voice, coupled with some calming strokes to the other side of his face, had the desired effect.

Whenever possible, I worked on teaching tap signals to Piglet at the same time that I was using my voice and gestures to speak with the rest of the pack. If it was mealtime, and everyone knew to sit in front of their dishes and "wait" until each one of them had been served, I'd start the process for Piglet of teaching him how to wait before going into his crate to eat his food.

I might say something like, "Everyone—wait. Look at me," and add a few reminders to "wait for everyone to get theirs," as I placed a food dish in front of each dog. Piglet's "wait" was a gentle tap from my open palm on his nose. This was my technique for getting the group to work together—in this instance, waiting until I gave them their verbal "OK," and then they could chow down. This wasn't something we did at every single meal, but the practice resulted in improved impulse control as every one of the six-pack learned to sit in front of their dishes with food in them until given the okay to eat.

If any one of them couldn't resist and had to scarf down food, I might laugh and say, "That was naughty, Zoey" (because she loved food so much), and the rest of the pack would love it because they knew they were doing it right.

Piglet seemed to recognize that the others were doing the things that he was learning to do, and he didn't want to miss out. With his powerful nose and ability to sense motion and breathing, he seemed very well aware that he was participating in group activities.

Mealtime in his little kitchen crate was a joyous affair, and because he was so tiny and couldn't eat a lot of food at every meal, I got into the habit of giving him lunch every day. The pink prince had to eat three meals every day. The others would look at me with glances of *Why does he get lunch and we don't?* To which I'd explain, "Because he's so little and needs to grow." Then I would give Piglity a "good dog" tap with a soft pat on his left side.

Traveling in the car began to improve. Piglet kept his noise level down, something I assumed meant that he knew we were going someplace good. He happily looked forward to getting a cookie when he got into his car crate, and without the high anxiety he suffered in the beginning, he actually was able to take long, relaxing naps as I drove around working for hours at a time. Some days I would reassure him, "You're going to go to work with your mom today," or "Ready to go see your girlfriend Monica?" and it would work to calm him even though he hadn't heard a word I said. No doubt, he was also picking up on the energy of the other dogs, who were listening and also getting very excited to be going to work with me.

In retrospect, the fact that I was already referring to myself as his mom and Warren as his Favorite Dad was really playing with fire, almost delusional. Warren went along with it because we were coconspirators in pretending that it would be easy to have a foster project that wouldn't cause enormous upheaval and believed in my ability to be reasonable, to do the right thing—the professional thing.

Of course, we were in so much denial. Reality told me that taking on the pink boy was going to be a never-ending responsibility. As much as I told myself I was preparing him to fit into someone else's life, he would always be at the center of everything, and that person was becoming harder and harder to find. Complicating those concerns was how deeply invested I had become in his future well-being and in how much progress we had made together.

Maybe the most unexpected piece of the latest developments was the reactions coming from so many quarters on social media. The funny thing was that I didn't use Facebook for myself much more than to post a few pictures of Warren, my kids, and my dogs and birds. Mostly, I just spent time following rescue groups and some of my high school and vet school friends. I had started a page for fellow house sparrow enthusiasts, so I was very familiar with how useful social media pages were for connecting to like-minded bird lovers. But after posting some of the pink puppy's earliest pictures and videos, I was totally surprised at how many people started liking and loving and sharing about Piglet/Bart. That's how I was first contacted by the many candidates interested in adopting him that I'd sent on to Gloria and Carolyn. That in itself was mind-boggling. But something else even more unplanned had begun to happen after I'd set up Piglet's own page on Facebook on April seventh. The numbers grew exponentially within days.

"Warren, Ellie!" I'd hear myself calling out, and when they came, I'd show them how many hundreds of new fans had "liked" Piglet's page. "We just got over a thousand fans. . . ." All the dogs' tails would start to wag, and Piglet, usually in Warren's arms, would yawn, oblivious to his drawing power. Ellie would look over and check out the page but then warn me, "Mom, I can't believe you're spending all this time on social media. Didn't you once say it was a waste of time?" I'd wave her off or remind her that I was using social media for something positive.

One night when Warren and I had sat together reading comments aloud and writing back, Ellie sat there at the kitchen table and shook her head before promising to do an intervention. "I can't believe my mom and dad are going to be *those* kind of parents on Facebook." Warren had reminded Ellie that this was how we were going to find Piglet's forever home, after all, and that it was well-known that if you wrote back to followers who made comments it increased engagement many times over. This was a convincing argument, but she still seemed mortified that her parents, especially me, would be poring over comments from strangers.

"Mom, you don't even watch TV!" Ellie exclaimed, hands up in the air. "You say it's just another noisemaker." She was right about that, but before I could answer, she was gone and I was drawn to yet another comment—this one from a woman who couldn't adopt a dog but felt inclined to tell Piglity, *I just want to hug you, sweet boy!* A video I had posted of Zoey playing rough with him had earned hearts and smiles and puppy faces with comments that ran the gamut from *Precious!* to *So adorable* to *This is so cute* to *He puts a smile on my face every day!*

Some of my posts were wordy and long in describing what it was that I found so fascinating about communicating with Piglet or how I admired his pluck and positivity. I wasn't conscious of creating a voice or trying to be funny or schmaltzy. I was just free flowing in the moment, and followers of Piglet's page were relating to His Pinkness through me. Maybe it was the anonymity of social media that let strangers pour their hearts out, I imagined, but some comments were unexpectedly private yet spoken in a public way. These were confiding less in me than in Piglet—about their depression or how he reminded them of a dog they'd lost or how they wished their mother, no longer alive, could have lived to see him. Piglet never gave up, many fans observed, and that inspired them to do the same.

🐾

After countless drafts aimed at creating an accurate description of our foster puppy, I sent off a final version to Gloria Andrews and her sister Carolyn to post on Petfinder.com—which is the most widely used directory of rescued animals in need of adoptive homes. Colbert Veterinary Rescue Services regularly updated Piglet's listing with new pictures and details about Piglet's special needs and care.

We had gone back and forth to make sure that we weren't scaring away the right kinds of adoptive families and also to limit applicants who wouldn't be the right fit or who had unrealistic expectations.

We replaced an earlier listing that showed Baby Bart at eight weeks old to now show him at ten weeks and settled on this even-handed write-up:

BART/PIGLET IS a male DACHSHUND MIX PUPPY WHO IS DEAF AND BLIND. He is sweet, friendly, loves other small dogs, is very active and playful, and is very smart. Unfortunately, he has no tolerance for crates and becomes very anxious when he finds himself alone in a crate or gated room. At times he can become extremely anxious to the point of vocalizing and running around aimlessly, which can last for well over an hour at a time. Bart will need a space (like a small gated room or large exercise pen) where he will be protected from potential dangers in the environment (such as stairs, larger dogs, household traffic). Gates are an absolute necessity to keep him safe. A small dog or dogs will be helpful if they can serve as guides and friends for him to play and sleep with. He needs a person to be with him most of the time for at least the first year while he goes through normal puppy stages, settles down, and adapts to his new family and home. He needs a very special owner who is willing to devote the time and energy to teaching him tap signals, interesting athletics like agility, and exploring other potential fun activities.

The word "owner" was one I preferred to avoid with reference to the human-animal relationship, not unlike the word "master." Those words raise the offensive suggestion that animals are our property, as opposed to the idea that we are their caretakers and surrogate family members. Still, I didn't want to start a semantics revolution when the goal was to find a wonderful, safe setting in which Piglet would thrive. So the above blurb was the description I sent to Carolyn, Gloria Andrews's sister, who lived in Rochester, New York, at the time but who regularly spent the spring months in Georgia to help her sister with the rescue work in an even more hands-on way. Carolyn took my description and posted it on Petfinder.

They were already getting applications from all around New York, New Jersey, Connecticut, Pennsylvania, Virginia, and Kentucky—which Carolyn would screen for any red flags and then forward the ones she found promising on to me. Not that many applications ever got to me because she had already eliminated most from consideration.

On the adoption site's post, we also let applicants know right up front that they would need to meet the following requirements before applying to adopt Bart/Piglet:

- Be 21 years of age or older.

- Be able and willing to spend the time and money necessary to provide training, medical treatment, and proper care for a pet for the entire life of that animal.

- Verify that all family members agree on this adoption. A meet and greet is required for any existing dogs. We will do home visits prior to the adoption and after the adoption to ensure that everyone is adjusting well.

In addition to being stringent about getting references for potential adopters, Carolyn requested that every applicant write an essay about their understanding of the causes of Piglet's disabilities and then describe their specific plan to care for a deaf and blind puppy.

I know, I know, it probably appears that somehow I secretly didn't want anyone else to work out. My mother, who had never said no to any animal I'd ever brought home—except the snake—confessed to being concerned by the number of hours I had to invest in the pink foster dog. The way she said the word "foster" led me to believe she was skeptical I'd let Piglet go in the end.

My father stood up for me, at least in the beginning. "If Melissa says she's going to do something, you know she does it!" he reassured my mother. Both of them were alarmed at Piglet's "vocalizations," as I'd put it, but they did agree he was ridiculously cute and very bright.

By the middle of April, Piglet's development had begun to spike as he explored the outdoors and zipped around, mapping the entire yard. The other dogs, especially Susie and Zoey, would check up on him and make sure he didn't get lost. Up until then, I'd been cautiously carrying him down and up the wooden stairs leading from the backyard into our house. It occurred to me that he knew where the stairs were and that it would give him a sense of freedom if I guided him up, keeping my hands on his back the whole time. He was super cautious, making small circles around the bottom landing, which was made of slate—until he was ready to go and I could help him center himself and then guide him up. He was so brave and determined to know the way.

Piglity later learned to go up so well, which gave him a feeling of independence. But he is so small that it actually is dangerous for him to be on the stairs alone. I almost regretted introducing the stairs at all because we always have to be behind him, spotting him, in case he takes a wrong step or gets distracted and loses his balance. Then, once he gets to the top, we need to be right there to prevent him from accidentally heading back down. He is much too small to safely walk down the stairs by himself, which is why we always carry him.

At the same time, I was so excited to see him aspiring to higher heights. In the midst of my excitement, I realized that the stairs—built like a stepladder—had no backs on them, and that made this whole challenge even more treacherous for baby Piglet, who could easily slip through and fall, hurting himself badly. In fact, the ladderlike wood steps were not so safe for any of us. Before we practiced any more, I scooped the pink puppy up and called my dad—or Pot, as the kids called him—to come over and tell us how to remodel the wooden steps so they could have backs on them. Unlike the contractors I also contacted—who wanted to reconfigure the whole staircase for a steep price—Pot proposed a simple and inexpensive solution.

When Rachael was all of ten months old, she couldn't say "Grandpa" or "Grandma," so she turned those sounds into "Pot" and "Bama." Those were their names from then on. We thought nothing of it until one day when my dad jotted down his new cell phone number on a piece of paper and left it on the kitchen table. It read *POT*, and then the number next to it. One of Rachael's friends happened to be over and raised his eyebrows with a nod, probably thinking we were cool parents for having the number of our pot dealer out like that on the kitchen table. Rachael clarified that the only Pot allowed in our house was her grandfather.

My father has always been available to fix anything. When he got started on fixing the steps for us, he didn't question the sudden interest in doing so for a foster dog who was going to get placed very soon. If he had thought to ask, I would have said that I didn't want the tiny boy to hurt himself in his couple more weeks with us. Besides, it would be better for the other small dogs, in any case. In a matter of days, my dad completed the project and we beheld a very safe staircase for our little pink boy and the rest of the family.

The theme of this same week for Piglity was getting him out of his comfort zone. I had decided it was time for him to have a couple of road trips and to change up some of the routines I'd carefully designed to give him structure and to calm him down. On our first outing—a hike in Holyoke, Massachusetts—Piglet joined Ellie, Zoey, and me for a challenging climb up a large mountain. This was Piglet's first time ever on a leash held by me while walking over rugged terrain. He only walked about twenty feet to pee, and then he kept going backward, but his nose was twitching away with the smells of nature and the thrill of adventure. Otherwise, he let me carry him the whole way, tucked into my nylon vest, which concerned Ellie but didn't bother me. In my mind, we were milking every moment that he had left with us.

Our next outing was to join Ellie for Accepted Students Day at Princeton. Ellie wasn't at all thrilled to have Piglet there that day. He was such a distracting conversation piece, and I understood. Piglet, however, was in heaven. Apparently, he loved Princeton and intended to return—as indicated by the mapping he did from the moment we got out of the car. He began making friends the minute he was noticed by Joyce Platt, who worked in the admissions office. An outgoing, welcoming woman with short blond hair and stylish glasses, Joyce was delighted to hold him while we filled out forms under the gigantic tent where we were all checking in. When she handed him back to me, Joyce said, "Oh, I could get used to having him to hug every day!"

"You want him?" I replied, sounding like my mom. "We're looking for an adoptive home."

Joyce laughed and shook her head no—with an expression that read, *I wish!*

Piglet was teeny, but for whatever reason, he immediately connected with the campus. I mostly carried him around because he was so young, and I initially didn't realize just how much he was paying attention. But then when we came back, just as he did with other places we had visited once, he was instantly comfortable and familiar with his surroundings.

By this point, I'd become well aware of how he used his nose and tactile senses to map his environment. He had figured out right away how to run around the plastic crate in the middle of our kitchen. He knew where the cocoon dog beds were, and he would go flying into them when he was overly excited while playing with the other dogs. He learned where his toys were and where the furniture was in the living room with very few bumps. He was always very careful. He really didn't like to bump. Depending on what he was doing and what he bumped into, he might bounce off happily and continue on like nothing happened. But other times, much less frequently, he would become very quiet and walk away slowly with his ears back. It depended on what his original mission was—playing, going to find a person or food, or something else that only he knew.

His development, after a month and a half with us, gave me much-needed information. Piglet was adaptable, and he would be fine, I told myself emphatically, to move on next to his forever home. When Gloria and her sister sent word that some suitable candidates had been found, my kids, especially Ellie, breathed a sigh of relief. So did Warren. Or so I thought.

APRIL 2017

Piglet had been with us a little over a month when Warren and I made the drive back to the Milford Petco for a reunion with the pink puppy's rescuers from Colbert Veterinary Rescue Services—who had come to town for an adoption event with a new batch of their most recent rescues. Everything about this day and the circumstances surrounding it were in stark contrast to the March morning five and a half weeks earlier when I had gone to pick up the hysterical Baby Bart.

The first time I'd driven by myself to go get the foster boy, it had been winter and the skies were ominous. By mid-April, we were enjoying a brisk and beautiful early spring.

No longer hysterical, Piglet/Bart was still prone—as I'd become fond of saying—to loud vocalizations. He still disliked going into his crate in the car, although we had made great strides in taming the dreaded crate monster for him by keeping a duplicate second crate in our tiny kitchen as his little eating cave. Associating the experience of being in a crate with eating, both in the kitchen for meals and in the car (getting a cookie as soon as he was placed in a crate), had a symbiotic effect on Piglet that enabled him to accept each crate as a positive place to be.

Until this day, I really hadn't realized just how tied up in knots I had started to become. Strong feelings were completely at odds inside me. He was so much work; I couldn't keep him, but I was so attached to him. The thought of him staying killed me; the thought of him leaving killed me again.

My sensible side grounded me. This was normal in some foster situations. He was ready to thrive somewhere else. That was the deal.

The thought of that inevitability caused a little stab in my heart and what must have been a worried expression. Warren picked up on my worry, as we pulled into a parking space outside the Milford Petco.

Warren remarked, "Melissa, they are not going to believe how he has changed. You're a miracle worker! It's all because you set goals, realistic goals, that you both enjoy working to achieve."

When I took Piglet out of the carrier and handed him to Warren, I did feel a wave of maternal pride. Piggy had filled out to over two pounds and had moved past that half-baked stage. Warren carried him into the store, tucked in the front of his jacket, with Piglet's pink face sticking out, his floppy ears waving in the wind, and roving pink nose inhaling the smell of spring.

Would he remember the trauma of being here the last time? The answer came as Warren, Piglet, and I entered the Petco and went to say hi to Gloria. Five weeks earlier, I'd grabbed the little screaming dragon and left so fast that we didn't even talk. This time, Piglet/ Bart rode in swathed in his Favorite Dad's jacketed arms, and the three of us were met by a beaming Dr. Gloria Andrews. Some of the same volunteers were there, all exchanging expressions of dubious surprise. Gloria petted Piggy, now in Warren's hands, telling him how proud she was of him and how strong and handsome he'd become. My foster boy sniffed the air and wagged his tail happily in a way that hinted he recognized his special rescuer.

Gloria beckoned us to follow her, saying as she went, "You've both done an amazing job with him. Thank you for everything you're doing to find the right home. Keep sending us potential candidates. Carolyn is continuing to screen applications."

The craziest mix of disappointment and relief fluttered through me. Warren heaved something close to an *I told you so* sigh.

Gloria let us know it looked like homes had been found for Piglet/ Bart's littermates after I'd listed him on other rescue group's pages. LT (Barrett), deaf and mildly vision-impaired, would be going to a home in Virginia where there were three other dogs and a cat. Josephine (Belinda), deaf and vision-impaired, and Napoleon (Blaze), who was not a double dapple and could see and hear, were going to a home in Virginia as well— where there were many other dogs, not necessarily optimal.

Gloria led us to a small pen, where I recognized Abigail, Piglet's canine mom, a tan-colored Chi/doxie mix with a faint dapple pattern over her back. Abigail had been placed at the adoption event back in March but soon after was returned due to behavioral issues. Ann Curcio, a longtime volunteer with Gloria's group and a devoted, capable organizer of other volunteers who helped oversee the adoption event logistics, had been fostering Abigail since then. Abigail loved Ann and a brother dog in the household and had so far adapted beautifully. She had no disabilities but was wild and edgy, apparently as much of a character as Piglet.

Ann mentioned that the rescue was still looking for placement for Abigail.

"How can you even think of giving her up?" I asked Ann. "She's so madly in love with you!"

If only I could have heard myself. Guilting foster parents about not adopting their foster dogs is disrespectful. As I well knew, fostering takes discipline and an understanding that the goal is to prepare a dog for a forever home. Maybe I was projecting. In any case, Ann would end up adopting Abigail not long after our conversation.

We entered the pen, and Warren placed Piglity on the ground so he could connect to his dog-mom without us forcing anything. Abigail approached tentatively. She had the same floppy ears, and same face as Piglet, though with big eyes and a brown button nose. I could see the signs of trauma, as she was wary of strangers. She looked closely at Piglet, a glimmer of recognition in her eyes, and then moved closer.

The reaction from Piglet as she approached him was almost instantaneous. First, he growled. No tail wag. Then he barked. Fiercely. He issued a warning: *Do not come any closer.* Abigail stepped back. He obviously sensed that there was no reason to continue barking, so he stopped.

Abigail wasn't in a defensive mode but looked like she could enjoy a spat with her prodigal son if the situation arose. Piglet wasn't having any of it. He stepped back again, not bothering to waste his time, so that I could pick him up. He relaxed in my arms.

The encounter was fascinating. Piglet knew who Abigail was. He definitely seemed to know that this was a mother who'd rejected him, and he did not like her. This same pattern would happen in other encounters when we brought the two together. Each time, Piglet recognizes her, and while he carries on with his nasty boy grumbling, he eventually pipes down and ignores her.

Of course, I had seen many such reunions in the past, and this was not so unusual. I'd also seen the opposite in all kinds of animal families, where offspring hear, see, or smell their long-lost mothers and show them affection instantly. Not Piglity.

"Interesting," I remarked to Warren as I held the pink puppy, comforted him, and followed Gloria to a quiet spot so we could talk about the ongoing search for Piglet's forever family. As we talked, Piglet cuddled up in my arms. Whatever was going to happen next, this moment told me explicitly that it wasn't going to be easy. I had to do the right thing. I just had to make sure I knew what the right thing was.

When Warren and I left the Milford Petco, that reality loomed over us like a massive storm cloud, but neither one of us was willing to admit it.

Gloria walked us out, thanking us profusely. "I am so impressed. His progress is unbelievable!" She had been so worried about Piggy's chances of even surviving. "Carolyn is working on some new applications, and one in particular looks good. We'll be in touch."

Chapter 6

FULL HOUSE

*Always do your best: Practice as much as you can, because
only through practice will you find out how good you can be . . .
Always try as hard as you can, always give as much as you
have . . . It's OK not to be the best. It's not OK if you don't try
your hardest. Make your best effort and that will get you to the
front, if not the top (of whatever you do).*

—An excerpt on doing your best from the Shapiro Rules (2004),
by Rachael, age ten, and Daniel, age eight, with Warren Shapiro

There are plenty of explanations I can offer as to how and why the
"two-dog MAX" rule had been broken on a regular basis by two otherwise very responsible adults and parents. The irony is that I'm not a
rule-driven person by nature, but I'm also not a rule breaker. Within
my own life, I've stuck to setting and achieving goals, rather than
making rules for myself. Maybe I had rules that I didn't call rules—
just commonsense ways to keep on track, stay safe, and make sure
that my life didn't roll out of control.

This is why, when we were starting out as parents and Warren proposed limiting the number of dogs in the household to two, I agreed
wholeheartedly. It was a safeguard against our potential for adding

an excessive number of dogs. It was also a good general rule for avoiding the ease with which animals seem to find their way into veterinarians' lives—the "too many animals" slippery slope. I had no desire to have a load of animals at any time—and definitely not in our early married years. I didn't even like birds when we met, and I was really happy with my one dog. For at least a decade, I'd been disciplined about not overcrowding the household with nonhumans.

Again, some rules—even the ones intended for the good of all—have to be bent, if not broken. That's the best way that I can explain how our animal population got a little out of control. Or maybe a lot out of control.

The lesson I learned in my own case was that sometimes what you gain by bringing the joy and beauty of birds into a home can be far more valuable than what you give up by avoiding too many animals. Even in a full house, everyone can be encouraged to be their best selves and live their best lives.

With that as a guiding principle, Warren and I avoided too many rules with Rachael, Daniel, and Ellie, preferring instead to enforce concerns that had to do with their personal safety. We stood accused of being overly protective. Warren may have exceeded me as far as safety rules went, but I ran a close second. Otherwise, we mostly had a basic philosophy (not so much rules) that prioritized our values about what was important, how to treat fellow beings and one another.

We wanted our kids to have self-esteem, to feel loved and encouraged to do the things that made them happy and that interested them. Somehow we never really got around to assigning household chores for them. We were completely lax about asking Rachael, Daniel, and Ellie to spend time on duties that might have taken away from their homework or from practicing their musical instruments or spending time outdoors.

Warren and I debated our parenting roles, individually and together, talking frequently about ways that would most encourage our children to become independent. We tried to lead by example, showing that it was possible for them to strive to be their best on their own terms. We had no preconceived ideas for what they would be interested in, what activities they would pursue, or what they would do later on in their lives. In my parents' tradition of enabling and enriching my brothers and me, I understood that each one of my children had their own unique talents and my job was to encourage, love, and protect them with all of my heart and energy, which is what I did. The fact that Rachael chose the piano, Daniel the French horn, and Ellie the violin was further evidence in our view that they liked being different from one another and weren't bowing to any peer or sibling pressure.

Warren and I worked together to provide what we felt was in their best interest every step of the way. We weren't always on target, and looking back we recognize many major mistakes. It's easy to second-guess decisions after the fact, so we try to remember that our intentions were always to give everything possible to make our kids' lives productive, meaningful, successful, and happy.

Warren would be the first to say that I believed everyone—be it a kid, dog, or grown-up—does better with goals and plans to reach those goals. I saw goal-setting as a key not only to individual success, but to the family's overall well-being. My list-making offers a daily reminder of the importance of little goals as well as big ones.

Most nights, I get out one of my small notebooks and make out a list for the next workday. That way, I wake up with everything settled in my mind. These can be related to things to do or just me spelling out long- and short-term goals, along with plans to achieve them.

Sometimes Warren will ask me a question and then see I'm making a list. He's always amazed at how much information I can pack onto a small blank page. I often joke, "My lists have lists."

Everyone has their own way of organizing their goals. It can be helpful to discuss them and have them in writing to refer back to their original intention and be reminded of the general direction we might take. After discussing ways to talk to our kids about values, Warren had the idea to engage them in conversation about creating guidelines toward being a happy, kind, thoughtful person, which was and is important to Warren and me.

We both saw values as a means of creating order and belonging and that it would be good to talk about what our values were—

especially once nine-year-old Rachael, seven-year-old Daniel, and four-and-a-half-year-old Ellie started having more and more activities. We imagined that putting something down in writing would provide rallying words to cheer one another on or just to create a good feeling.

Warren enlisted all three of them to come up with the Shapiro Rules. Ellie was probably too young to contribute at the time, but presumably Rachael and Daniel took her concerns into account. After multiple drafts and some help from Warren, they emerged with a wonderful overview of how to live a meaningful and productive life as a Shapiro. Their sections included "Be Smart," "Stay Healthy," and "Be Kind" with suggestions to be nice to everyone, including those who might be younger, or different, or who don't necessarily fit in with the most popular groups or who might have disabilities, and not to show off or brag and "Never ever be a bully."

And a section headed by "Be Tough":

> Don't let anyone pick on someone else; stand up for your
> friends. Stand up for what you know is right.

> Control yourself when you get mad, but don't be afraid to
> get mad. Sometimes you have to get mad to stop people
> from being mean (but be polite).

And "Be Clean":

> Don't leave junk around your room, you will trip on it.

> Don't litter, it's not fair to animals.

On the list of Shapiro Rules, there were no household chores mentioned, but in the section called "Always Do Your Best," the importance of practicing instruments was right at the top. So instead of chores, eventually their main job was to aim to practice every day for a minimum of two hours.

As time went on, I was happy when they chose to practice even longer. By that point, each of the kids had outgrown music teachers who had given them great foundations and then sent them off to lessons with some of the top teachers in New York City. Even though Daniel was the only one to later go on to become a professional musician—and I saw that the girls would not ultimately go that route—my feeling was that they should take advantage of their talents to be as good as they could be. There is nothing more gratifying than achieving a high level of any skill and feeling the rewards of hard work.

Daniel, logical and linear, who read Civil War histories and hefty nonfiction works that weren't even assigned to him, set his goal and designed his routine for five hours of daily practice of the French horn—with short breaks on the hour to recharge. Rachael had a much different approach. When she sat down to practice the piano, she did so for the sheer joy of it—with so much abandon that she might play for hours on end or for only a short period of time. Ellie's meticulous method for practicing the violin was first suggested by her teachers at Juilliard Pre-College (which Daniel had attended as well). Ellie would start with scales and progress to tackling a difficult piece measure by measure and phrase by phrase, repeating each series of notes over and over to perfection, blending feeling and precision.

There was so much we both loved about how each of them made their practice time matter and how they played with distinction, beautiful tonality, and finesse. Rachael threw in surprising elements. For example, when she was practicing the piano portion of a chamber music piece, Rachael would sing the violin and cello portions too. It was so much fun and so settling after a demanding day to listen to her play a wide-ranging repertoire. We didn't need a CD player. With her musicality and polish, I had the feeling of attending a private concert. The same went for the other two for different reasons. Whenever I heard Ellie on the violin, the pieces took me back to my own days of playing, and while I was never near to Ellie's level, I appreciated her accomplishments and talent all the more. The real surprise was Daniel's playing of the horn. We had worried that the big brass sound would overwhelm our house, but as soon as Daniel played his first note, it was like the missing resonant tone to join in with our household.

I never once took it for granted that we had three children who practiced with serious discipline and passion for their craft, filling up the different levels of our house with beautiful music for hours, every single day. There were several occasions when I had to jump on the phone to order vet practice supplies, and I chose to invite my favorite sales reps to listen along with me. My main medical supplies representative, Pam Conkey, has listened over the years as the three developed into serious young musicians. She and I have never met in person, but we continue to be great friends as well as work colleagues, and she still follows the adventures of the young Shapiros with great interest.

As our three reached and even surpassed their musical goals, we made it a point for us all to find times to enjoy music for its own sake. Sometimes we went to classical concerts as a family, and other times, like on road trips, we would all sing almost the entire Beatles catalog or Queen's "Bohemian Rhapsody" and not even notice the hours and miles flying by.

Over their developmental years, the more that I thought about how different Rachael, Daniel, and Ellie were from one another, how differently they had learned to be their best and managed to find their own brands of brilliance, the more I thought about how the various members of our dog pack had learned in unique ways to shine individually. That would lead to a question that would have later relevance for Piglet. After all, in the right environment, with encouragement and patience, why couldn't a blind and deaf puppy who could sit in the palm of my hand also learn to live his best life?

Even though all the words weren't explicitly stated in the Shapiro Rules, I could see how certain values were also implied—the importance of being yourself, standing up for the rights of others to be themselves, and caring for animals and others who needed compassion and kindness.

From childhood on, these were certainly values that led me to have a deepening interest in caring for animals with disabilities and special needs. Interestingly enough, it was around the same time the Shapiro Rules were being written that I found myself on the slippery slope of growing our numbers in our already full house—this time with a class of birds otherwise completely unprotected.

My history with birds was much different from my lifelong experience with dogs, although it probably was rooted in my passion for animal rescue that went back to childhood. Though I really had no interest in keeping birds, I unexpectedly found myself wanting to learn about wildlife rehab, which happened to include raising and releasing baby birds.

That's my only explanation for how, in the spring of 2003, when the kids were in elementary school, I was seized by the bright idea to get involved in wild bird rehab.

Baby bird season runs from early spring through the middle of the summer, and it is well-known in bird circles that many of the babies don't survive a whole host of dangers. Again, I wasn't and am still not an expert in avian veterinary practice or in wildlife rehabilitation, but I quickly learned that legally protected species are required to be brought to a licensed rehabilitator. House sparrows, pigeons, and European starlings, however, are not protected by federal law, so in most US states, anyone can step in to help them. Unfortunately, not being protected does leave them vulnerable to many levels of abuse. When I learned about the plight of these three unprotected species, I was drawn in and wanted to help. It was not a question of *why* I'd spend time caring for birds but *why not*.

There is a vast amount of research conducted by an array of interdisciplinary experts that says there is a measurable increase in happiness in the people who have birds in their home or who observe and hear birds outdoors. Humans are said to be healthier and less prone to illness in the places where environments support the health of diverse species of birds. When people are exposed to birds, these scientists say, they have a greater connection to nature and, as a result, are generally happier and healthier.

I can attest to the fact that our birds, as well as our dogs, helped deepen our children's love of animals, as well as an interest in animal welfare that was a common thread for all three, starting early on. After I rescued four baby house sparrows, took care of them, and prepared them for release back into the wild, eight-year-old Rachael assisted me in the process and wrote a memorable essay about the experience called "Baby Birds Fly to Freedom." In the fifth grade, she insisted on making an emergency call home from her elementary school about an injured bird, a dove, she'd found in an enclosed courtyard. After school, I met her at the entrance, and she led me to the spot so we could rescue the bird. It was a young dove with a wing injury that we took care of briefly at home before bringing it up to the wildlife center for release.

All of our birds were in love with Daniel, who had always been a science and nature buff, reminding his grandparents, Bama and Pot, of me at his age. Even as a baby he loved to gently touch trees and leaves, curiously connecting to the natural world around him. At the age of three, he wanted to read adult science books with tiny print for his bedtime stories.

At an early age, Daniel also was the first of our children to raise the issue of eating animals, when he pointed to our dinner of chicken and looked around at the family as if we had not realized something that had suddenly become obvious: "You know that is *shicken*, don't you?" We nodded as he repeated with his funny pronunciation, "We're eating *shicken*." Shortly thereafter I adopted a mainly plant-based diet altogether. Daniel did not, but he had a mindful approach to eating that started young.

When Daniel was in the third grade, I took him on a day trip, just the two of us, in our kayak. We brought money so we could stop at a little store along the river to get some snacks. I waited at the dock and watched Daniel run up to the little market alone to buy cantaloupe. When he returned, I resumed paddling up the river as he slowly ate every bite—absorbing the sights and sounds nearby.

At one point when we came to the bay, after he had been paddling with me again, Daniel asked, "Can we stop paddling?"

Concerned, I asked him, "Oh, are you getting tired?"

No, he said, he just wanted to stop to look at the scenery. And then while we were sitting and resting in the middle of the peaceful bay, he gave our surroundings one full glance and turned back to me, saying, "This is the best day of my whole life!"

It was a perfect day.

Daniel had always shown a special connection to all the birds we'd had—starting with Feather, a rescued green Quaker parrot who had been injured at the beach. Feather's permanently broken wing prevented him from being released back into the wild. Between his loud and noisy though mostly unintelligible monologues and his apparent dislike of Warren, Feather said one thing quite clearly: "Be quiet!" We all thought it was really cute and revealing because he created so much noise that we were constantly telling him to be quiet.

I loved Feather and hated to join the ranks of so many who abandon their beautiful parrots, but he eventually wore out his welcome with Warren. The truth is that most people are not equipped to deal with the noise and temperaments of most parrots. In our case, we were lucky that my good friend Patty Hochman, whose late husband, Dr. Howard Hochman, was an avian vet, and the veterinarian for the Beardsley Zoo in Bridgeport, had me bring Feather to her. She assured me that she would keep him herself until she could find him the perfect home. It took a year, but eventually Feather went to live with a friend of Patty's, where he shared a large room with another parrot friend. They were not kept in a cage but flew freely in their room, building nests and enjoying a very good bird life.

Later, when an injured robin I raised started to fly again, he would land only on Daniel's head. Dakota the pigeon, who had a severe head injury, would sleep on Daniel's hand. When we had several baby birds in the house, Daniel helped me feed them once they were stable and growing. Usually, this is not a suitable job for a young child because baby birds are so fragile that they can aspirate food if it's not administered very carefully. Yet this process revealed that he had a knack for this kind of meticulous care.

For my kids, caring for birds in our home enabled their all-around interest in animal welfare and general love of helping care for pets. When Ellie was very young, instead of leaving her with a babysitter, I would have her join me as my adorable toddler veterinary assistant. Her job was to wipe the runny eyes of our dog patients with cotton balls I kept in my supply box. Ellie developed a practice of holding an old chewed roll of adhesive tape as a distraction for puppies when I gave them their vaccines. She remembers this vividly and reminds me of this sweet memory whenever we talk about her coming to work with me. She also helped me by eating breakfast with my clients during house-call visits and thoroughly enchanting them. With her long, curly golden-brown hair and twinkling blue eyes, she charmed humans and nonhumans alike. Ellie could sit and have a conversation with anyone of any age, much like her older siblings.

Like Daniel, Ellie was interested in caring for two baby birds I brought home. It was so sweet to see real human siblings caring for two infant birds who became surrogate siblings in our home.

Of all the birds who joined our household at different stages, Lukita stole Ellie's heart when he arrived during her high school years. I'd first seen Lukita, our blue foreign-speaking debonair parakeet, in a Facebook post with a picture of him lying on his belly. I'd already begun saying *no more birds*, but Lukita was destined to be the last I would bring home.

Feather the green Quaker parrot had given me a taste of what it was like to fall in love with a bird. But it only took one tiny baby bird to make me fully appreciate what I'd been missing for my whole life! My bird rescue crusade kicked into high gear on July 5, 2003, when Warren, the kids, and I were driving back home from a vacation in Maine and I heard from Diane, a vet tech back home, about a baby bird in rather dire shape. Diane told me about the newborn house sparrow, saying, "She was found two days ago, baking on a hot sidewalk." A kind individual had picked up the near-death baby and brought her to the vet hospital, where Diane took her in, started feeding her, and treated her injured right eye.

Wary, I expressed concern about diving in all over again, after having lost a baby grackle a couple of weeks earlier.

Diane assured me, "This one is a survivor."

My first glimpse of Baby Bird, as I soon named her, was not so comforting. She was a featherless pink prehistoric tiny creature with a sparse few pinfeathers coming in on her wings. She had a severely infected right eye and mangled crooked legs. Yet she managed to look right up at me with her good eye—with a wink just about that seemed to say, *What took you so long?* It was as if she knew I was the one who was supposed to come get her.

When Baby Piglet arrived in March 2017, he looked like a
baby pig, a piglet, which is how he got his name!

Baby Piglet's toys were as big as he was.

Melissa at six years old with her new mini schnauzer puppy, Pretzel.

Warren and Melissa with their sweet dogs Jamie
and April at Compo Beach in 1991.

Melissa with April at the Foodmans', in Westport, 1990.

Rachael, Daniel, and Ellie, at ages seven, five, and three, swimming at the Hilton Garden Inn in Freeport, Maine.

Baby Bird sitting on eight-year-old Daniel's shoulder while he did his homework at the kitchen table.

Rachael with Zoey and Susie at our favorite Compo Beach in 2016.

Sweet Susie comforting Baby Piglet when he first arrived in March of 2017.

Monica cradling and singing to Baby Piglet the first moment they met at Norwalk Veterinary Hospital on March 4, 2017.

Daniel with beautiful Gina on our front porch in 2019.

Odd couple Piglet and Zoey celebrating Valentine's Day, 2018.

Dean and Gina in our backyard with Ellie, April 2021.

Melissa Shapiro

Melissa Shapiro

(Above) Piglet and his Inclusion Pack sitting together on a stone bench at Longshore Club Park in 2019.

Piglet with his extra special veterinarian friend and rescuer, Dr. Gloria Andrews, reunited in September 2017 at an adoption event in Connecticut.

Melissa Shapiro

(Above) Ellie with Piglet
and the "travel team" girls
at Piglet's favorite college,
Princeton University, 2018.

Melissa Shapiro

Piglet in his stroller.

Piglet on the A-frame with his mom spotting him at the
Special K9 Games in Columbus, Ohio in 2018.

Piglet sitting in front of the first ever Piglet Mindset poster, created by third graders in Plainville, Massachusetts, in the fall of 2017.

Piglet is proud of his stickers that grace water bottles all around the world!

Piglet, Susie, and Evie doing a tap-signal demo during a class visit in 2019.

Piglet saying hello to teacher Ms. Tricia Fregeau during the
first Pink Party in Plainville, Massachusetts, in June 2018.

Piglet dressed in his Superman costume doing his tap-signal demo for third graders during our visit to their classroom with the *NBC Nightly News* team in November 2019.

(Above) Favorite Dad Warren with Piglet in front of The Lemon ce King of Corona in Queens, New York, July 2018.

Seven dogs in our kitchen all waiting for a treat!

The handsome pink Piglet at Compo Beach, 2020.

I spent many hours warming her, cradling her, and allowing my hand to become her favorite napping nest. She had a hearty appetite, and once she started eating on her own, delicacies like Special K cereal, bagels, and cream cheese became her favorite treats. She took baths in a little yellow bowl, and skillfully flew around our living room and kitchen area despite the loss of her right eye. Like most birds, she was set in her ways and did not adapt well to changes, like a new chair in the living room, a change in the type of cereal, or the location of her favorite perch.

Baby Bird was forever a baby, in need of holding, petting, and comforting. She was unbelievably precious. She made me unbelievably happy. She made everyone happy. We had no plans to have any more birds, except for rescued babies that would be released. But plans, like rules, can sometimes change, and I took in my second house sparrow when Baby Bird was about two years old. Rescued by Wildlife in Crisis, a wildlife rehabilitation center in Weston, Connecticut, the three-week-old baby house sparrow—whom Warren named Bobby— had come to me to help rehab for a poorly healed leg fracture. He was drop-dead adorable with his little yellow baby sparrow beak. Bobby was friendly, very social, and loved music.

Bobby came to stay. His injured leg had healed in the most inconvenient position—sticking straight out to the side. He would not have survived if released.

Warren looked at me and, having seen the futility of saying no, reluctantly nodded an *okay*.

For the next week, I continued to feed Bobby by hand every hour on the hour. Bobby's unnaturally healed leg limited his movement so that he could hop along and kind of fly, maybe fifty percent of the time. The challenge was that his wing feathers would get scratched off when he contorted to be able to scratch his head. He also had trouble getting good footing when landing to be held on my arm or on flat household surfaces. After observing how, in the cage, he would stand next to the edge so he could wedge his foot up against the side bars, I covered the perches with paper towels so he wouldn't abrade his leg and foot on the hard wood. Eventually, I started wearing fleece jackets and shirts so he could snuggle without slipping. In no time, I collected quite the wardrobe of bird fleece, which I wore every day.

Bobby was also sort of a flirt. It wasn't just that he sang perfectly in my direction but that he made kissing noises to me. If I kissed his head, he kissed me back in the same rhythm at the same time.

Unexpectedly, Bobby turned out to be a musical prodigy. Because he lived downstairs in the den—then also occupied by the piano where the kids would play—after a few months, Bobby started to sing his own renditions of Bach, Haydn, and Mozart. At first, I thought he was chirping along and only sounding like he knew the music, but with time it became apparent that Bobby had memorized the works of different composers and was chiming in at key parts in the music with his own original chirping patterns and sequences. He would sing along at precisely the same point in the music, each time.

"Do you hear what he's doing?" I whispered to Warren, who was as flabbergasted as me the first time we caught on to what a musical prodigy he was.

Warren whispered back, "He's adding his own trills and long notes that are part of the melody!"

Bobby's abilities were quite elaborate. Rachael later did her eighth-grade science project about the biological processes in bird song development that allowed him to master so many classical music pieces.

Like each one of our birds who joined and/or followed Baby Bird, Bobby was such a quirky character. At about three months of age he was out of his cage, sitting on my shoulder one afternoon, when nine-year-old Daniel walked into the den wearing his red sweatshirt, sending Bobby into a dramatic fit as he dove into his cage screaming at the top of his lungs. We couldn't figure it out until Daniel took off his sweatshirt and Bobby calmed down. He was freaked out by the color red. From then on, I told everyone, "You're wearing red, you're not coming in the living room."

Weirdly, Bobby developed a major fascination with my portable ultrasound unit. He would sit on my shoulder and look at the computer screen whenever I reviewed the imagery, before hopping back and forth from my left hand on the controls to my right hand, which held the probe on the dog.

Right around this time, I "accidentally" adopted two more house sparrows. The first was Stevie, who had been brought in to the vet hospital at about six days old without any identifying information. Two days later, after being pampered and fed all day by the vet techs—who named her Steven, unaware yet of her sex—I volunteered to take care of her briefly. From the minute I saw her, it was obvious she was already completely imprinted on humans, and she was determined to be with people every minute of the day. I took her home with the sincere intention of bringing her straight to the wildlife rehab center, where I was hoping she would go back to being a bird. We were set to go, packed and planning on it, but I had to delay the trip due to family obligations. By the time I could take Stevie up there, we had fallen in love with her, and I made the decision to keep her until I found a companion for her, knowing well that imprinted birds do not do well when released into the wild.

Rather than adopt her for good, I found Betty, an available sister sparrow—who was exactly the same age—so that I could do a soft release in the backyard with the two birds together. When I first made the introduction, Stevie was not having it. She threw a four-hour chirping tantrum, standing in her box as far away from Betty as possible, as if the new bird friend was invading her wonderful life. Before too long, miraculously, the babies bonded into an adorable pair. What began as a cautious interest in each other soon led to their learning to fly together—the most euphoric sight to see. One baby learning to fly is extraordinary; two babies flying together, alternately struggling and soaring, pushing each other past their fears, is magic. In their case, our living room was their flight runway, which was quite the sight. Stevie and Betty slept and snuggled together, and shared food, attention, and activity.

Ornithologists and experts in social aspects of avian behavior have suggested that under certain circumstances birds exhibit traits of generosity that are noble and even uncanny. Most of the birds who visited and/or stayed with us were not as social with one another as Betty and Stevie. Their friendship was epic. The bonded pair spent their first summer and winter in a small bathroom, flying free during the day. They slept in their cage at night for safety reasons. We established their various morning and evening rituals while they were in the house.

Betty proved to be a most comical bird who was not inhibited about expressing her strong opinions. She loved to chatter, especially in the springtime. She was an alarmist to the point that after I got new eyeglasses, she wouldn't come near me for weeks. A new black shirt with pink lettering sent Betty into a tailspin, and when I put on snow boots in the winter she became hysterical.

Once it became clear that Stevie and Betty were Shapiro birds, I wasn't sure where to keep them in our already crowded house. Baby Bird was in one spot in the living room, while Bobby was in another, both bonded to me as individuals. In an effort to avoid further fallout from breaking the unspoken rule prohibiting too many animals, I had an epiphany that we could avoid the madness by commissioning a beautiful outdoor aviary just for Betty and Stevie. The birdhouse of my dreams had to be predator-proof, and it had to have heat in the winter. Most important, it had to be spacious enough for them to fly free, and for me to sit and visit with them.

We began this relatively small-scale project in the summer of 2008, and I threw myself into it as though I were my mom planning a wedding (which, by the way, was not something I might ever do, not being a fan of all the wedding excess). For weeks I spent untold numbers of hours researching and designing the safest housing for Betty and Stevie—comparing materials and choosing a location in our backyard. Getting it built became a nightmare! My original lavish budget of $1,000 crept steadily up to $3,500. We began with the help of a friend, and then a handyman finished the work. My father added an electrical outlet at the end so that the birds could have heat during the winter. After many fits and starts, when The Bird House (as it was lovingly named) was finished in the spring of 2009, it was exactly what I wanted for my two tiny brown birds.

On its first official night of use, Warren and I, fourteen-year-old Rachael, twelve-year-old Daniel, and ten-year-old Ellie walked out to behold the Girlitas in their outdoor newly completed Bird House.

Warren commented, "It's like a fortress!"

The kids nodded in agreement. Relieved, I could sleep now knowing they were going to be safe.

It was a big transition for Betty and Stevie, as they had to adjust to a new climate, new sounds, and a new set of perches. We kept some of the old routines and created new ones. They took baths in their bathing bowls, which were placed on the bench during the warm months. They had their afternoon carrots and apples on the bench and in the open cage. In the evening, they roosted on the door, where I found them waiting for me to hold them in my hands before I put them on their respective perches in the cage for the night. The cage got covered with a sheet in the summer and fleece in the winter. When the weather turned frigid and unbearable, or if there was a big storm, they came into the house temporarily. The Girlitas had the best of all worlds. They had each other, they loved people, they loved the outdoors, and they loved being pampered.

Throughout the time the two lived in The Bird House, I went out anywhere from three to four times a day to feed, clean, and visit the birds, day after day, year after year. We sat in the peaceful calm of The Bird House enjoying one another's company while I made work phone calls or created new lists or, on occasion, found a peaceful place to cry about a variety of cry-worthy events.

In the summer of 2011, Bobby became very ill. Despite everything I tried—including a number of meds and treatments—he stopped eating and I knew the end was coming.

Out of desperation, I put on CDs of Rachael playing, and he became alert and happy and began to chirp along. (She was away at camp or she would have played for him in person.) That moment let me offer him, and me, some comfort, although I knew he was not going to recover. Bobby died in my hand at the age of six years old. He is the reason that I own so many fleece shirts and jackets, and why I still never wear red. His favorite, a purple North Face fleece jacket, especially reminds me whenever I put it on of how much joy our sweet little Baba brought into our house.

In this same period, seven-year-old Baby Bird was also in decline. The precious girl became ill and languished for so long that I had to accept it was time to let her go peacefully. My job had taught me to be accepting in those times when it was necessary. There was no debate. Baby Bird was in constant pain, and her quality of life was fading. But on the same morning when I'd planned to put her to sleep, her desire to have breakfast with me was so strong that I decided to wait just a little bit longer. That gave us time to change her medications, and add road trips to her list of favorite activities.

Two weeks later, our first opportunity to travel came along thanks to a trip I'd planned to take Rachael for her first college visit—to Oberlin in Ohio. I packed Baby Bird up, not knowing how it would turn out, but I knew I couldn't leave her home with Warren. In fact, she was so fragile that I brought euthanasia solution with me just in case things turned south. But she was immediately rejuvenated with the Beatles song "Ob-La-Di Ob-La-Da." And we were off onto a new chapter in her life that centered around traveling with me wherever I went.

Warren was stunned by this reversal. "You're telling me that Baby Bird wants to do more traveling?"

I couldn't explain it, but, yes, I knew it was the right thing to do. That's what we both wanted. Besides, I wasn't going to leave her after seeing how much she'd enjoyed our trip.

Over the last five years of her life, Baby Bird came on countless trips with me to other states. She traveled in a tiny carrier, which became her regular sleeping spot as well. When in the car, she chirped to old Beatles music. She waited for me every night to visit with her—a space of time when finally I could sit down once my kids were all in bed and the house was quiet. We'd share a bowl of Special K cereal with cow's milk, but eventually, we graduated to organic multigrain cereal with almond milk. She would eat her cereal and then go to sleep in my hand. It was a quiet, peaceful time we shared every night for twelve years.

Baby Bird had just gotten out of the woods when, in July 2010, I noticed that Stevie was suffering—the result of an illness that was due to an egg that was stuck. After weeks of lubricants, Metacam, Clavamox, and a lot of worry, she was still swollen and straining. I brought her to my zoo and bird veterinarian friend, Dr. Hochman,

who collapsed the egg with a needle. This alleviated the pressure in her abdomen and allowed her to eventually pass the eggshell. In anticipation of losing her, I adopted five-week-old Sunny so that Betty wouldn't be alone. Fortunately, Stevie survived the egg ordeal. When I brought Sunny out to be with the girls in The Bird House, Sunny only wanted to chase them and have bird brawls. So Sunny moved back into her room upstairs in our house, later joined by a blind sparrow named Willie.

Our bedtime routine with the Girlitas in The Bird House was the same every night for eight years until November of 2016, when my little Stevie was in her final decline. Despite my greatest efforts and a massive amount of tears, there was little else I could do. Deep down I had known that she wasn't going to recover. Unfortunately, I had to go to New York City to attend Ellie's November orchestra concert at Juilliard. I really didn't want to leave Stevie but felt comfortable that at least she was with her sister, Betty, in their sleeping cage in the bird-house. We got home around eleven, and I ran out to check on her. She was huddled in the corner, struggling to breathe. I picked her up and held her to my lips. She took another two to three breaths as I felt her relax peacefully in my hand. I was crushed but relieved for Stevie. She was bonded to Betty, but her true bond was with me. Stevie gave me the incomparable gift of her own brand of a calm that only a special little house sparrow can share.

Unwilling to leave Betty outside alone, I still wasn't sure how she would do, moving inside with Sunny and Blind Boy Willie, both house sparrows. Betty had been inside for a winter a few years before, as well as during a few severe storms. But for the most part she and Stevie had been outside year-round.

Much to my surprise and relief, it only took a day or two for Betty to settle and accept her new home. By 2017, when Piglet became our foster dog, the four birds who lived inside with us in our full house were Betty, Sunny, Willie, and Lukita. It had only been a year and a half earlier, on August 5, 2015, that the time had come for me to say goodbye to my dearest, beloved, beautiful Baby Bird. After her miraculous recovery five years earlier, I knew she had been living on borrowed time.

Baby Bird's final illness was a rapidly growing abdominal tumor. It was one of the most heart-wrenching times of my life, even though I had expected it. She had just turned twelve and had made two last summer trips with us to Maine and Western New York State before her pain became too great. She was as connected to me as any dog I've ever loved, and she was one of the most pleasant, precious, and special little friends I could ever wish to spend so much time with. During Baby Bird's years with us, we had increased the bird population and filled the house with the music of their singing and chirping, and they were all delights and funny, lovely, animated characters who gave us all joy. Still, when Baby Bird left, she took a big piece of me with her. Less than two years later, I hadn't nearly recovered from the loss enough to begin to imagine allowing another to occupy the same place in my heart.

So when Piglet showed up, in need of so much care, I could only choose to give him my all, teach him all that I could, and then, as Ellie voiced so often—expressing feelings the rest of the family shared—find him his forever home.

That was the right thing to do. We would find him a place where his new family would be ready for a deaf blind pink puppy, somewhere wonderful where he belonged, that would give him his very best life.

Chapter 7

DOESN'T PIGLET
HAVE A SAY?

*Five little puppies dug a hole under the fence and went for a walk
in the wide, wide world. . . .*
—*The Poky Little Puppy*, Janette Sebring Lowrey (1942)

(The top all-time best-selling children's hardcover book in English, and
my favorite as a child and as an adult.)

APRIL 14–MAY 3, 2017

For a hot minute, Warren and I had given in to thinking that our
best bet would be to place Piglity with someone we knew personally.
That way we could see him and check up on his well-being. There
was a flaw in that logic, but we went with it. Sure enough, through
a musician friend and professional violinist named Darwin Shen,
we connected to another musician friend named Andy Armstrong,
a concert pianist, whose very pregnant wife, Esty, had fallen in love
with Piglet on Facebook. After Warren saw Andy one night at a concert I didn't attend, he received an email with a passionate declara-
tion of his wife's desire to adopt our foster puppy. Andy wrote:

Crazy question for you. I was trying to guess how serious Esty was about Piglet. Turns out she was totally serious. I'm planning a date of surprise things for Esty (like a pottery session) in Westport for next Saturday. So, outrageous question, mightn't Piglet still be with you in 5 days and mightn't we stop by to visit you for a short while some time during the day? I'm a bit of a dreamer, and can't help fantasizing about a scenario where we are the perfect home to give Piglet tons of adult/kiddy/and-other-doggies-LOVE. Though I am fully prepared to be rejected. You and Melissa know Piglet so well of course, and you will know what is the perfect life for him . . .

This was charming, of course, and somewhat glamorous but raised a few red flags. Inviting them to stop by (how could I say no?), I let him know in advance that Piggy would need a great deal of attention and that a small child and big dogs (which they already had) were not compatible with such a teeny disabled dog.

The visit ought to have discouraged them but when Andy and Esty dropped by, all the dogs, including Piglet, were delighted to see them. Led by sweet Susan, they crowded our guests in a swarm of tail-wagging enthusiasm. In my arms, Piglet was on his best behavior.

Watching this scene play out put the progress of our household into greater perspective. Warren had a theory that Susie's ability to set the tone came from her great aspiration to surround herself with a diverse group of dogs who would be kind and accepting of one another. Somehow Piglet had helped expand that capacity. Zoey had learned to share me with Piggy without losing her own cuteness crown. Evie and Annie, tentative at first, had stepped up when needed. Evie would goad our foster baby on during our walks, while Annie, shy as she is, would go over to him occasionally to calm his anxiety. Gina had avoided Piggy for weeks but at one point decided he was fun, after all. She understood that she was so much bigger than him so no matter how rough he tried to play with her, she stayed gentle. Dean was the last holdout, keeping his cool—though not happily—with his only competition for female attention. Still, if he detected a note of fear in his foster brother or a possible threat from another dog or human, Dean would let his barking presence be known.

After the dogs said their hellos to the Armstrongs, little Piglet gave them his own very warm greeting. They asked a range of questions, as I shared our thoughts on what the ideal Piglet home would be like. They were smitten and Andy followed up the visit with an email of continuing interest, but I knew it wouldn't work.

In my emailed response, I went over my concerns—including the fact that Piglet would really need one or two small, kind dogs for friendship and snuggling, and that with a baby on the way, I knew their time was going to be limited. In all honesty, I wrote:

> . . . I greatly appreciate your interest in this very special
> puppy. I'm having a very hard time even considering handing
> him over to anyone. But when the right match comes along,
> hopefully it will be clear and relatively easy for me to give in.

Two years later, Andy offered hearty, belated thanks that I had not given them the go-ahead. This was after he realized the incredible rigors of a newborn baby! But at the time, I asked, "Was I too harsh?" as Warren reread my email the next morning. He said, no, then read aloud my line about my having a hard time "even considering" handing him over.

Warren just looked at me.

"I know, I know. Gloria has a new candidate who looks like a match," I reminded Warren.

Just then Ellie walked into the kitchen to grab her packed lunch and sensed something was in the air.

"Mom! Dad! No . . ." It was like she had discovered us having a relapse of some sort. She said a lot of things that made perfect sense to me, all along the lines of *How could you turn down the opportunity to give him to a concert pianist and his family?* Under her words were loving concern for her parents. She didn't have to say, *Do you really want to have a severely disabled dog hermetically sealed to you 24/7?*

Warren grabbed his stuff for work and followed Ellie toward the door, reassuring her, "The rescue group in Georgia has a really promising candidate. They know what they're doing."

He said it really loud so I could hear it too.

The minute I loaded up the car for my house calls later that morning, my brain attempted to switch into hyperfocus mode. My four-dog travel crew for this day—Evie, Zoey, Gina, and Piglet—were all in their respective places in my very large Honda Odyssey minivan, ready to roll. As I started down our street, the rain began.

To my fellow passengers I announced, "Well, that's going to make a mess of traffic!" But in a way I welcomed the rain. I was in the mood for mellow seventies rock. But I settled on some more lively bluegrass.

Piglet was making some honking-type barks, and I just wanted to enjoy the music and think about our next stops and said loudly to the pink boy, "Could ya keep it down?" Then I felt bad, even if he couldn't hear me. About to say something apologetic, I realized all of a sudden, *Oh, he's not barking. Or whining or screaming.* We drove another ten minutes. Not a peep. Was he okay? Had he fallen asleep? At a stoplight I checked on him. He was awake, alert, along for the ride, and, as I'd told everyone their job for the day was to visit with some of my favorite clients after my appointments, he seemed ready to do what was asked of him.

"What a good boy you are, Piglity!" I praised him. Of course, I had to tell each of the girls how good they were too. They were! The rainy drive had been a chance to feel grateful. Fostering Piglet for longer than expected had taught me so much. We would be fine letting him go. We would be. We had to be.

For no obvious reason, it was then that a memory popped into my head of an incident that took place when I was in vet school, when I volunteered to decorate the bulletin boards at the Tippecanoe County Humane Society with information about spaying and neutering dogs and cats. Vet students like me routinely volunteered there in Lafayette to do exams on shelter animals, and while I was there I'm sure my mother's teacher influence had something to do with my needing to fix up the bulletin boards with colorful, attractive, informative posters. This was early practice for later jazzing up my kids' school poster projects.

At the time, the pet overpopulation was exponentially worse than it is today—a change that happened in large part thanks to organizations like the Humane Society of the United States, Friends of Animals, and Petfinder.com. Wanting to help, I was there stapling my colorful display outlining the benefits of spaying and neutering dogs and cats onto the bulletin board in the rather dreary but clean entry area when an older, short, stocky, balding man came in with a beagle.

My attention was drawn to this good-looking, healthy, reasonably well-behaved dog—who, it became immediately clear, was being dumped at a shelter for no apparent rational reason. That powerless feeling I had of not being able to help was a heart-wrenching experience that still makes me cry these decades later. Dumping any animal that has been a family member at a kill shelter is beyond my wildest imagination.

The man brought that sweet dog up to the desk, and as he handed her over, he said quietly, "My grandson would kill me if he knew I was doing this."

Too upset to stay much longer, I finished quickly, ran out sobbing, grabbed my bike, a light blue Schwinn Continental that I used for transportation in those days, jumped on it, and sped off. Distraught as I was, I kept an eye on the road. But, as I was riding down a long hill that ran down the middle of Lafayette, where there were cars parallel parked along the side, I didn't notice the door of a white Camaro opening right in front of me. Though at the last second I swerved to avoid hitting it head-on, I did hit the edge of the door and literally went flying into the middle of the street.

Landing in a heap, tangled in the bike frame, I looked back with relief to see there were no cars barreling down the hill toward me. In an oddly vivid moment, I watched as the driver—a young woman with long, dark hair pulled back who was dressed in a short skirt, boots, and a short fur coat of some sort—approached me.

"Are you okay?" she asked.

"Yes," I said, trying to be calm as I struggled to untangle myself from my bike.

Relieved, she turned and walked away, muttering a barely audible "Sorry."

Zero empathy. Just like the man who was getting rid of a dog whose future would be completely uncertain. Not a shred of compassion.

The bike was a wreck, but I was able to get it fixed at a nearby bicycle shop. It lived and so did I, despite a badly banged up leg. The experience had sharpened my belief about living up to our responsibilities to the animals we bring into our homes—keeping our promises to love and protect them as best we can. Happily, that facility later became a no-kill shelter and was taken over by a nonprofit called Almost Home Humane Society.

The memory reminded me that while I had lived up to my promise to foster Piglet—and had helped turn a screaming, anxious, needy puppy into a much calmer, loving, amazingly adaptable dog with rapidly improving coping skills—it was critical that we find him a *committed* forever family soon. It was essential that such a family appreciate him for the wonderful, quirky character that was emerging, and who would be there to help him thrive as he grew out of his puppyhood and into the full-fledged dog that he would eventually be.

As I reviewed our destinations for the day, I paused to appreciate the evolution of my practice. House calls are a naturally good alternative for a wide range of veterinary needs, but in-home care is particularly well suited for older pets. From the start of my career, I'd always enjoyed working with elderly dogs and cats. So much so that in 2014 I created Your Senior Pet's Vet, a subdivision within Visiting Vet Service to formally address the needs of senior pets. I had always offered end-of-life care but formalized the service, making it much easier for pet parents to understand how I could help when their pets were aging and when they were nearing the end of their lives.

Though I have never tallied up the number of animals I have euthanized over the years, I do remember many of the encounters I've had with people who were absolutely devastated in the very last moments they were spending with their beloved pet. Most think that those euthanasia appointments are the worst part of being a veterinarian. The responsibility for guiding families through palliative care, quality of life assessments, and then finally choosing to allow their pet to leave them in a kind, peaceful way is a tremendous responsibility. There are no other professions that routinely put humans in a position to legally take a life.

From my earliest professional days, I knew this and accepted that the custom care provided to senior pets and their families invariably culminates in loss, very often in that final decision and procedure—euthanasia. The pressure to be skillful, compassionate, and have the ability to improvise, is real. But rather than this being the hardest part of my job, I have found it to be one of the most rewarding pieces of my life as a veterinarian—being there for people in distress, and giving the gift of a peaceful death to a beautiful animal who has given all he or she can.

I generally don't cry with my clients, but I do comfort and support them, validate their decision to have their pet euthanized, and afterward, I encourage them to take out their favorite pictures and write about their pets.

Sometimes, after we've finished and we're standing outside by my car, clients might want to cuddle with my dogs—who are always so sweet, allowing the person going through such a painful passage to cry more or to laugh or dream again of parenting another animal.

Once I had my Your Senior Pet's Vet website up and running, I did a mailing out to area vets informing them of the expanded reach of these mobile services, and many began referring their patients to me. I also got lots of word-of-mouth referrals from previous clients and friends who knew that I offered in-home end-of-life and euthanasia services. The main challenge for me as demand has grown is that it can be an unpredictable business. I get calls at all hours of the day and night, during the week, and on weekends. Usually, euthanasia appointments can't be scheduled too far in advance.

One Friday night, I was finally sitting down to tackle a large pile of records and invoices when I got a call from a distraught dog-mom. She had been given my name earlier when the family golden retriever showed no signs of improvement after being diagnosed with a bleeding splenic tumor. Her college-age kids had come home to say goodbye, and though they'd thought their sweet dog Harley would make it to the morning, she had begun to deteriorate and was having some labored breathing.

The woman tearfully apologized, saying that it would mean so much if I could come to their home for euthanasia rather than having to bring Harley to the emergency clinic. "I'd been dreading making the decision, which is why I didn't call earlier. I'm sure it would have made it easier for you." It was late, but there was something about her anguished voice that made me say, "I'll be there as soon as I can."

With my supplies and a couple of small dogs loaded into the car, I plugged the address into the GPS, and off I went. Upon my arrival, I found a beautiful family of five huddled around their sweet golden retriever, who was definitely ready to move on.

"We'll make sure that Harley is comfortable and at peace," I promised quietly. It was heartbreaking. They were all crying as each of them said a goodbye and a thank-you for being their best dog ever. That Harley was one of those amazing all-around family dogs who was loved by all who knew her. The family's three sons moved her into the back of my car so I could arrange for her cremation.

A couple of years later, I was walking with my dogs down our street when a car stopped next to me. The woman introduced herself and proceeded to thank me again for being there for Harley that night and for her and her family. These are moments—when former clients stop me on the street to say "thank you" for helping them during their most difficult times with their pets—that make my job rewarding and reaffirm that my efforts have had a lasting impact on so many people whose paths have crossed mine.

Out on my rounds on that particular day, when I'd reminded myself that I wasn't going to be the one to find Piglet's adoptive future home, I knew there was an elephant in the living room—or rather, a tiny pink tornado of a puppy who could neither see nor hear and who had stolen my heart. The clock was ticking. We couldn't keep putting off the inevitable.

By the end of the day, the rain had subsided, the appointments had gone smoothly and, as a special treat for Piglet, I decided to drop by Norwalk Veterinary Hospital for supplies, and to say hi. The minute I got Piggy out of his little crate and bundled him into my arms, he knew exactly where he was and started sniffing madly in the exact direction of the side entrance he'd used before. Mr. Amazing! The urgent ping of a text message made me pause, hug the pink baby, and glance down to see that Rachael's name had come up. Apparently, she had just heard that Piglet wasn't going to go to the Armstrongs:

> Please tell me that you aren't considering keeping him, Mom! You can't have seven dogs. You can't! Please end the chaos!

That's it, I thought. *I'm going home, and I will read over everything and look closely at the latest candidate from Gloria and Carolyn.* But first, Piggy Lee was going to go see his best girlfriend Monica, not to mention Emily, and a growing number of the female vet techs and assistants he was adding to his list of friends.

We'd barely gotten in the door before Monica and Emily were at our sides, whisking Piglet away from me, both of them surrounding him in a huddle that gave him a cradle as he dove headfirst into Emily's pocket for a treat and then, munching still, flew up Monica's arm and down her shirt.

As always, she chatted and sang to him in a mix of Spanish, English, and gibberish, and as she did, I had to take a video. "Now that he likes pocket diving, pretty soon he's going to outgrow shirt diving," Monica warned. "He won't be a baby for too much longer!" With that, Piglet poked his head out of her top and brought his nose right up to her mouth, inhaling her breath. "See, I told you," she reminded me, "it's the cilantro!"

Dr. Charlie Duffy, an animal whisperer if there ever was one, dashed past us as he bid farewell to a canine patient eager to head home. "Wow," he said peering down to take a closer look at Piglet. "He's doubled in size! It's hard to believe he's the same puppy; he seems so much happier!"

Monica walked Piglet and me toward the exit. "Everything okay, Dr. Shapiro?" she asked. She knew that we were running low on options for an adoptive home and could see what was happening.

"Absolutely. You just can't be too careful."

Monica nodded in agreement and then shrugged, saying, "And you know what? If you decide to keep him, there's nothing wrong with that."

I loved that she said it, but a big message flashed across my brain—the email I'd sent to Warren that read, *Foster project?* I mumbled my appreciation and admitted it would be hard but it was for the best.

"Yeah, I'm sure," she agreed, though she didn't sound so sure. She handed Piglet back to me and gave him a last nose rub with her nose. "But if you change your mind, or don't find the right place, don't stress—I got your back, girlfriend."

Piglet didn't seem to pick up on any of my turbulent energy as I carried him out to the car. Why would he? In his scope of awareness, I'm certain he believed he was exactly where he was supposed to be. In my arms.

MAY 3, 2017

Everything came to a head almost two months exactly (less one day) from when Baby Bart had unexpectedly taken control of every minute of our days. Minor events seemed to take on added weight, pushing me one way or the other. There was a visit to New York City to see Rachael that included a walk with Piglity in her neighborhood. As we passed a few clusters of tourists on the street, we both noticed that the pink pup was getting a lot of stares and compliments. Someone said, "Omigod, is that a tiny baby pig?"

Rachael, gregarious always and quite charismatic, said, "No, it's a puppy whose name is Piglet."

Soon he had drawn a small crowd. Piggy did a little twisty dance and showed off in response to the attention he could only sense, not see or hear. The reactions were identical to those that I'd get on social media. "He's adorable!" "Precious!" "So sweet!" Smiles, laughter, and tearful shakes of heads—because he was so cute and not at all dismayed by his disabilities. The thing that struck me most, though, was how much trust he had to have in me to let so many strangers come close. He knew he was protected. Not only that, but he seemed to enjoy the attention. That was something of a revelation to me.

We walked on.

Rachael started to speak. "Mom, I understand how hard this is, but—"

"We'll have someone," I interrupted. "It's down to two applicants. . . . One of them looks really good."

She looked at me and smiled with love. Instead of telling me what to do—because she had already made her point—Rachael acknowledged that she knew saying goodbye was not going to be easy.

A few days later, I was surprised to see Ellie arriving home with one of her friends from school. This was something of a rare occurrence, and I was glad that the dogs were all relatively quiet when the two of them arrived. Ellie led the way into the kitchen, where Piggy Lee was happily playing with a chew toy. Not screaming or being obnoxious.

"Oh, your puppy is so adorable!"

Ellie shrugged, admitting he was cute, but added that he was a foster dog, and, "We aren't keeping him."

Her friend seemed incredulous. Why would we not keep such a little adorable dog who must not be any trouble at all?

Working at the kitchen table right nearby, I tried not to laugh or appear to listen too closely.

Ellie explained that he had severe disabilities and that I'd been getting him ready for a home where he was going to be much better off.

At that moment, I was working on invoices to clients. Though I was concentrating, Ellie's comment sent a jealous pang through me.

I wondered, *Why would he be better off anywhere else?* All kinds of other issues had been tugging at me, but this put everything into its simplest and purest form. What was going to be best for Piglet?

Days earlier, Daniel had dropped by to visit and had asked if I could see Piglet being happy at the homes of the two people still in contention. When I showed him the profile of one of them—a woman who lived in the country with a large amount of land, as well as several dogs, including a blind dog whom they took very good care of and who would be a nice companion for Bart/Piggy—Daniel took a close look at some of the pictures she had posted on her own Facebook page. The setting was gorgeous, and there were absolutely sweet pictures of her grandchildren, but Daniel pointed to one outdoor photo, saying, "There's no fence."

"What?"

"Maybe I'm missing something, Mom, but I don't see a fence."

Immediately, I contacted the woman and asked about fencing and she said that she would absolutely install a fence that would keep the pink baby boy safe. The more I thought about it, though, the more nightmare scenarios I considered. The dealbreaker came when more detective work revealed that she ran a day care in her home. For everyone's safety, one of our stipulations was "no small children."

That had left one more contender. After two full months, the vetting of countless applications and Carolyn's interviews with many potential adopters and combing through their references, we had turned away many capable and lovely people who desperately wanted Piglet. But the rules mattered to me—no young kids, someone home a good deal of the time, safety measures in place, small companion dogs in the household, fenced outdoor areas, and a willingness to learn tap signals to communicate with him.

This last applicant met much of the criteria. Once we said no to the woman out in the country, I was able to focus on the match that made the most sense—a young woman who had just graduated from college and would be starting grad school in the fall. She wrote a beautiful essay about how she would care for Piglet, noting that she would be studying at home, and she even had another little doxie. Warren and I reviewed everything together, and we could see that he would be given the love, attention, and resources he would need.

We more or less were ready to say yes and began to make a plan for handing Piglet over.

We reviewed our fostering past together—how we had managed to successfully say goodbye to animals we had loved. In a couple of instances, we were relieved. In two of those instances, we did not do well and regretted our decision not to adopt.

Then, when reviewing her application more carefully, I realized

that the young woman had asked if it would be all right if we kept him for the summer while she visited him and got to know him better. Her logic was that she wouldn't be able to move to her new place until she started grad school in September. This was about what was convenient for her, not for Piglet and not for us.

Ultimately, I could not have been more relieved. At first, I didn't know whether to laugh or scream. This was the final straw: there was no way we could keep him for another four months, have him settle in further, and then uproot him. My response was that this would not be a consideration for a number of reasons. We wouldn't be able to manage the emotional upset that would create. But the bottom line was something I had yet to phrase out loud until I turned to Warren and asked, "Has anyone talked about what this would do to Piglet?"

Warren, who was holding him as I said that, nodded solemnly. He may have said something along the lines of *He would be devastated!* Or *Back to the drawing board.* Or *Piglet's not a college dog anyway!*

Saying nothing, I went to bed, knowing full well that the search was over. The request to keep him for the summer had made me realize we couldn't keep him for even another week, have him bond to us further, and expect him to thrive elsewhere.

Before I could say anything to anyone, I had to sit with my decision alone. That's me. Once I make up my mind, there are no do-overs. Most foster dogs are placed. That's the whole rational idea behind fostering. Most foster dogs do just fine in their forever home. But Piglet wasn't most dogs. Piglet would have been crushed beyond my ability to contemplate if he had been sent away. He wasn't like other dogs, other than that he barked. His connection to his people and his environment is unique due to his complex disabilities and how he adapts using his own means of processing.

The following evening, I attended a county veterinary meeting in Stamford and left Piglet at home with Warren. When I arrived, I realized that the two months of tension and stress were no more, even if I hadn't told anyone yet. All along, I had forgotten my own ability to listen to the one being whose future was most at stake. Finally, I'd been forced to ask, *Doesn't Piglet have a say?* He'd been telling us all along! So loud it just sounded like screaming!

Before leaving I emailed Gloria to tell her my decision:

> I'm going to send you an adoption fee and the contract. Just do me a favor, take him off of Petfinder but don't formally publicize that he has a home. Just let it be. I don't want facebook or our e-mails swarming with comments right now. Everyone thinks we're nuts and we don't need to invite the sarcasm.

She emailed back:

> Thank you and give Bart a snuggle for me. Both he and your family are extra special and so deserving. No regrets at all.

My response:

> Warren is home alone with the dogs as I'm in a vet meeting. I think he's going to kill me when I get home! The puppy won't settle down. He has his issues. But he's as cute as a button.

And finally, from Gloria:

> Please forgo the adoption fee. You have done so much more for him than we did. He is where he needs to be and we very much appreciate that. Thank you.

Ah, I wondered with a laugh, *was this a setup all along?* Before driving home, I sent Warren a note apologizing for the decision I had just made without formally consulting him. Piglet was not going anywhere. He was already in his forever home, and we were his mom and dad.

When I got home and snuggled up with Mr. Amazing—the deaf blind pink puppy we'd named Piglet—and his Favorite Dad, I felt a peace that had been long in coming. How crazy we had been. Piglet had been home from the moment he arrived. Warren pointed out that

there is no other dog who so directly and personally connects with you. He draws you in, smells your breath to know that it's you, and then kisses you on the mouth.

We would keep our promise to love and protect him. Without fail. This was objectively part of the decision to formally adopt Piglet. He would be here with us, and I would care for him and about him, and of course, keep him safe. The reality is that I think about him constantly, night and day, every single day. But there was something else that required a different kind of commitment.

Piglet was now a Shapiro, and as a member of our family, I promised that from this moment on he would have a productive, meaningful life. I didn't need another lapdog. He didn't need to prove to the world how cute and irresistible he was. He was going to serve a higher calling; he would have a purpose.

That was not the explanation as to what had happened that I gave to Ellie—who may still secretly be looking for Piglet's forever home somewhere else. We were in a bookstore a short time later, and some friends of the family approached, asking if our puppy was ever placed in a good home.

With a shrug, I smiled and threw a bit of an apologetic squint at Ellie and said, "Yes, we're keeping him."

Her reaction was somewhere between *Are you kidding me right now?* and *I knew you'd never let him go!*

Warren broke the news on social media a short time after that, posting a photograph of himself holding Piglet, captioned, as he put it, *Me and my son.*

PART TWO

PERFECT PINK BOY

Chapter 8

PUPPY ON A MISSION

WARREN SHAPIRO: "What can I say, he's a 'failed foster.'
We had every intention of finding him a home but in the end we
couldn't give him up."
MELISSA SHAPIRO: "I am not forcing you to say this, right?"
WARREN SHAPIRO: "I feel like this is a Senate investigation.
No, my response is: I was not coerced in any way and I've made
these comments of my own free will."
—Comments on Favorite Dad's Facebook confession
that Piglet was here to stay

MAY 2017

When I announced to my parents, "I asked Gloria and her sister to take down the listing. Piglet's going to be staying," they lovingly pretended to be surprised.

Piggy and I had stopped by in person, bringing their beloved granddog, Susie, along with us, only to hear my mom's "You did? Oh, well, what do you know?" With that, she turned to my dad, who confessed, "We can't believe it took you so long to adopt him yourself. We knew that nobody else could care for him the way you do, Melissa."

My mother, always positive, went further: "I think seven dogs is a better number than six. Piglet's your Lucky Seven." From then on, that was her special nickname for Piggy—"Lucky Seven"!

Their *What took you so long?* was the general consensus from most everyone close to us—family, friends, many of my veterinary clients, and, of course, Piglet's BFFs (and my colleagues) at Norwalk Veterinary Hospital. On the same day that I went there to announce the news, a few afternoons after the fact, as Piggy and I were on the way inside, he sat up at attention, almost wriggling out of my arms, his nose twitching with anticipation.

This was all part of his systematic mapping—which was my term for how he learned his way around. Whether in our house or our yard or on outings like this one, when he was being carried, he'd take it all in that first time, a function mostly of smell, touch, and memory. The next time, he'd immediately navigate the route taken without guesswork.

The more I studied how Piglet used the abilities he did have, the more I suspected that he was forming "pictures" of just where he was, and where he was headed. He paid rapt attention every second and put all the pieces together as they came to him. For a sighted dog with hearing, these observations would have been par for the course. The only difference was that Piggy was doing it mainly with another organ: his nose. The effort of this mind work had to be tremendous, but I understood that he was motivated to gain his bearings because he didn't want to feel alone. On top of that, he was genuinely interested in engaging in his own world and the world around him. He did this more and more efficiently and effectively as he built on previous experiences. It was particularly remarkable that the runt of the litter, who may well have been "half-baked"—as Gina, the vet tech, had once described him—would turn out to be such a powerhouse thinker.

Sometimes he reminded me of a pink puppy Sherlock Holmes, making inferences about where we were and how to recognize humans and animals. He could smell their breath and other telltale scents about them, recording the details on his spreadsheet of friends, kept in a mental directory.

Mapping for Piglet wasn't continuous, just when encountering a new environment or when there was a change in a familiar setting. Invariably, he forgot nothing and could navigate exactly where we were going if we'd been there before. In this case, because he hadn't had all of his vaccines, I chose not to let him walk on the grass or sidewalks outside NVH. Until the last set of puppy DHPP vaccines, it's always advisable to avoid letting a puppy walk around in places where lots of other dogs congregate or travel through. Once young dogs are fully immunized, they can safely be on the ground in such settings.

Whether or not he could feel my excited energy about announcing that Lucky Seven was here to stay, I didn't know. What I did know was that he was an extraordinary thinker and that I had yet to see all that he could do with his mind.

"You know, you are a smart one!" I told him, both in words he couldn't hear and with a loving hug he could feel.

When we got inside Norwalk Veterinary Hospital, all I had to do was enter grinning and most everyone understood right away that Piglet was going to be a Shapiro after all. Piglity at once began to frantically sniff the air for the smell of familiar cilantro, almost trying to lurch from my arms in the direction of where Monica was usually stationed but was not there at the moment. Before he could get too upset, he picked up on the presence of his other girlfriend— Oneida (Monica's cousin), who worked out front as a receptionist.

Two months earlier, Oneida had stopped over to visit with Monica and her husband, Armando, the day they were babysitting Piggy, who was smitten with her ever since. Oneida was not as effusive as Monica, but she happily took the elated pink puppy and began exchanging nose rubs and kisses with him. Oneida whispered, as if it was a secret, "You aren't letting him go?"

I shook my head no, and she let out a huge, thankful breath of air. Regrettably, she had to return to her desk, handing him back to me, saying, "That's the best news ever!" as she walked away. We looked around for Emily, the vet tech Piggy knew had treats in her pocket, but we couldn't find her. We did, however, find Jessica and Mallory, who made a royal fuss over him. When I told them that we were officially adopting him, they started oohing and aahing over the pink puppy boy so happily that Monica and Emily picked up on the buzz as they walked through the treatment room door.

"Oh, my God, yes, thank you!" Monica said loudly. "That's the best news!" With that, Piggy's tail kicked into an even higher, faster wagging gear and, remembering she was his true BFF girlfriend, he scrambled to leave my arms, launching over for Monica to hold him. She smooched him on one side of his face, then on the other. Monica let Piggy dive down her shirt, all the while cooing and singing welcome songs in a mix of languages, both real and made-up. Emily joined the happy cluster and soon had Piglet in her arms. His nose twitched as he did a windup for pocket diving. Our huddle was like an impromptu adoption party.

The vets were congratulatory but not at all surprised. Dr. Janice Duffy came over and gave me a big smile, telling me she was happy that I'd kept him because "Now we get to see him grow up." Dr. Charlie Duffy laughed and looked at me with a nod and eye roll, as if to say he'd known this was inevitable even if he did think I was a little bit crazy.

I know there were other colleagues who may have thought that too, but only one said it out loud, quite a few months later. She really couldn't believe I'd keep yet another needy puppy in addition to the six dogs and four birds that already took up most of my time and energy. Her exact words were, "You need to have your head examined."

The comment was off the cuff, not meant to be mean, but it took me by surprise. She may have been projecting because a lot of vets don't always have self-control when it comes to adding just one more.

I paused and then asked her, "Why do you say that?"

She mumbled something about having my hands full, at which point I handed her Piglet's newly printed business card, assuring her that there was nothing crazy about the advocacy work we were able to do for other dogs and pets with disabilities.

I didn't have to say anything else or state out loud that, of course, who better to advocate for such issues as these than a cute dog who was deaf and blind but living up to a calling this meaningful? Nor did I have to say that as veterinarians we should be the first to help spread that message.

She later visited his website, was quite complimentary, and offered a sincere apology.

Becoming an animal welfare advocate was the main mission that we had in mind when I made Piglet's adoption contingency promise that he would have a productive meaningful life. By "we," of course I meant that "I" had decided our simple goal, initially, would be to raise awareness and money specifically for organizations that rescue and help place pets with disabilities.

The overall mission grew quickly to encourage spaying and neutering of dogs and cats, to educate people about the severe consequences of double-dapple (and double-merle) breeding, and to encourage the adoption of special-needs pets.

The other comment that really haunted me was the one that had come from a work associate of Warren's who was also a dog breeder. At the time, Warren had been talking to co-workers about how amazing Piglet was, showing them pictures and saying that the puppy was deaf and blind. This work associate understood that we had seven dogs, each of whom had come to us from rescue groups, and then he let it slip to Warren that they didn't sell puppies with disabilities. "We cull dogs with that type of defect because they don't have a good quality of life."

To him, and to some others in the breeding world, it was accepted that the puppies with physical or developmental deficits were not adopted out or even given away. What, then? Warren couldn't even say it. Neither could I. When Warren first told me about it later that night, I was seething. Even thinking about it now makes me sick to my stomach.

At the same time, it added extra fire to my modest goal of enabling Piglet to be an ambassador who could encourage changes in those practices.

This was when I really embraced my role as teacher/enabler, not to push the pink prodigy to do things that other dogs without disabilities do, but rather to meet him where his desire to learn would take us. That meant following his lead. This entailed doing what all enablers do best—to set him up for success and give Piglity the chance to show us what he could do and how far he wanted to go. I would start by shining a light on his gifts that existed not in spite of his disabilities but alongside them.

Piglet was no different from all the other dogs who genuinely love to learn because they love to bond and communicate back and forth with their person. They thrive on praise and encouragement from the person who provides comfort, security, food, and companionship. Lots of dogs are food-motivated, so treats are an initial gateway to connecting with a new dog who might be fearful or shy, or just unsure about themselves.

Over his first two months as a foster puppy, thanks to tap signals, Piglet had already quickly learned basic skills that had given us a common language. Now we advanced to refining his "wait" or "stay" that involved having Piglet understand that I was asking him to remain still. I stood in front of him, not moving, and after only a few seconds, when he didn't move, I gave him his "OK" signal, and then a treat. Once he realized I was asking him to stay where he was, I was able to move back a step and then right back into him. Then when I stepped away, I delayed going back to him for a few seconds, a minute, two minutes . . .

He got it. His wheels were turning. I was able to teach him "come" with a food lure and a gentle swipe forward under his chin. Then we did "down," which was a little bit more of a challenge because he wasn't one to want to lie down in what some dogs consider a vulnerable position.

All of this was coming together by the summer of 2017. In time, we would move on to more sophisticated tap signals such as "go to your bed." Some of these behaviors took a year or more, but they all happened as Piglet built quite an impressive means of communicating solely using his sense of touch.

My approach, whenever any of my dogs were working on mastering their individual basics, was to use any opportunity that presented itself to create a teachable moment for everyone. By incorporating their skills into their everyday activities, they would practice and have a means for applying what they'd learned. The same was true for Piglet. No sooner would we arrive home from work than Piglet, knowing the routine, would appear at my feet, ready for class to commence. We'd usually head outside and enjoy the warm evening air, staying out as long as we could.

Instead of opening the back door for the dogs to run out like a pack of wolves, I created another routine. Once learned, they all knew to sit and wait for their name to be called—alone, in smaller groups, or all together, something they learned from the time they were little puppies. This is a routine with purpose. That wait period lets me scan the yard to be sure there are no wild animals waiting for my dogs, make sure the gates are closed, and allow the smaller dogs to get down the stairs without the bigger dogs running them over!

Once outside, we practice various "sit, stay, come" routines with individual dogs and in groups. There was no special lesson plan or set time for our Piglet School, but Piglet had lots of individual practice out in the backyard, and he really enjoyed doing his tricks with the whole group.

The dogs also understand "wait" when I open the car door. My dogs know they are not allowed to jump out of the car when the door opens. It's a helpful safeguard when we're near a busy road or in a spot where a car might appear out of nowhere. When we're ready for them to come out, we call each dog's name. The big ones know it's their signal to jump out of the car, and the little dogs know that they will be lifted out and placed on the ground. The little ones aren't allowed to jump out on their own.

In the car at the beach, Piglet is most often in his little car carrier, so there is no need for him to do "wait" as we pick him up, put his harness on, and either carry him or (after his last puppy shots) set him onto the ground to walk on the sand with the others—never a completely successful operation. Walking down the road wasn't much better. Piglet might race to the front to lead the pack and then stop to sniff something, causing a pileup, with everybody having to sniff too. He really was a tripping hazard for me, which required extreme concentration to avoid going flying or accidentally stepping on him! After his stop, he'd pick up again but might zigzag or slow down to almost a standstill, circling and becoming disoriented. The other dogs were very patient as they would stop and wait for me to either coax him along with a tap signal for "let's go," or pick him up and carry him for a little while. I think that they differentiated their "real" walks from the walks with the pink boy.

The ongoing lesson of teaching Piglet to apply what he knew of "wait" and "stay" to being able to leave food in his food dish in front of him was much more complicated than any of the other tricks. Generally, when we teach a dog to "leave it" they are never to have the item, food, or other object that we are telling them to leave. In Piglet's case, it was more of a "wait before eating" than a "leave it."

There are different methods to teaching "leave it" to dogs. We started with my holding a treat in my closed fist. When he tried to get at the treat, I held my hand closed. Eventually, and it didn't take long, he would look away, somewhat frustrated because he couldn't get the treat in my hand. The second he looked away, I would give him his "OK" tap and a treat. He quickly realized that when he looked away from my hand that held a treat, he got a different treat. I labeled his looking away with a tap to his forehead, which signaled him to look away from whatever he thought he should have.

In short order, we were able to transition to Piglet looking away from a full bowl of food placed down in front of him. After being given the "leave it/wait before eating" tap, Piglet will actually dip his nose into his bowl to smell his food and then quickly look up, as he waits for the "OK" to dive in! Watching Piglet put all these steps together and delay gratification, just as the other dogs did, was one of the most fascinating dog teaching experiences I've had.

"Let's go," a soft draw over his shoulders and neck, became a universal type of signal. It could mean "let's go inside from the backyard," "let's go into the kitchen from the living room," or "let's keep walking" when he would stop and get a little bit confused on one of our neighborhood walks. He was able to apply it to many different situations, which showed just how much thought he was putting in. "Good dog" (a calm pat with my whole hand on his left side) was reassuring and comforting, as well as straightforward praise. Learning these taps did not involve food rewards. They were signals that led to an action and a connection. He was well aware of our communication, which, after a while, became second nature. I spoke to the other dogs and I tapped Piglet. He was so eager to learn, and always very responsive.

Piglet being so receptive to trying new things was like a border collie, only in a pink dachshund suit. He spurred my creativity. At one point during my late-night list-making, I started coming up with tricks to teach him in the future, and mentioned to Warren, "I'll bet I can teach Piglet to 'shake.'"

"Does anyone know how to 'shake'?"

Gina and Dean had learned "shake" when they went to dog classes. But none of the other dogs were interested. My hunch was that Piggy Lee could pick it up in a flash—which of course eventually happened.

At times, I would "mark" fun behaviors that he was already doing, like going to sit on his bed. He loved to race to his bed for a treat, so I very easily added a tap, a gentle squeeze over his mid back, tapping both sides of his rib cage, while he was already going to his bed. This marked the command "go to your bed" with a tap signal. After a few days of practice, he connected it with going to his bed and he would respond appropriately from anywhere in our living room or kitchen area.

I'd also find ways to teach Piglet in response to negative behaviors he had developed. Yes, the tiny pink one can be very naughty. Whenever we ran the vacuum cleaner or even worse, the carpet steam cleaner, within seconds Piglet would become hysterical, carrying on and barking wildly like the machines were invading from Mars. In his attempt to show them who was boss, he'd growl, bark, and attack the machines in dragon-like fashion. Zoey did this too, which led me to believe that she'd signaled this behavior when Piglet was very young. He then began to associate the smell of the cleaners with their tag team carryings-on.

One day Warren was getting ready to vacuum, but before he could turn it on, I watched Piggy walk past it, then turn around and start chomping on the hose! My teachable moment radar was on full alert, at which time I corralled both Piglet and Zoey and asked them to sit and wait, only a foot or two away from the dreaded machine. If they both waited without barking, they'd get a cookie. Soon "kill the vacuum cleaner" became "sit and wait patiently while Favorite Dad does his vacuuming."

At approximately three-and-a-half months old, Piglet was progressing in all respects. His physical dexterity alone was remarkable, especially given how fast he was growing in size. This can often make puppies trip over paws too big for their bodies, but not this tiny one. He was growing not just in size but in stamina and strength. The first picture I'd ever seen of Piglet had him at one pound. When he became our foster pup, he was already one and a half pounds, and two weeks later he'd gained another half pound. At the end of April he was 3.3 pounds. Two weeks later, on May eighth, after another visit with me to Norwalk Veterinary Hospital, I posted a picture of his handsomeness, commenting:

> Weigh-in today—4.1 pounds. At this rate of gain, he is going to end up being a giant.

A few weeks later was Mother's Day 2017. Our family tradition for many years was to go hear Daniel play in the Norwalk Youth Symphony's annual Mother's Day Concert. When the kids were younger, we'd go over to Bama and Pot's for brunch and then to the concert in the afternoon. In more recent years, we would just convene at the concert and then go out to dinner afterward.

Ever since Piglet had appeared in our lives, the reality was that he needed to be with us most of the time—meaning no restaurants unless Warren and I took turns. This year I had warned my mom that I wasn't sure about going out for dinner on Mother's Day. She understood that attending the concert was about all I could manage with logistics that had to be arranged for Piglet. If we tired him out earlier in the day, Piggy would sleep in his crate in the car, along with a couple of his dog sisters snoozing in their crates. But trying to go to a restaurant was pushing it.

"We can all come back and eat here," my mom suggested on the phone. "I have enough food for everyone. Would you make a salad?"

I laughed. My mother knew that if she was going to cook for everyone, that would usually mean not much to eat for the two vegans—Ellie and me. My mom didn't want to make me feel bad, adding quickly, "You make the best salads." She's never been able to figure out how my salads somehow taste better than the ones she gets from Costco.

"I'd be happy to make a salad, Mom."

My mom's problem-solving approach was always to come up with a plan to accommodate everyone. After teaching for over fifty years (thirty-two of those years for the Norwalk public school system), along with the attainment of multiple advanced degrees and the receipt of more honors for her work than could be counted, what distinguished her was her knack for helping students thrive individually and making everyone in the class feel included.

Mom had her own story of "when the teacher is ready, the student appears." In her case, in the later 1970s, her first response was "I'm not ready!" when her principal announced that they were starting a policy of immersion and she would have a new student with special needs in her class. The idea was to teach students with and without disabilities at the same academic/educational level in the same classroom. Immersion was also seen as a form of inclusion. Students with and without disadvantages could learn from one another's daily challenges and advantages.

The Norwalk elementary school principal informed her, "Oh yes, you are ready."

Arline Foodman immediately went to work to learn about accessibility and how best to adapt her classroom for her new third-grade student with spina bifida, a condition that affects the spine and can make walking difficult if not impossible. As my mother later described it, she and her student had a beautiful collaboration. My father was the one who told me, "The newspapers covered this story and before long your mother and her student were local pioneers helping change educational trends."

My mother wasn't a crusader for a cause. She was a problem solver. If that student was going to be in her class, she excitedly pulled out all the stops to create the same opportunities for learning that she did for everyone else. The best teachers, I learned from her example, are always educating themselves to better enable students at every level to succeed.

Snippets of recent conversations with my parents were running through my mind on that Mother's Day morning as I carried Piglet down our recently remodeled back stairs to the yard.

Studying Piglet's changing profile before setting him down on the grass, I could see the puppy in him already giving way to the young dog man to come. Piglet's soft pink ears no longer obscured most of his brow like a nun's floppy habit. They lay on each side of his head as if they were pink wings picking up air currents and setting off the cuteness of his face. His nose—that active GPS system perched front and center on his face—had now grown into more of a canine profile.

"Go pee," I said aloud, as I gave him a little tap to his right armpit. As Piglet took off on his own, I had a minute to inhale the day, a beautiful Sunday morning, while surveying the yard for the other members of our little dog group, who were busy running around the yard for their first of many outings of the day.

Warren followed me outside, watching Susie, Evie, Zoey, and Piglet enjoy their romp in the fresh-smelling spring air. The sun was already up and burning off the morning fog, although it had rained the day before and the grass was wet and a little slippery.

We watched our resident den mother, Susie, hovering close to Piggy, who was being unusually rambunctious. Warren repeated his now-familiar theory: "We never had a choice, you know; it was always Susie who wanted a brood."

I smiled as I saw Susie approach Piglet, who was getting too close for comfort to a fence post. Piglet sensed her, slowed down, and paused, head up in the air. Instances like this one had lately been making me wonder if maybe he had some minimal sight in his left eye after all, but I was pretty certain that at most he could only make out shadows.

Multitasking as usual, Warren and I each scooped up poop, chatting as we planned out the afternoon's events. Evie, recently bathed, all white and fluffy, and one of the most good-natured and well-behaved doggies ever, came bounding over for a hug from Warren. He praised her, "Good girl, Evie," and gave her what had become her favorite massage on the underside of her neck.

"Oh." Warren turned to me. "Happy Mother's Day!" He added quickly, "I can get everyone fed and take them back out in the yard again, if you like, and you can relax. Or go for a walk without the whole mob."

We both laughed. I wasn't much of a relaxer. There was always too much to do. Besides, like our dogs, our birds, and our kids, I needed my routine. Just like the counting. Rounding this group of four dogs up, I counted Evie, Susie, Piglet, and . . . but that was only three. Where was ZoZo?

"C'mon, ZoZo!" I called. "Time to go inside." Hearing that, Evie and Susie sped to the steps. Piglet, smelling them, I guessed, followed their trail to the base of the steps.

No Zoey yet. I couldn't find her. Hearing a rustle behind me, I turned around to see the funny little chocolate Chihuahua/Yorkie-Maltese mix, standing right behind me, looking at me innocently, as if I'd never look for her there. Even though this wasn't the height of acorn season, she had that look that she got whenever she had scooped up contraband she wasn't supposed to have. She was obsessed with finding and hoarding acorns—something she'd been doing since she was a little puppy. Early on, Zoey would pick them up, hide them in her mouth, and walk along nonchalantly so I couldn't really tell. Eventually, I noticed that when she was walking next to me, her head would be held just a little bit forward with her nose pointed down, and that usually meant that she was hiding something.

Our routine was for me to ask, "Do you have something in your mouth?" and then follow it with a long-drawn-out "DROP!"—sort of singing it to her, and she would usually drop not just one but multiple acorns at a time. Zoey had never swallowed or eaten any, but these acorns posed a serious choking hazard to a six-pound dog.

This time it was only one large green acorn, and the message of "drop it" was the charm, another reminder of why this was one of the lessons I made sure to practice regularly with my dogs and highly recommended to all of my dog family clients.

"Melissa! You don't want to miss this!" Warren's voice was almost a stage whisper, as if some vibration in his projection or breath might distract Piglet.

As soon as I looked in his direction, I saw what he was talking about. Piglet, that handsome pink boy, was intensely focused on pulling himself up, like an inchworm, from the slate at the base of the stairs up to the middle of the first step. All on his own. I hurried over, Zoey in my arms, and watched breathlessly as he made it to step one. Without pausing, he began to feel how much room he had before stretching up to the second step. Surely that was enough for the day. But no, he wanted to do it again, putting one tiny paw on the back of the step and then reaching up with the other paw before launching himself up with his back legs.

Handing ZoZo to Warren, I stood next to Piglet to spot him if he slipped but, for the first time ever, didn't guide him with my hands on his back.

Two steps! This was what I had taught him to do on a daily basis for weeks. He was using his memory of what he had practiced, doing it independently. It was a supreme effort, yet his motion up the stairs accelerated. Warren had gone up to the top landing, and I was right behind Piglet following him up when, on the third step, his paw missed and he tripped. He caught himself before I had to grab him, then he continued to the top. As Piglity hit the mat in front of the door, he did a grand victory dance—a twisty turn on the textured mat, or two for good measure, before placing his right foot on the door saddle. He lifted his chin in my direction as if to say, *What's next?* I almost cried.

Warren was just as excited and proud of Piglet, on top of the fact that Favorite Dad didn't have to worry about doing anything more to make sure I had the best possible Mother's Day celebration with all of our babies, including our newest.

WESTPORT DOG FESTIVAL

As much as I had begun to have a clear sense of *what* Piglet's mission was going to be, I honestly had very little knowledge about *how* to create meaningful momentum for it. Somewhere in my planning brain, I'm sure that I'd contemplated having him make public appearances—as an example, say, of why people should support the work of rescue organizations like the one that saved Piglet's life.

About a week before the pink boy's feat of going up the stairs on his own on Mother's Day, we were given our first opportunity for a public appearance, of sorts. This coincided with a talk I'd agreed to give on pet safety at the second annual Westport Dog Festival. The year before, I'd been an exhibitor and though I liked seeing fellow vets, there wasn't much foot traffic. But beause this was a fundraiser for local animal rescue groups, I was happy to lend our support and decided to reserve a booth for the day. Informally, I could chat with members of the community who stopped by and learn of their pet needs. For those with aging animals, I could let them know about Your Senior Pet's Vet, along with the rest of my in-home veterinary services.

My thought was to bring Piglet, have him hang out, interact a bit, and see how he did. Upon arrival, Warren and I struggled to get our booth's tent assembled. We were not alone, as we discovered from vet friends from Winslow Park Veterinary Hospital, a vet practice located right next door to where the event was taking place. We were able to joke about how hard it was to pitch the tents as we set up for the day.

As always, I had come prepared. That's what a house-call vet does. For weeks I had gathered materials, collecting all sorts of informational pamphlets about products and services available to senior pets—special harnesses, nonslip booties, ramps, orthopedic bedding, and pee pads. I had printed handouts that I use for my own clients that would go along with my prepared talk about pet safety. A few other vets had also signed up to give thirty-minute talks about a variety of topics. In good company, for the talk I even made a pet safety poster, border and all.

In addition to Piglet, we had also brought Evie—my demo dog whenever I did talks to a range of audiences. She loves children, especially, but is almost as fond of seniors. If it was a veterinary workshop for kids, I'd show the kids how I put on my stethoscope and listened to her heart and lungs, how I checked her teeth and coat, and basically run down the main aspects of a typical physical exam. Evie, poised and polished, loved playing patient, as well as socializing with the audience while I gave my talk. It seemed like a good plan to me that Evie would be able to show Piggy the ropes of going out and being at a public event. Why I felt so nervous about how he might react to crowds of people I can't explain, but I had butterflies on the pink puppy's behalf. Just in case it was too much for him, I had all kinds of treats, food, and blankets, and a couple of toys to give him. For when he needed downtime, I'd brought his little crate.

At the start, Piglet sat contentedly on a blanket with Evie in the front of my partially shaded booth. As I talked to people and passed out information, the dogs seemed delighted with the activity, though I watched the sun to be sure Piggy didn't get sunburned. Lots of people came by, and of course most were interested in learning about the tiny deaf blind pink puppy. He was gracious and friendly. He really seemed happy to be there meeting new friends.

Following Evie's lead, Piglet was in fine form. He was especially happy to meet many children who sat on the blanket with the two of them. At one point, appearing to have had enough, he went into his crate to take a nap.

When it was time for my talk, I moved away from the spot in front of our booth and went into a little open area with benches to sit on, where I greeted a handful of spectators, mostly my vet clients. With a lot of competing noise in the background, I went through the main pet safety points I'd prepared and then turned the conversation to Piglet. My client and longtime friend Pamela Clark was there to support my veterinary talk but mostly to meet the tiny pink puppy.

"I'm so glad you came!" I interjected before starting my informal talk.

"I wouldn't have missed it," she said. "And I had to meet this Piglet I've been seeing on social media." The first time we'd met, she had brought her dog Alexis and her one-year-old baby boy to the animal hospital in Stamford where I worked then. Many changes had gone on in our lives since those days.

Pamela greeted Warren, who handed over the tiny pink boy. Piglet was so comfortable in her lap, she ended up holding him for the duration of the talk—which went well except for the sun in my eyes and some competing background nose. Piglity didn't mind. In fact, we had to peel him out of Pamela's arms when it was over.

"Thank you again for coming," I said as she rose to leave. "We didn't really get to catch up."

"Are you kidding? I wouldn't have missed it," Pamela exclaimed. "I got to sit and hold Piglet, the deaf blind pink puppy! I'll say that I knew him when."

I laughed. The thought of him being famous or a public figure with a big following didn't register as real to me, although it was sweet that when we packed up and took our things to the car, a lot of the festival attendees were calling out, "Bye, Piglet!" and a little girl said, "I love you, baby Piglet!"

He couldn't hear their words, but I was sure that the expression on his face was a smile.

Even though I hadn't planned on it being anything special, Piglet's public debut at the Westport Dog Festival in May of 2017 was somewhat auspicious—giving me surprising clues about his comfort level in front of crowds. I'd had no idea that he would like interacting with the public so much or respond in the cool, relaxed way he had. Warren and I both saw it. Evie appeared to be a proud big sister, trotting along with us as we carried Piglet and my supplies to the car.

She looked up at me and over at Piglet and gave me her white fluffy head shake, assuring me, *Oh yeah, he's got that "it" factor, just wait.*

Evie was right. Little could I have imagined how completely different Piglet's next opportunity to reach the public was going to be—less than a month later.

Chapter 9

DOG TALK

"He knew he was home before you did!"

"Wow has he grown! What a handsome brave boy he is. There is a special place in our hearts for little guys like him and the loving people who give him the chance to be everything he can be and more. Thank you"

"Piglet was not a mistake of nature. He was born to make others caring and happy."

—Early comments from top fans on Facebook

JUNE–AUGUST 2017

Summer came on strong. For us, though, school was in session and the world was our campus. Piggy Little, whose nicknames were proliferating by the day, was attached to my hip—literally, most of the time—and managed to memorize not only his routine to a tee but mine as well. He had already been riding along with the rest of the three-dog travel team on my work rounds, but once he was fully vaccinated, he was able to have more contact with my clients and patients and proved to be an asset. Sometimes he was a comfort and an example of hope for clients whose dogs, cats, and other pets had a diagnosis or prognosis of concern. Sometimes, when I'd tell his story and how we decided to adopt him, clients who were still debating whether or not they were ready to adopt after the loss of a family pet would feel inspired to at least look into fostering. Some even wanted to look into the possibility of fostering or adopting special-needs pets. Little Piggy Lee was already gaining a kind of purpose.

Heading out for a couple of routine calls a week or so after the Westport Dog Festival, I had a sudden *aha* moment about why people seemed much more interested in hearing about Piglet than in showing up for an informative talk about pet safety or to hear about caring for senior dogs at my booth. It wasn't just because Piglity was so precious and pink, although he was fairly irresistible. What captivated people was his unlikely story—one that was yet to fully unfold but was quite interesting already. People were not drawn to him out of pity. Just the opposite. There was something about Piglet's story—his uncrushable spirit, his huge appetite for learning, and how he optimized what he did have—that made him compelling.

That welcome realization caught me somewhat by surprise, leading me to pull the car over for a quick list-writing stop. If we were going to gain traction for the important goals of our mission, it was going to be up to me to improve my skills of storytelling and communicating our concerns—with Piglet as our standard-bearer. Three quick thoughts that came to mind were 1) learning more about how to use social media, 2) coming up with a list of interesting dog-related topics (why take a dog to classes, dog safety, adopting vs. buying dogs) that general audiences would find meaningful—staging "conversations" for Piglet and the six-pack to help illustrate, 3) implementing strategies that would change public perception about dogs with disabilities.

The last note on my list sent me into deep thought as I said, "Of course!" out loud to the travel team. Ignoring their curious barking and grumbling, I wrote down an important sentence—*Don't feel sorry for Piglet.*

In my head, I started to construct a response to anyone who saw certain animals as destined for a good life and others cursed not to have one. Later I wrote these thoughts down as one of my first attempts at telling the story of the deaf blind pink puppy, beginning with the prompt *So, why shouldn't we feel sorry for Piglet?*

> As I sit and write the list of what Piglet can't do, I realize that the list isn't very long at all. There really isn't much Piglet can't do. I frequently think back to a flippant remark made to my husband by a dog breeder acquaintance. He suggested that dogs like Piglet should be euthanized because they have no quality of life. In fact, Piglet leads a very happy, active, and full life despite his small size, and lack of two of the five senses.
>
> With thoughtful, careful accommodations that suit his special needs, we give Piglet the opportunity to adapt and use what he does have. Yes, it would be nice for him to be able to see our smiles and hand gestures, and it would be easier to call to him and have him respond to our voices, but Piglet has learned to optimize the senses he does have through positive as well as negative experiences he has as he immerses himself in his daily routines. He builds on his always growing skills to explore new environments and meet new friends as he travels near and far with his human and dog family.
>
> Instead of voice or hand signals, Piglet has a growing tap signal vocabulary. He understands taps for sit, stay, wait, come, ok, up, go pee, and come along. He is comforted with massages over his back and neck, and he loves to be held and cuddled. His sense of touch is his physical connection to his people and his environment.
>
> Combining touch with his sense of smell, Piglet recognizes his family and friends, and he eagerly meets new people

by smelling their breath, as he logs them into his internal experience database. He can tell when a new person or dog has entered a room even when he is fast asleep, wrapped in a blanket, on our lap. We watch his nose wriggle as he constantly scans for new input to process.

Piglet smoothly maneuvers around in familiar places like his backyard to the point that some question whether he is truly blind. He quickly maps out new environments so he can be comfortable in new places when we travel and visit friends.

Piglet's mapping skills are shockingly high level. When we visited our friends in New Hampshire for the first time, Piglet had their house mapped out within minutes so he could find his water dish, his toys, and obstacles to avoid. Most remarkably, after just two walks up and down their neighborhood road, he led us down the correct driveway to go back to the house.

Piglet leads a happy life filled with love. In fact, he is more in tune with what's going on around him than most dogs that can see and hear. There are plenty of animals to feel sorry for. Piglet is not one of them.

This was a piece I went on to update more than once as Piglet's story evolved and took unexpected turns down the road. The flow of it, however, had formed in my mind by the time the we arrived at our first stop in Rowayton, a very nice friendly neighborhood right in the center of the upscale waterfront section of Norwalk. When I'd first gotten started building my vet house-call practice, two of my first clients (and friends), Amy Kamisher and Erica Merrill, lived in Rowayton and over the years referred many of their good neighborhood friends to me.

On this day, our visit in Rowayton was with Karen Pace, a kind, caring teacher and mom to two handsome, sweet sons. The adored family dog, Daisy, a pampered, affectionate little Cavalier King Charles spaniel, was now a senior, and greeted me with a subdued tail wag before the exam and dreaded nail trim began. The moment Karen and I got her up on the couch, Daisy began to shake while pretending to be somewhat stoic. We moved through our visit as quickly as possible so that Daisy could get on with her usually relaxing peaceful day.

Once her exam was done and nails were cut, Daisy heaved a sigh of relief and leapt off the couch, but stuck around as she recognized that I was putting my supplies away.

"Daisy's looking good, considering all," I reassured Karen and made recommendations to keep her that way. We talked about how she was doing and weathering the transitions in her life before she asked me about how I was handling my first taste of an empty nest.

"Oh," I admitted, "it's quite a mixed bag." No matter how nice it could sometimes be to have the extra time and a little less commotion, it was not easy facing up to the reality that a very big life chapter was about to end.

"The funniest thing is that I probably hear from Ellie more often than the other two." I laughed when I reported she was away in Switzerland at a prestigious music festival, yet still checked in daily. "She worries I'm spending too much time on social media!"

We both laughed. Of course, Karen had been following all of my Facebook posts about baby Piglet and said that she hoped I wouldn't stop them any time soon. "He's addictive!" she said.

"The truth is that he takes up a lot of time, so I don't have any left over to think about the empty nest."

Having parked in the shade with the windows down so the four dogs inside could rest, enjoying the summer morning breeze, I let them all know, "Everyone's going to get a turn to say hi. Piggy first." I was excited for Karen to meet Piglet in person.

After taking the little sleepy pink boy out of his carrier, I handed him over to her. She had a look of such tenderness on her face as she held Piglet, whose eyes were still sort of closed.

Quietly, I said, "He wants you to hold him up to your mouth so he can smell your breath for future reference."

Karen held Piglity to her face as he inhaled his new friend's breath and decided then and there she was welcome into the inner circle. Then she snuggled him into her neck, and she too closed her eyes—no doubt experiencing the pure bliss that comes with holding a relaxed Piglet.

I snapped a shot of the two of them and later texted it to her, which made her day, probably year.

Karen handed Piglet back to me, and I got him settled back into his carrier. Then I let Evie and Zoey out of their car crates so they could have their chance to say hi. Evie, of course, took great joy in meeting every person who would pet her favorite spot under her neck, which Karen was more than happy to do. Zoey, on the other hand, said her usual quick hello before retreating back into her crate in the hopes of receiving a prized cookie. Finally, I opened the back hatch so Gina wouldn't feel left out.

As I said goodbye and got into my car, I joked, "It seems like we spent more time outside talking about my dogs than we did inside with Daisy." We agreed that Daisy was happy to have her house back to herself and was more than happy that the focus had shifted away from her. Karen thanked me for sharing my Piglet and the others with her.

We said our goodbyes and I started the car, ready to back out when she waved at me to stop because she had a question. Karen said, "I just can't believe how well-behaved all of your dogs are. How do you do it?"

I kind of took it for granted. But as I thought about it, I answered, "I've had a lot of practice."

🐾

If there had ever been any such thing as the Foodman Rules, at the top of them would have been my parents' passion for providing education to all inhabitants of the family. So it was only natural that our dogs were also given classes. Starting in the eighth grade, I began my own enrichment as a teacher, in the world of dog training, by accompanying our dogs to class. From then on, at every stage of my personal and professional life, unless I was bringing home a dog that had already been educated, I made sure to carve out time to take every one of my dogs to learn the basics so important for his or her well-being.

As a vet, I encourage all of my clients to look into classes for their new dogs. Some ask me for recommendations for where they should enroll, and others choose to do it their own way. High on my list of "dog talk" topics, my main premise is the belief that an educated dog is more likely to be a well-adjusted, happy dog. The reasons for formal classes are many: bonding, safety, intellectual stimulation, manners, limits and boundaries, routines, and more. Dog school or private lessons with trainers should preferably happen soon after we bring a dog into our lives—whether as puppies or adult dogs, rescued dogs with baggage, or turnkey dogs that come from a stable background. Some need time to decompress before heading out to dog school, but all dogs benefit from learning with their person or people.

The fact is that dogs' brains need intellectual stimulation. Directed activities are helpful to avoid boredom, anxiety, and undesirable behaviors. A lack of direction leads many dogs to destructive behaviors that land some in animal shelters, looking for new homes. Starting out with the basics—"sit," "look," "down," "come," "wait," "stay," "leave it," "drop it," and an emergency recall—serves as a good foundation and is a nice way to establish positive communication and a healthy working relationship with a dog. To be clear, I'm not talking about instruction as a dominant or authoritative kind of interaction.

My first exposure to dog school came at the age of thirteen, when I took our family's standard schnauzer Zig to classes, and it was a nightmare. Difficult to handle, he was poorly socialized and aggressive toward our friends who innocently entered our house. In those days, dog training was referred to as dog obedience classes—very different from the positive reward-based approach we have these days.

The classes I attended with Zig required that we bring food, but the dogs also wore choke-chain collars, which I later viewed as unnecessarily harsh. The dogs were meant to learn not to pull after only a few pops on the choke chain. Once they went through the initial pops to their neck, they mostly didn't have to experience the choking sensation, unless they and their handler weren't connecting on the message—in which case, the dog continued to pull and choking ensued.

Although Zig learned the basics, he never learned to be a well-mannered dog. Despite his thug-like behavior, he stayed with our family because a) my father couldn't conceive of euthanasia as an option for preventing our dangerous dog from hurting person after person, and b) as my mother realized, having Zig, who was a great guard dog, gave her a sense of security when my father traveled for work. Ziggy was so crazy no one in their right mind would enter our house with that lunatic ball of fire charging at the door!

Whitney, the dog I adopted from the Norwalk pound in the summer right before I was to start vet school, was sweet but wild, and she had severe separation anxiety, which made it difficult to have her with me while starting vet school. After bringing her home at Thanksgiving time to stay with my parents—which I chose to do so that I could adopt April—I returned to Connecticut the following summer and enrolled Whitney in classes given at the high school in Westport. The main goal was to help address her separation anxiety. Whitney did remarkably well, I thought. The training still relied on the choke-chain collar, but Whitney was a very sweet dog and didn't need much "correcting."

On the last day of class, my parents came to watch the "recital." At the end, we had the dogs sit and stay behind a curtain. All the dogs stayed except my Wee. She came walking around slowly, peering out from behind the curtain.

Whitney loved my father, her Favorite Dad, and knew Harold Foodman was in the audience. The separation was too much for her. But other than that exercise, she came through with flying colors. She lived happily with my parents until she was fourteen—when she died from liver failure.

While classes are good for dogs and their people to deal with

issues like aggression or anxiety, I'm also a fan of taking well-adjusted puppies to class for fun and all-around development. When Rachael was two and Daniel a baby, back in the golden years of having just two dogs—Wendy, a whippet puppy, and Lucy, a border collie puppy—once a week my parents came and stayed with the kids while Warren and I took Wendy and Lucy to their Tuesday night class in Fairfield. Methods were now moving toward being reward-based and were taught by an exceptional dog trainer.

For the first time in our history as dog parents, Warren and I had chosen to bring home purebred dogs who came from reputable breeders. This was an overreaction to a difficult biting dog we had previously rescued. With Wendy and Lucy, who absolutely loved their Tuesday night classes, we went with breeds known for their intelligence, athleticism, and gentle temperaments, and for being good around children. We had a great experience and could not have found two better dogs for us at the time, whom we loved very much. That said, if I had it to do over again, I would have adopted two rescues. I'm still surprised that I generalized one difficult experience that I felt I couldn't adopt another rescue when my children were young.

When Susie came along, I had decided that even though she was cute and lovable, and already a young adult dog, I needed to bring her to classes. The major concern was Susie's obsession with chasing chipmunks. Something in her terrier mix DNA or her Tennessee upbringing released a single-minded focus on the pursuit of chipmunks, which generally meant that she would run across our busy road, risking her life for a little chippy.

Not leaving anything to chance, Susie and I went over to the nearby Dog Gone Smart for classes. We also had a dog trainer come to the house to assess the layout. She had been running out our front door, and actually left briefly through a hole in the back fence, which Ellie had warned me about earlier in the day. Thankfully, Susie returned unharmed about fifteen minutes later, but we knew that we needed reinforcements. We heeded all advice and installed an invisible (electric) fence around the full perimeter of the backyard fence, which came around to enclose the front of the house.

Susie couldn't leave that way anymore, but none of these measures ended her obsession with chasing chipmunks and other animals like skunks when we were outside or even inside our doubly-fenced back yard. This is why it was crucial for Susie to learn a reliable emergency recall.

For this effort, I first had Susie wait with someone else holding her leash, letting her become very excited about a must-have treat like chicken or some other meaty type of food I had in my hand. Then I would walk about fifty feet back away from her, at which point I'd yell, "HERE!" and wave my arms around in an enthusiastic, welcoming manner. The person with the leash would let go and Susie would come racing toward me. As soon as she reached me, I would give her the food she was running for. It only took a few times to make it clear to her what "HERE" meant.

The emergency recall is not for the everyday "come"; unless I am reinforcing it to keep it meaningful to the dog, it's something I would only use in the event of a real emergency. And it works: Susie has turned on a dime and come right back to me when she was almost nose to nose with a skunk, and when she was headed toward a busy street. With dog safety a priority, I taught all the dogs the emergency recall—in addition to their regular manners. Unfortunately, a couple of our dogs have been a bit blasé about the emergency recall, but most come racing to me the instant they hear the call.

Before Piglet arrived and I became his main teacher, each of the other six dogs had been to classes where we'd covered basic manners up to more advanced dog obedience work. This was all positive reward-based training that used clicker techniques where we marked good behavior with a click and a treat. The dogs love the activity, they feel special, and it is an opportunity for bonding with their person or people—us.

My continuing education for each of them, individually and together, is to mix it up and make learning fun—something I've cultivated from years of reading lots of dog-trainer blogs, websites, and books. One of the best pieces of advice that resonated with me was from top dog blogger and author Susan Garrett, who recommends making everything into a game. This way the dog stays

fully engaged and is learning while having fun. That's what I had in mind when I chose to enrich our dogs' education by taking them to fun, noncompetitive agility classes taught by my dog trainer friend Betsy Schwartz. In addition to creating games and contests, Betsy made it clear that agility required using everything the dogs had already learned in their basic dog school classes or at home with me. I then set up a small-scale agility course in our backyard, which everybody liked, especially Gina, who is very athletic and agile, despite her vision and hearing deficits. She can weave magnificently and fly over hurdles. They all really love our nylon tunnels—including Piggy Lee.

Everyone but Annie loved school. She was too shy and really preferred to be working with her other dog sibs in a group at home rather than alone in the formal classes. In fact, when she went into the agility tunnel at a class and did a little pee, I let her know then and there, "It's okay, Annie—no more classes for you." Annie benefitted from the basics, but everyone has a different learning style, and dog school wasn't for her.

Zoey had specific needs when I took her to Dog Gone Smart. She already knew the basics of "sit," "down," "stay," "come," and "wait," but I was concerned about her resistance to listening whenever anything fell on the floor and she'd hoover it up within a split second. This was the issue we had with the acorns. ZoZo missed nothing, and as the smallest and fastest of our group, there was always the danger that she'd grab something potentially toxic, like a grape or raisin, or that a larger object might get stuck in the back of her throat. This made it especially important for Zoey to recognize and respond reliably to "drop it."

As I often underscored in my dog-talk topic of pet safety, we dog-moms and -dads have to be knowledgeable of such issues as the deadly dangers of certain everyday foods like grapes and to be ready to act in such cases. It happened one day in our house when I was washing grapes in the kitchen sink for my birds. Somehow one grape bounced off the counter onto the floor. My reflexes had me immediately dropping to the floor to pick it up ASAP. Unfortunately, Zoey's reflexes are much faster than mine, and she is much closer to the floor.

The grape fell right in front of her nose! My instantaneous "NO!" and then "Drop it!" came just as the grape entered her tiny little mouth. Within another split second, to my relief but not surprise, the grape dropped to the floor with another little bounce. I picked it up and gave Zoey a big, safe reward!

Chalk up another victory for dog school and follow-up reinforcement. Not everything, however, is fixed one hundred percent by classes and practice—like ZoZo's typical little-dog aggression toward dogs she doesn't know. It can be disruptive and keeps me from taking her to events where there are going to be lots of other dogs. Otherwise, she is a perfect dog!

This is all to say that during the summer of 2017, while Piglet's learning curve was kicking in, mine was too. After a lifetime of going to hundreds of dog classes, I'd come to the fast conclusion that training a deaf blind dog was surprisingly similar to working with dogs who can hear and see. What voice and hand signals do for sighted/hearing dogs, tap signals and, later, blowing a stream of air could achieve for Piglet. The key with all dogs is motivating them to have a desire to accomplish a clear goal and then communicating the achievement of that goal. In any language, "good boy," or "good girl"—spoken with a loving, complimentary tone—can work wonders for animals and humans alike.

The other running theme in dog education is to identify strengths and build on them. With Piglet, I had almost forgotten how we began—that he had entered our lives with no form of communication other than instinctive carrying on and screaming. Instead of focusing on his sensory deficits, I was able to steer myself to an obvious but sometimes overlooked strength. He was an avid snuggler, which was also an instinctive trait in both breeds in his mix of dachshund and Chihuahua. Both of those breeds are into being held, burrowing under blankets, and bonding deeply with their people. Piglet had all of that under control—as did his Favorite Dad, who took up most of the evening snuggle detail.

Piglet also loved practicing what he'd learned alongside the rest of the Shapiro dogs. Whenever I practiced with him by himself, I'd notice the other dogs attentively watching and wanting to get in on the act. After I'd made a conscious decision to incorporate all of them into demonstrations to go along with my talks about teaching tap signals to Piglet, somehow the idea of a show evolved without any preconceived ideas of its scale or reach. When Warren arrived home from work or if any of the kids or Bama and Pot came around, I'd wave everyone over to gather around, either outside in the yard or indoors in the living room, and we'd show off our seven-pack's command of the basics. This was what was meant by fun and games for dogs. The time had been well spent for boosting confidence, listening skills, impulse control, and positive group dynamics.

I continued to incorporate these group tricks into their daily routines—like waiting before everyone starts to eat their food, or waiting to be called one by one out the back door when I am standing out of sight. Piggy, still in learning mode, somehow knew that he was excelling and appeared eager to move to the next level.

They were so infectious in their enthusiasm that I thought it would be fun to maybe go and perform for local community groups—a senior center or an area preschool. This was how, at some point, I'm not sure when exactly, I started calling these demos the "Piglet Show."

Piggy Lee was such a tenacious worker whenever learning something new, his exuberance was contagious. I had my camera out all the time because I wanted to capture moments of Piglet's perseverance as he worked on new skills—how determined he obviously was and how it felt to me observing. In some magical way, we began ever so quietly to have a sort of dialogue that let me be his voice and vice versa.

It just happened. And in the process, the people who were following him on social media got to inhabit his experience and feel happy. This discovery was subtle at first, but the comments that were being left on his posts took on new depth—how seeing him learning agility jumps with the other dogs had reminded them of their lives and given them the boost they needed.

The more often these reactions happened, the more I knew that connecting our mission to Piglet's evolving story was the key to getting our message of advocacy out there. To that end, I was still learning, very much a work in progress.

Two significant events happened in July. Both involved social media. Ellie, calling and texting from Switzerland during her rare phone breaks, continued to caution me against spending too much time online. Daniel took a middle-ground, "wait and see" stance, not sure if much would happen beyond where we were. Rachael, trekking home on a weekend to come see everyone—always a holiday for the Shapiro dogs—was more enthusiastic about the ways that Piglet's story was a good one for raising awareness for rescue groups, special-needs pet adoption, and the importance of spaying and neutering.

Rachael agreed with Ellie that spending too much time on social media ran the risk of being a huge time destroyer. However, if I was going to do it to raise awareness and gain followers and a larger platform, Rachael went so far as to encourage me to expand my use of social media.

"How?"

"Well, right now you've got your personal page on Facebook and Piglet's got his own page. That's great, Mom. But you should also be on Instagram." Her argument was that a lot of Facebook users were migrating to Instagram and that searchable hashtags were helpful for brands, organizations, and other causes to establish themselves. Rachael also mentioned that I should probably look into getting a YouTube account.

Rachael showed me some adorable pet pages on Instagram that she called "influencers."

I had no idea what that meant, although I was shocked to see that some of the really cute animal Internet celebrities had massive followings, complete with merchandise, ads, and sponsorships. That didn't interest me, except that being competitive, I thought Piglet was as cute as any of them, plus he had an amazing story and a mission.

I made a note to explore Instagram per her suggestion. In the meantime, one thing I'd been pursuing was having Piggy's story picked up by The Dodo media company. They produced short videos with heartwarming animal stories, usually having to do with a harrowing rescue—by an animal rescuing a human being or vice versa. Piglet's "rescue" story fit their profile. When I showed Rachael the story I'd written about Piglet, along with some of the videos I'd sent to The Dodo, she was sure they'd be head over heels and run his story.

"But I haven't heard back at all and I've sent them to several different admins. Not a word." After I mumbled something to the effect that I was giving up, Rachael looked at me skeptically.

"You? Give up?" She gave me a hug and a grin that said, *No way*.

Looking back, I'm not sure why I had so much trouble finding the right email address for sending the story and the videos of our adorable pink puppy. Trying one more time, I landed on what appeared to be a trustworthy link for submitting stories and, one more time, sent in my write-up of Piglet's story.

A short while later, just before the July Fourth holiday, I was reading over comments on Facebook about Piglet's funny antics when an email popped up that was a notice from someone at The Dodo that they were going to run the Piglet story I'd submitted.

We were pumped and announced to the family and a few friends to be on the lookout for a Dodo video about Piglity on Facebook. Three days later, on July 6, 2017, The Dodo video titled "Blind And Deaf Puppy Rescued From Hoarding Situation" ran on their platform.

The numbers were incomprehensible. We had by this point accumulated thousands of followers, and that was crazy enough. Shortly after the video's release, it accumulated about thirteen million views and over four thousand comments. I had heard the expression "going viral" before but I had never imagined my pink Piglet actually going viral! As a result, Piggy's Facebook page grew by the thousands overnight. And it wasn't just the Dodo clip. Knockoffs were soon being released (sometimes without anyone notifying us), but every time they were, another wave of followers would "Like" Piglet's Facebook page. A few months later, The Dodo rereleased the same video as a setup to another video about Piglet finding his forever family (as part of The Dodo Impact series), this one adding another initial million views. And the following spring a third video was released about Piglet as part of their "Little but Fierce" series that costarred the rest of his dog siblings and underscored the message of hope and positivity he was bringing to the world. It came out in May 2018 and soon earned fifteen million views and eleven thousand comments. Those many millions of views continue to multiply exponentially to this day.

In preparation for that video, I had done a Skype interview but had no idea they were recording it to include me in the video that would eventually air. When I sat down to watch it, I was shocked to see that I was actually in it. All I could think was how fortunate it was that I had taken a shower and washed my hair before the interview!

Even when we saw the first video and learned that there had been thirteen million views, we were still in the bubble of the Internet, with lots of followers and comments but from people we didn't really know. By the time fall came around, however, Piglet was starting to be recognized on the street.

He took it all in as if he had known all along this was going to happen. Warren and I kept expecting for the hoopla to fade and for us to go back to our normal life of a regular family in the suburbs with seven dogs—one of whom was a deaf blind pink puppy. But that didn't happen. Not by a long shot.

As overwhelming and exciting as it had been for Piglet to have a public outing on the global platform of The Dodo, in a video that drew in a mammoth-sized audience, something even more important happened in July—even if I didn't yet know how important it was.

That was when I first responded to a comment from third-grade teacher Tricia Fregeau of Plainville, Massachusetts, who mentioned she was going to share Piglet with her students to show them "the amazing things that can be accomplished no matter who or what stands in your way." I had offered at the time to create a personalized video for her students. In the process of making that video, I decided to do more and create a full PowerPoint presentation in video format that told the pink puppy's story in language that I knew would be accessible to them.

In the fall, Tricia had followed up to say how much her students loved it and how they had brainstormed about Piglet's growth mindset. This was at the center of an educational program she was developing for her students, along with activities and lesson plans.

With all my goals and intentions to guide Piglet to his purpose, elementary school education hadn't been in my thinking. In fact, I honestly had no idea what a growth mindset even was—although in time I was going to learn all about it.

Chapter 10

PIGLET ON THE MOVE

You cannot get through a single day without having an impact on the world around you. What you do makes a difference, and you have to decide what kind of difference you want to make.

—Jane Goodall, primatologist, anthropologist, author

AUGUST–SEPTEMBER 2017

"Job!" I called to sweet, shy Annie the tan terrier mix, on a sweltering August afternoon, letting her know with just that one word that it was time to go get the mail. Annie loves her job so much, the mere mention of the word is enough for her to hop off her bed, which is on top of a dog crate, onto the adjacent chair, so I can pick her up to go outside. As usual, I cradled her so that she could sit on my left arm while I hugged her in with my right arm, all nice and snug. We headed out the front door and down the steps to the mailbox, and I chatted with her as we walked.

"You're doing your job, Anna, such a good girl, getting the mail."

She looked pleased with herself, always a nice sign to see her get a confidence boost from having pride in purpose.

"Oh, what do you know?" I said as I retrieved a padded envelope from National Pen, the company I'd chosen to make up our first item of Piglet merchandise. It had been hidden under mostly lots of junk mail.

Annie's ears pricked up, as though she was as eager to see the contents as I was.

We hurried back into the house, still following our protocol for getting the mail, which requires me to set her down to go back up the front steps on her own. This was always Annie's "job," and she did it to perfection.

Once inside, the moment I sat down at our old country kitchen table to go through the mail, Piglet decided that meant it was time to play. He started nipping at my feet, grunting loud enough to get some of the others to join in with him.

Even with the AC on, it was really too hot for any of us to get so worked up. Telling the group, "Settle down!" I quieted everyone except for Lukita, the blue parakeet, who decided this was his time to say a thing or two in his foreign bird talk. Deciphering his chatter as best I could, I took him out of the cage and gave him his favorite ear massage. He continued on with his monologue as I sat back down and proceeded to open the package.

For a flash, I felt oddly out of my depth. There were lots of things that I knew how to do well or even sometimes extremely well, or that weren't too hard to figure out, but the whole process of coming up with merchandise to raise money for Piglet's mission was forcing me out of my comfort zone. Sometimes I felt that I was learning from him, basically borrowing from his skills for mapping. If something was new, I'd dip my toe in, asking for expertise from others, but then have faith that I could navigate new terrain on my own, learning to trust my own instincts.

The larger, more unexpected piece of all of this was that though I had envisioned raising money to donate to the rescue groups we wanted to help, I wasn't exactly sure what that would entail—especially because our community was worldwide not local. I had heard and seen many organizations and influencers selling "merch," but I didn't know which companies were best to work with, and which had the highest-quality merchandise. I had ordered personalized pens from a company called National Pen for my vet practice, so I frequently got catalogs from them in the mail. The most recent catalog had a number of items I was interested in, so I called to find out the details of customizing a logo and placing a bulk order.

Phone case wallets were trending at the time, and they would easily fit in an envelope, which would make shipping very simple. I chose hot pink, with a white line drawing of Piglet in the center, and the words *Piglet, the deaf blind pink puppy* underneath. They were adorable, and as soon as I posted the picture on Piglet's Facebook page, I had orders coming in by the dozens.

Ellie, ensconced in her upcoming new life as a college freshman, was beside herself. "You're selling merchandise?!"

"It's our first Piglet fundraiser, this time to benefit Colbert Vet Rescue Services, the group that saved our tiny pink man!" I explained that I was making it easy by starting with a small, flat item that I could send all around the world in a regular envelope with a stamp. I wouldn't even have to go to the post office.

By the time this first effort concluded, I'd sold hundreds of Piglet phone case wallets, which I individually placed into envelopes, stamped, addressed by hand, and recorded. I collected the funds via PayPal, and when all was said and done, sent about $1,200 to the rescue.

The enthusiasm for Piglet merch was overwhelmingly positive. Selling the items was a big commitment, but I was excited to be able to donate a nice sum to Colbert.

Next, I went for pink oval car magnets, which, again, I did by hand. Ellie again chimed in with her concern that I was spending countless hours selling small items, which was not the best use of my time. I agreed as she muttered something about "What's next, T-shirts?"

I had, in fact, already been speaking to a rep from Bonfire.com, a full-service T-shirt/merchandise company used by many nonprofits for their fundraisers. They help with the design, take the orders, print the shirts, and ship directly to the customers—in our case, Piglet fans.

"It's all for Piglet's mission and I don't have to do anything but post about it. This company does the rest, and then sends a check with my profits."

Ellie's concern was that the Piglet project would keep ballooning out of control and that my life would be consumed by him.

I laughed and asked her, "Would you like me to order a Piglet hoodie for you?" Realizing Ellie was truly concerned that I wouldn't make time for myself, I assured her that we were having fun and that we were raising much-needed money for rescue groups who care for pets that might not make it otherwise. Ellie couldn't argue because she had also done fundraising for a dog rescue a few years earlier. She was familiar with the impact large donations could have.

Later, Ellie would recall there was a turning point around this time, not only because of my passionate goals for Piglet, but also because she could see that I was enjoying the process. The real shift for Ellie took place after I'd sent off the first PowerPoint of Piglet's story to elementary school teacher Tricia Fregeau from Plainville, Massachusetts, who planned to use it to teach growth mindset to her third-grade students.

Ellie's reaction took me by surprise. When I mentioned the lesson to her, she actually agreed that connecting with this innovative creative teacher through social media was kind of cool and, also, that using my time to develop teaching tools for children—based on Pigli- ty's story—put my efforts in a different light.

Tricia had used the term "Piglet Mindset," so I had assumed it was primarily about facing challenges with a positive attitude, just like Piglet. But later on, as I began honing the presentation, I learned that there was much more to teaching growth mindset, which was somewhat new in elementary education. Eventually, I came across a TED Talk and the writing of Carol Dweck:

"In a growth mindset, people believe that their most basic abili- ties can be developed through dedication and hard work—brains and talent are just the starting point. This view creates a love of learning and a resilience that is essential for great accomplishment," (Carol Dweck, 2015).

The fundamentals resonated for me and were in keeping with val- ues at the core of our own Shapiro Rules. I loved how Piglet person- ified the idea that even without all of the five senses, he used what he had—with determination and perseverance—to do virtually everything he needed to do to engage happily and confidently with his people, his dog pack, and his environment. In teaching growth mindset, each of the five stances—optimism, perseverance, resilience, flexibility, and empathy—were addressed individually, and then together. I could see how Piglet's story illustrated those positive growth mindset ideals.

Yet nothing prepared me for the front page of the school's newspaper, which Tricia emailed me in early October. Front and center was a photo of her entire class, each student holding a photo of a pale pink handsome young Piglet under their smiling face. A second photo showed the huge poster with the top heading of "What is a Piglet Mindset?" Each student had contributed her or his own descriptive word or phrase.

The caption under the pictures mentioned that after watching the PowerPoint, they'd discussed his story and "have decided as a class to use him as a role model and face each day in a 'Piglet State of Mind' to grow as students and individuals."

In this completely unexpected way, Tricia Fregeau gave Piglet a plank in his mission that had been missing—educational outreach. Calling it a happy accident that we had met through Piggy's social media, Tricia not only coined the phrase "Piglet Mindset" but immediately got busy developing lesson plans and activities that I was able to share on our website, along with my educational PowerPoints, so that they could be used and accessed by teachers everywhere.

A few weeks after that newsletter was published, in honor of their pink mascot, Tricia's class sent Piggy a box full of gorgeous, handmade Halloween cards, addressed to him, all with sweet messages and drawings, many of them telling Piglet that they were his number one fan, how much they loved him, and wishing him a "pawsome" Halloween. There were also toys and treats for the others in the six-pack to share, including a Halloween eyeball-ball attached to a red rope that is still one of Piggy's absolute favorite tug toys.

The arrival of that box coincided with an unexpected call from my high school friend Kathy Stumpp Lopes, who invited Piglet to lend his presence at what would be his first charity event appearance.

"Oh, and you and Warren, of course!" Kathy added as she went on to tell me more about the Halloween parade fundraiser for Woofgang & Co—a new nonprofit founded by parents and champions of disabled young adults that focused on connecting them to meaningful jobs. Their business centered on employing these young adults to bake dog treats and craft dog blankets, along with other products, learning the ins and outs of selling these goods in a small storefront in Fairfield, Connecticut. Kathy had become involved with the nonprofit after her charming son Chris—an avid dog lover with Down syndrome, as well as a professional actor who had already appeared on Netflix, Off Broadway, and in several national commercials—had begun working at Woofgang & Co.

I said, "Yes, we'd love to come!" almost before Kathy finished telling me about the work of the nonprofit and then mentioning what appearing in the parade for Piggy (and perhaps one of his sister dogs) was going to entail. More than anything, I was happy to support the work of an organization that focused on such issues near to our hearts as job creation, employing/elevating young adults with disabilities, and tying it all into a love of goodies for dogs.

The parade was to be held on October twenty-eighth, at Jennings Beach in Fairfield at eleven a.m. About two hundred people were expected, and there would be refreshments for dogs, as well as for their humans. Warren and I decided that Susie should accompany Piglity to the parade and that they would go as two absolutely adorable matching orange pumpkins with green felt collars.

Some dogs do not like clothing. Such was not the case for Piggy Lee, who had become something of a clotheshorse. When he was a puppy, it didn't occur to me that he should wear a sweater or coat unless he was going outside on a cold, wintry day. I had never dressed my other dogs, and wasn't planning on starting with Piglet. He was so adorable, pink, and tiny, he looked perfect without any adornments, which some Facebook followers described as "going nakey."

Earlier in the summer, some of Piggy's fans started sending him tiny T-shirts that their dogs had outgrown. He seemed to really like them. He'd sit on the couch, nose pointed up in the air, waiting to put his head through the neck hole while I pulled his shirts on and put his little feet through the sleeves. When colder weather set in, his wardrobe expanded to include various sweaters and coats, which, as he filled out, suited him much better. He looked handsome in every color, and I thought the clothes made him look quite dashing in his photos. The T-shirts and sweaters kept him warm in cold months and, in warmer months, helped keep his skin from burning.

Piglet was in high spirits, dressed in his pumpkin costume, as was our sweet Susie. The two pranced out the door, probably aware of how cute they looked, while the rest of the dogs exchanged dubious glances. They were all in disbelief that they were being left behind, but were not jealous of the costume part of the impending outing.

When we arrived at Jennings Beach, it was a crisp, classic New England fall morning, and I was impressed at the amazing turnout. Everyone was mingling around the large roped-off parade area with their dogs dressed in costume. Some people wore outfits that matched or complemented their dogs' costumes and everyone was smiling. One woman was dressed as a magician's assistant in smashing red and black, while her scruffy dog escort was the magician with a red-and-black cape and a shiny red hat perched on his head. A grinning hound dog wore a taco costume, and a skinny golden with long legs had on a pink ballerina tutu.

Susie was on her leash while I carried Piglet over to the information table and spotted Kathy helping sign people in. She whisked us over to introduce us to the founders and organizers of Woofgang & Co.

They all thanked us for bringing Piglet—and Susie, of course—and asked about the educational outreach we'd been doing. I explained that we were just in our early stages but that our program that focused on growth mindset was already becoming popular with teachers and students around the United States.

As we went to find our places at the starting line for the parade, the energy and enthusiasm for this kickoff event were infectious. It was touching to see so much goodwill and support for the cause. Just before the parade began, Amy Stern, one of Woofgang's founding moms, welcomed everyone and named some special guests, which included, "Piglet, the deaf blind pink puppy, who is an ambassador for disabled animals and people, raises money for animal rescue groups, and also has a new Piglet Mindset educational program."

The big crowd applause and recognition of Piglet was humbling, not expected, and somewhat overwhelming. My focus was on giving exposure to their work, which, after learning of it, was now on my list. My wheels started to churn as to how I could work with Woofgang and other organizations that focused on people with disabilities, imagining we could collaborate on ways to educate, gain support for shared causes, and have enough impact to uplift our communities.

The parade route was an expansive circle inside a large square lined with spectators. Each of the parade participants was given lots of space to walk, one family and their dog or dogs at a time. They had planned this thoughtfully to avoid dogs crowding together and getting into any kind of potential dog conflicts. When it was Piglet's turn, he held his head up, strutting forward quite confidently alongside Susie. He seemed to enjoy the enthusiasm and excitement of the crowd. Saying as much to our new friends at Woofgang, I told them, "Please let us know if we can be involved in any of your future events. Maybe we can collaborate in some way." And then I added, "And we can't wait to come and shop at the store. We have seven dogs who all love treats."

"We'd love that," said one of the founders and, speaking directly to Susie and to Piglet, added, "Thank you for being in the parade! You both helped make it a big success." After a beat, she added, "You know, I forgot that Piglet can't hear me. We're just so happy he could come and make it more special." She shrugged and said with a smile, "I guess you'll let him know?"

"He knows," I assured her. I didn't know how he did it, but he absolutely knew that he along with Susie had done a really good job for a very good cause.

FEBRUARY 2018–JUNE 2018
NEW YORK CITY

How does he know?

Whenever Piglet reacted appropriately to new situations that would stress most hearing and sighted dogs, I'd ask myself that question. It was very much on my mind when he and I boarded the train for New York City on a freezing-cold Thursday afternoon in early February 2018. Specifically, how did this little pink one-year-old handsome-boy dog *appear* to know that this, his very first train ride from Westport to Manhattan, was happening for an important reason?

For Piggy, always fastidious about his routines, this was unlike any outing or events we had attended in the past. Just getting to the train station was a big challenge for me for several reasons—starting with the fact that I had to transfer all of his supplies from the tiny gray backpack I use locally to the new roomier, lightweight one I had just bought. The bigger pack had extra space for his blanket, an extra sweater for me, and whatever items we needed to bring back from New York. Piglet was very attentive and curious about the new smells of the platform and then on the train. He was exceptionally calm and composed, and absolutely adorable, which, in turn, gave me the early confidence I needed to feel that we could do whatever we'd set forth to do.

The truth is that I had worked myself up to the point that I was an absolute wreck after worrying in the two days leading up to this departure. I wasn't sure if I could bring a tiny dog on the train with me, whether he would be happy in his little carry bag, or if I could keep him on my lap wrapped in his blanket, and whether that was even safe? Piglet's calm grounded me as he did what he does—which is to exceed all expectations as he adapts and adjusts to new situations. For that reason, there was no question that he knew this was something special.

After sniffing the cold winter air outside the train station, Piglet patiently let me wrap him in an extra blanket, and then, with a look of composure and confidence, he ate his little treat, and curled up in his carrier, as I zipped him in. He let out a few grunts and squeaks as the train pulled out of the station, and I couldn't tell if he was unsettled by the movement over the tracks or entertained by it. Still, the reassuring message he relayed was *Relax, we're going to be fine.*

This whole expedition had only come about two days earlier, after I received a message at twelve forty-five p.m. on Piglet's Facebook page from Loren Morrissey of Stamford, Connecticut:

> Hi, this is very late notice but you just came to my attention.
> We are hosting the New York Pet Fashion Show this
> Thursday February 8th at the Hotel Pennsylvania from 6 till
> 10 p.m. We would love to have you and Piglet participate if
> you are interested, and would put together something very
> simple and easy for you . . .

The moment I read Loren's message the first thing that came to mind was, *I'd never be in a fashion show!* But after calling and finding out what exactly this would entail, I was happy to hear they were not inviting me to be in the show. They were looking for Piglet, up-and-coming star, to participate as an ambassador for rescue dogs.

I learned that the annual fashion show and fundraiser was going into its fifteenth year and that "when it comes to rescues, pets, and fashion" this was *the* iconic event of the NYC social season. The two powerhouses behind the charity were the chairman, pet media guru Gregg Oehler (president of Oehler Media Inc.), and cochair Ada Nieves, a world-renowned pet fashion designer and rescue advocate. In addition to raising money for rescue groups, the purpose of the show with pets (some of them animal celebrities) in top-of-the-line couture fashion was to change public perception of rescue animals.

Of course, I loved the cause. The main beneficiary of the event was the Mayor's Alliance for NYC's Animals, which is "dedicated to providing a higher quality of life & 'Forever Homes' for our companion animals."

It also happened that I had no work scheduled on Thursday, so we could easily take the train to be there at five p.m.—with enough time to get up to the ballroom on the eighteenth floor of the Hotel Pennsylvania. I'd be able to get Piggy Lee situated and all dressed up in his cowboy fashion and still have time to attend the very crowded media gathering before he went on at seven thirty.

It was flattering to say the least. This was the first request for Piglet to make a public appearance at such a large fundraising event, and this would be his New York debut.

On the train ride, I recalled how Warren had urged me to attend but declined having me get a dog sitter so he could come with us.

"Of course you should go to the fashion show. Piglet should hob-nob with all the fashionistas," Warren said. He thought my going alone would be an adventure, and a timely one for networking, now that Piglet had his own business cards, stickers, buttons, and magnets that I could bring to the show. I almost decided to wear one of our new Baby Piglet T-shirts but broke down and wore real clothes for the fashion show. I didn't know what to expect, so I conformed that year!

After saying we would be happy to attend, I sent the pink boy's bio and lots of pictures—including group shots of our most adorable seven-pack of dogs with Piglet in the middle. They would use his bio for the script to tell his rescue story as he was walked down the run-way. Trying to cover all bases, I reminded Loren that this was going to be a new experience for Piggy, with tons of new dog smells, in a new environment, not to mention that he would be working with someone he didn't know and who didn't know him. Loren assured me that we would address all those concerns. When I emailed the press materials, I also wrote:

> "I'll wait to hear from you re what I need to do next. I can measure whatever you need me to re the outfits. He is petite and long. And he is extremely handsome."

Loren wrote back in a flash:

> "OH MY GOSH he is adorbs! He weighs 5.5 pounds? Am I correct?"

I confirmed to her that was his correct weight, Loren let me know that she would be the one walking Piglet and that she would be dressed as a "Rhinestone Cowgirl" to go along with his "Country Couture"—which sounded like an audience grabber. I had to ask every possible safety question, letting her know that I'd need some coordinating time with her to make sure she and he were comfortable with each other. I reminded her that while he was incredibly adaptable, being deaf and blind, it would take a little time for him to acclimate to the new environment and to her.

Loren's response was so reassuring, predicting that Piglet would enjoy himself and "who knows, he may choose to become a runway model":

> "We will figure it out together—you, Piglet and me! The runway is raised, so Piglet would need to be right at my side or I'll hold him the whole time, maybe put him down for a moment at the end on a short leash for photographs. Safety, comfort, happiness first."

Even with her encouragement, a somewhat unfamiliar side of me came roaring to the fore—protective stage mom. Whenever my children performed in high-pressure settings, I knew they would soar—because I knew they were prepared and had the love and passion for what they were doing. With Piglet, I never wanted to do anything that would make him feel uncomfortable.

There were also the daunting logistics of traipsing around New York City with an almost-six-pound Piggy in a carrier that I would try not to jostle and a backpack full of all his supplies—extra shirts, food, wipes, treats, coats, and baggies. Ten years earlier, no problem. But in February 2018 and to this day, this wasn't ideal for my back and shoulders. There was also the issue of finding a spot where Piglity would pee and poop. Being on the eighteenth floor of the hotel without easy access to a grassy yard was another complication.

As I learned later, most of the fashion-show dogs were little Chihuahuas and other small breeds. Most of them happily used pee pads. Not my country dog, who was only going to go outside on grass. Piglet stopped using pee pads when he was a teeny baby.

Once we were on the tracks on our way to the actual event, with a sleeping Piggy in his carrier on my lap, I made a decision to stop stressing and just have an adventure. One of the Halloween cards from a boy in Tricia's third-grade class had commended Piglet for his courage, despite his lack of hair. He said that he always tried to get into a Piglet State of Mind when he needed to feel more brave. There was no reason I couldn't do the same thing.

Upon our arrival at Grand Central Station, Piglity immediately recognized that we were in a very new place. Even before I took him out of his carrier so he could stretch his legs a little bit, he barked and carried on, reacting to all the scents swirling like a *Wizard of Oz* tornado, until I put him back in his bag. It really did feel like we'd landed very far from our home in Westport, Connecticut.

"C'mon, big boy," I said, not caring what strangers thought as I talked to my dog carrier and hit the street on a dark, cold February night to look for a Piglet pee spot. There was no grass anywhere in the vicinity of the train station.

At last, we found the promised land, not far from Grand Central, in the form of a patch of dirt outside the New York Public Library. From then on, that spot served as one of Piglet's reliable pee places whenever we were coming and going from the train.

When we arrived at the hotel, we went straight up to meet Loren in her hotel suite. She was in the middle of getting dressed, so Piglet made himself at home, mapping the small room in her suite—first by walking the perimeter a few times, next by making small then increasingly larger concentric circles. Once he was satisfied, I fed him his dinner.

Loren, a vivacious blonde, joined us and was dressed just as she'd described to me in one of her emails with an attached photo:

"... as The Rhinestone Cowgirl in honor of the late great
Glenn Campbell! I will be wearing white with gold sequins
(mocking rhinestones) mini dress and boots. Notice the
boots. one of them says RESCUE. Ada and I blinged them
over the past 2 weeks."

She was smitten instantly with Piggy, giving him a snuggle and a big hello. He liked her at once, returning her hello with his signature tail-wagging greeting and a sniff, registering her in his growing memory file of friends.

"Piglet's going to steal the show," Loren pronounced. We planned to meet up again when the preshow media event was taking place. He would get his little cowboy T-shirt right before his call time.

Before anything actually kicked off, Piglet and I went to the main room and were soon connecting with various folks and pets in the fashion and rescue world. The combination was interesting. This was my second experience with dog fashion. Some years before I'd been a guest on *Pet Talk with Lauren Collier*, a Connecticut cable show, where I'd been invited to talk about senior pet care and the use of laser therapy for helping arthritic dogs. Evie—who had just arrived in our household—accompanied me onto the show. The *Pet Talk* guests after me had dogs wearing elaborate holiday outfits. Evie glanced at those dogs and did a little doggy double take.

At the New York Fashion Show, I was dazzled by the ornately designed costumes for animals and the models and celebrities with them. There was a model carrying a chicken (both dressed as showgirls), a bearded dragon looking like some kind of outlaw, lots of cowboy and cowgirl hats, plus dogs with ukeleles and tiny guitars, and plenty of gingham, feather headdresses, and bow ties.

When we reconnected with Loren, she took Piggy in her arms, proving that he was comfortable with her as they practiced the runway walk—the timing for how she would come out holding Piglet, while the emcee told the deaf blind pink boy's story, and then walk with him, in her arms, to the end of the runway, where she was going to pause for pictures. All my stage-mother nerves soon calmed down. This was going to proceed beautifully.

We then stayed with Loren for the preshow and she held the pink boy as we talked to press and to some of the VIPs. After all of that, I felt very relieved.

We set a time to meet right before Piglet's turn so that Loren could mingle, and then he and I went to find a calm spot where we could chill until he had to change.

Every time I thought, *Hmm, maybe we should go out and get him to pee before his turn on the runway*, I got distracted which delayed getting him outside. Piglet didn't complain as he sometimes would, because he was also distracted by all the commotion. But before he could warn me that he needed to get to a pee spot *fast*, he had an accident that landed him and me covered in urine.

Of all the things to worry about, this was an unfortunate one but not a crisis. "It's okay, Piglity," I comforted him with reassuring strokes and pats, not taps, and lots of kisses, as I located a restroom.

Accidents aren't common for Piglet, but when he is in a new environment, he tends to become overstimulated, and needs to pee more frequently. Fortunately, I was prepared—I had been packing extra supplies for my kids for the past twenty-some years and was ready. I cleaned him up with the baby wipes I carry for him, washing myself up, and changed his little shirt.

"Not a big deal, Pinky," I said to him, knowing as always that he couldn't hear, but certain he could feel my reassuring touch. He wasn't wearing his fashion show shirt yet, so all was fine.

Then it was time. I went to get his Western cowboy costume on him, wrapped him in a blanket, and then handed him to Loren just before his turn. Holding my breath, I watched as the cue was given and she unwrapped him so he could "walk" with her down the runaway, at which point he popped out and was ready. He was extremely adorable, my little handsome boy. It was a very unusual feeling for me to watch someone else whom I had just met handling Piggy. Wide-awake and alert, in her arms he was evidently poised and ready—showtime!—like a tiny cowboy angel. At the moment when she paused at the end of the runway, Loren held him up in a spotlight so everyone could see his little cowboy outfit: a blue T-shirt, red bandana, and a little cowboy hat that slipped down around his neck. (He does not like hats.)

This was uncharted territory for us. He was calm and went along with the whole scene, being photographed like he was a true star, serene in his confidence with cameras flashing away. I ran through a tightly packed crowd to get to a place so I could take a video of him at the end of the runway. I was surprised that this had turned into such an emotionally charged throwback to all those instances when I'd taken pictures and videos of my kids at their music concerts.

Audible reactions to his cuteness rang through the room. The emcee read the summary of Piglet's rescue, his being a double-dapple doxie/Chi mix, and that he was deaf and blind. He even included a mention of Piglet Mindset educational outreach. Wrapping up, he further thanked Piglet especially for "your work as an advocate for other rescue dogs with disabilities," as the audience broke out into applause.

Loren, the Rhinestone Cowgirl, and Piglet, the perfect pink cowboy dog, turned around so all could get one last look, as I glanced at all the smiles in the large ballroom. We had ventured into a world of fashion and pets that was like going to Oz, and we'd made a lot of new friends, so much so that we were thrilled to return to the event the following two years.

In the meantime, I made an important decision on the way home that meant we were going to be on the move more than ever.

🐾

Once I form a strong stance, there's usually not much that will change my mind. But in keeping with the principles of growth mindset, Piglet helped me see that sometimes reconsidering and being flexible can be a good thing. In this case, I had to let go of an old idea that I wasn't a dog-stroller mom. The Pet Fashion Show goodie bag (full of party favors, samples, Piggy's costume, and accessories) was too much for me to carry on top of everything else I had brought. If I was going to be walking—and I like to walk—I couldn't go into the city or anyplace else where I had to transport Piglet in a carrier and carry a backpack filled with supplies. My shoulders and back had protested too fiercely this time around.

At the fashion show, I had seen lots of little dogs in strollers, and they seemed to really enjoy their comfy coaches. The dogs had plenty of room to ride in style, there were storage baskets underneath, and I could almost imagine Piglet napping peacefully, all snuggled up in his favorite blankies, in a stroller. Whatever old ideas I had about the stigma of a dog stroller, I knew it was time to let them go.

When I got on the train, I googled dog strollers and came up with a few options to consider. I tucked the idea away because we had no immediate travel plans. But sooner or later, with more trips on the horizon, a dog stroller was definitely on our short list.

Being self-employed gave me the freedom to set my own schedule, which meant that travel for events with Piglet wasn't too much of a problem. The challenge came in making arrangements for the care of the other dogs and the birds and, in the case of pet emergencies for my clients, letting them know I'd be away and who to contact with concerns. Also, even when Warren stayed home to take care of our menagerie, we still had to have vet techs who could be there to help when he was at work or had his own work travel.

As we all knew, Baby Piglet loved his Favorite Dad most of all, but he was good to go with his mom, me, when we were heading out for activities. Even when I invited him to come along, Warren usually said, "No, I'll stay at home and hold down the fort." Then with deadpan delivery he'd add, "Don't forget to text pictures and videos."

Under most circumstances, whether we were flying, going by train, or driving, I didn't mind heading out with just Piglity alone. But there were certain times when I was really happy Warren agreed and was able to join us, as was the case with a long-planned trip to the very first Special K9 Games, to be held in Columbus, Ohio, in May 2018.

Toward the end of April, I took the plunge. It was a dramatic move in and of itself, though I tried to be prudent, telling Warren, "I'm just ordering this cheap jogger-style stroller for Piglet." My logic was that I shouldn't get anything really fancy because I probably was not going to get much use out of it.

The day the stroller arrived I was very excited to try it out. My first jaunt brought back fond memories of the blue Baby Jogger I'd had for running and walking with our young Shapiros when they were babies and toddlers. The spin also revealed that the stroller's canopy had a faulty zipper that kept sliding open, something that could be a real issue for Piglet—he needs the canopy to stay closed so that he doesn't accidentally bounce or climb out. Sometimes you have to be ready for a little trial and error when it comes to pet supplies, but once I found the right model, we were in business.

Piglet loved his stroller right from the start. It was the perfect size, it folded up easily, and it wasn't too heavy. Our ability to travel was transformed. It was one of the best purchases I have made for my tiny pink dog. His stroller lets him feel comfortable and very safe. It's his private chamber, allowing him downtime with real privacy. It is all his.

Piglet was on the move, no question, and his stroller went everywhere that he did, including to Columbus, Ohio, where we experienced a series of more firsts that I later captured in an article about our adventure:

With the theme, Be Brave, the Special K9 Games were created to encourage people with special needs dogs to become active with them, step out of their comfort zones, build trust, and enjoy being with their dogs. The special dogs who attended with their devoted moms and dads were there to learn new skills, improve their current skills, and then compete. The dogs came with varying abilities and training, but embraced the spirit of joining in and moving past their individual challenges. Events included agility, nose work, lure coursing, frisbee, and tricks.

Our little Piglet was the smallest dog attending. He was one of only a few deaf blind dogs. I decided to bring him to this first Special K9 Games because I wanted to meet others who were involved in taking care of and advocating for special needs dogs. I wanted to broaden Piglet's world, give him new experiences, and see just what he was capable of.

Piglet cautiously tried the agility equipment on Saturday during the workshop. With each run-through, he became more comfortable with each obstacle. On Sunday morning, we arrived to "watch" (he's blind) the competition. It seemed a far reach for Piglet to actually complete the agility course in a reasonable amount of time. The organizers encouraged us to sign on to have him compete. It didn't take much convincing. Piglet's name and credentials were added to the roster.

Piglity enthusiastically completed his first special games agility competition run. He did not do the tunnel because I wasn't willing to crawl into the tunnel to guide him through. But he jumped over jumps, went through a short tunnel, sat on the platform table for the required 5 seconds, walked over the dog walk, jumped through the tire, and scaled the A-frame before he finished his run with an adorable happy prance and a final sit. He won a 2nd place ribbon in the deaf blind agility division and he left lots of smiles in his path.

Reflecting back on our inspiring and motivating experience at the games, relative to current world events, having my 5½ pound dog participate in a dog agility event seems rather trivial. But in our own little world, which we still do live in, witnessing our profoundly disabled Tiny Man Piglet participate and enjoy an activity meant for the finest of athletic dogs was quite a heartwarming thrill. We met over 40 dogs and 100 people at the first Special K9 Games, all there with their deaf, blind, deaf blind, and mobility impaired dogs, for similar reasons. The fact is that at every level, dogs enjoy learning, participating, and bonding with their people. Special needs dogs are no different.

After the first day of the games was over, we headed out to downtown Columbus to find a place to eat dinner. We had just parked our car and gone to look at a menu outside one restaurant's main entrance. Not finding anything of interest on the menu, Warren turned to walk over to the next restaurant when out of nowhere, a woman stopped directly in front of him and exclaimed, "I know you!" Warren initially thought it was someone he had met at a national sales meeting from work but then she said it again, and as she looked at me, added, "I know you too!" Before we could respond, the woman practically shouted at us, "You're Piglet's Favorite Dad, and you're his mom!"

Warren and I looked at each other, probably both thinking that she had seen our Piglet shirts, but they were underneath our jackets. She actually had recognized us!

The woman signaled to her two embarrassed friends—who by now were nervously smiling as they watched their friend approach complete strangers on the sidewalk in downtown Columbus.

"Oooh, come meet the Favorite Dad of Piglet, the deaf blind pink puppy," she said loudly to her friends. She told them and us how much she loved Piggy and was dying to meet him. "Is he back at the hotel?" she asked.

Warren and I looked at each other, looked at the car, and pointed. It had begun to rain, but not too hard. We shrugged, and across the street we went so she could meet the tiny pink man.

"You know, I'm a dog person," she admitted, mentioning that she worked as a dog groomer. When we got Piggy out of the car, he gave her his signature tail-wagging greeting, kissed her, and recorded her smells into his friend database. Zoey and Evie came out to say hi as well.

After we took lots of pictures, our new friend kissed him good-bye and gave hugs to me and Warren, telling us, "I've been following Piglet since he was a tiny little foster puppy. Meeting him in person tonight will keep me smiling for a very long time! What an amazing surprise this has been. I'm so glad you kept him."

On the trip home, Warren and I talked about the fact that Piglity had without a doubt added meaning, purpose, and, yes, character-building challenge to our lives, far beyond what might have seemed possible a year earlier. The beauty of having a family pack of dogs as we do was recognizing how each of them had achieved their own identity and manner of contribution to the greater good of the others, and us. That understanding got us onto the subject of how our dogs all had a designated role that they played in the family. We hadn't consciously set out to do it, but the practice had evolved naturally around the time that we started saying Annie's job was getting the mail. When we say that each dog has a "job," it means that each has a little thing that we do with only them and no one else. It's something noticeable that they do that is unique to them. Warren and I agreed that it's important for the dogs to feel like they are special individuals.

Neither one of us could remember when we started identifying these "jobs," although it very well may have been an extension of the Shapiro Rules—which, looking back, were actually a variation of growth-mindset thinking before that term existed in our household.

Evie, the most people-friendly of the entire seven-pack, had long excelled in her top job as a demo dog for my veterinary workshops, and was the anchor of the travel team—which was composed of her, Zoey, Piglet, and, whenever possible, Gina. Even though Evie is not a certified therapy dog, she could certainly pass the tests required. Whenever we meet anyone in need of comfort and calming, Evie takes on that job instinctively.

On one family trip, Rachael noticed that a family couldn't get their daughter to stop crying after she had fallen on the boardwalk. We brought Evie over to work her magic. The little girl took one look at Evita's big, black, concerned eyes and grew silent. The next thing we knew, she was petting and hugging our white fluffy poodle mix, her tears long forgotten. On that same trip, we also met a disabled woman who was sitting at a picnic table next to ours. Evie insisted on meeting her, and the two became instant friends. The woman, because of her limited mobility, started to pet Evie with a pounding motion, apologizing: "I'm so sorry. I hope I'm not hurting her."

We assured her, "Evie likes the attention! She knows you're just showing her love. If you were hurting her, she would move away."

Now that Piglet was with us, Evie's responsibilities had expanded to being part of the Piglet Show when we visited schools and classrooms, not just during the act but before and after. She was like a magnet for students who enjoyed hugging and petting her soft, fluffy white coat, never minding how many were doing it at the same time.

Zoey also has a few jobs—being on the travel team and adding delightful bits of humor as a member of the supporting cast of the Piglet Show. Her main job, though, is as my special first lapdog. In hindsight, I think that she also assigned herself the job of making sure that Piglet didn't steal all the focus in the household—just by remaining the quirky, authentic chocolate-chip character that she is.

Beautiful Gina has the job of riding in the car with me whenever possible. She knows it's her job and never complains; even if it means she will spend time waiting for me in her crate, she is fine with it. She clocked countless miles accompanying Rachael and the rest of us on college tours, followed by well over fifteen trips to Ohio once Rachael became a student there. Riding in the car with me is not just about physically being a presence in the back; Gina's job is also to lend her loving, healing presence to me when I'm on the go. Maybe it's because she has always reminded me of April, not only in looks but in her connection to me, but Gina is a thinking dog. She takes time to observe and react to the way I'm feeling. I generally don't see dogs as having empathy, but if they do, Gina is definitely an empathetic dog.

Most of the time, Gina was part of the travel team, but once Piglet came, he bumped her to the home team on those instances when we can only bring three dogs. When we were unable to take her, I'd tell her, "Your job today is to be part of the home team, Gina, so help Dean while I'm gone."

She never took the news well. She has severe anxiety when I leave her. But she adapts and is flexible about whatever is asked of her. Then again, "helping Dean" to her has usually meant barking at him whenever he starts to bark.

I was still working on convincing Dean that barking wasn't his job. His actual job was sitting on the couch.

Warren wondered at times if we were treating Dean as an underachiever.

My response to that, as I remarked on our drive home from Columbus, was, "That's just his obvious job." Less obvious was the responsibility of being sweet and keeping the other home team members, Susie and Annie, happy. Dean knows he has a little posse of girls and is masterful at that job. The three loved one another deeply, and they included Gina in that mix—thanks to Susie, our nurturer in chief, making sure that no one ever felt left out.

That, after all, was the job Susie had given herself from the start— to be our resident den mother and to make sure everyone felt wanted, needed, and included in the family.

In the course of this drive home, Piggie had been silent until, from his carrier, he went from his deep state of sleep he did so well to barking urgently enough that I assumed he needed us to stop. Warren veered toward an exit, glancing at me as we left the highway to ask, "So what's Piglet's job?"

"Piglet's job is to be Piglet."

Warren couldn't argue. One year earlier, I had set my own goal to ensure that Piglet's life be productive and meaningful. In that short amount of time, he had fully embraced his role as an ambassador for his own mission, which would eventually include:

- Advocate for and support rescued animals through education and fundraising.

- Inspire and motivate others to adopt special-needs pets.

- Facilitate Piglet Mindset educational outreach to teachers, students, and others in the community.

- Encourage acceptance, inclusion, empathy, and kindness through the example of Piglet's Inclusion Pack.

- Put smiles on faces all around the world.

Being Piglet also meant touching people emotionally, giving them a space to laugh or cry or wonder how he does what he does, finding his pink, wiggly way into their hearts, and reminding everyone how special they are too. Besides all that, he's a celeb and he's cool.

He looks good in clothes, holds himself with dignity, poses for pictures with strangers, and knows how to enter a venue like a prince. He usually rises to whatever the occasion demands, making sure that he gives his all.

Most unexpected of all, his job was to educate the world about each of our own capacities for living productive and meaningful lives, by bringing out the best in us or challenging us to be better and even to change. That was something that I hadn't really appreciated until we made our unforgettable trip to Plainville to surprise the third-grade students in the class of Tricia Fregeau—who had first conceived and taught the Piglet Mindset.

Chapter 11

THE POWER OF PINK

"A lot of people with disabilities are tired of the word 'inspirational.' I teach people to see disability as an asset . . . to see the story of disability driving innovation, inspiring new technologies, bringing people together and connecting everyone—not just being 'inspirational' . . . Perhaps we should stop asking, 'How the heck do you go to the store?' and start asking, 'How do we make sure others with deaf-blindness can graduate from law school?'"

—Haben Girma, author, inventor, leader, disability rights advocate, and first deaf blind graduate of Harvard Law School

SUMMER 2018

The more I learned about the theories of growth mindset in general as being similar to the Shapiro Rules, the more I appreciated how our kids and Warren wove in the ideas of accepting and understanding others for who they are and being willing to include them in your circle of friends—regardless of their differences. What was also woven into the framework, as it was with Piglet Mindset, was self-acceptance—regardless of your differences.

This was a concept I applied in several contexts in my life but especially when it came to my competitive streak. In general, I compete with myself, but every now and then, even when I'm out to have a good time, I still find myself setting my sights on winning. That happened not long after Warren, the travel team, and I had our first Pink Party and met Tricia Fregeau's students in Plainville, Massachusetts, and decided, on a last-minute whim, to enter Piglet, Evie, and Zoey in the tricks competition at the annual Westport Dog Festival.

After two previous years of sitting at a booth and realizing it wasn't really the right venue for giving my veterinary talks, I'd opted not to go as an exhibitor. I still wanted to show up for the community and the good causes that the festival benefitted so that's how I found myself registering Piggy and his sisters to compete the very next day.

Just getting into the spirit surprised me. Somehow having three kids out the door already in college/the real world and being the dog-mom to seven well-behaved dogs had not softened my intense competitive side. In spite of telling myself this was just a local dog tricks competition that I was participating in to give the dogs a fun experience, of course, thoughts of winning surfaced in my mind.

I added a fresh element to our "sit, stay" routine and rushed out to buy Piglet a large, soft, hot pink towel to serve as his little stage and a plastic box that was about six inches high to be placed under the towel. It looked like a tiny throne for His Pink Majesty to sit on during the sequence of tricks. I also bought matching hot pink bandanas for the dogs to wear.

When we arrived at the festival site of Winslow Park, I was impressed by the turnout of what the count later said was 2,400 people and over 1,000 dogs. The festival atmosphere was in full swing with vendors, food trucks, face painting, and other activity areas for children, plus signs directing spectators toward demonstration areas that mentioned demos by police dogs and guide dogs, plus frisbee-catching and agility shows. The most competitive event was a preset obstacle race course, promising the fastest dog a full year's supply of dog food as a prize. When I signed us in and got our time, I saw that in addition to a category listed as Best Trick, there were other competitions for Best Tail Wagger, Best Dressed, Best Kisser, and a

Dog and Owner Look-Alike contest. The panel of judges was composed of state and local officials.

Warren and I chatted with friends and others who were there for the tricks competition. Just before it was our turn to head into the ring, he walked over to the side while I huddled up with my three dogs, Piggy, ZoZo, and Evita, telling them, "Your turn is coming up. They're going to call our names soon. Let's do it!"

They all looked remarkably relaxed. Not me. I could feel a tinge of butterflies as I discreetly glanced over into the ring to check out the other dogs who were performing in front of the judges. It was the usual fare of very talented, well-trained dogs and their people, along with a few who hadn't prepared but were simply there to participate—a herding dog who did an army crawl, a wiggly tail-wagging puppy who wouldn't sit even for a treat, and a small dog who was part of a magic act that ended with the dog jumping into his mom's arms. At that point seeing how much fun the others were having with their dogs, it hit me that my main goal was to make sure that my dogs and I enjoyed sharing their skillful adorableness with one another and with everyone who was watching. My dogs are not flawless, but even when they don't perform perfectly, their spirit is infectious!

There was a large fenced area where each team of contenders would go in to do their tricks and the rest of us would watch outside the open entryway while we waited for our turns. Warren, now about twenty yards away from us, held up his phone, "You sure you trust me to video? You know I'm not that good at this!"

"You'll do fine!" I encouraged him. (Just in case, I asked a friend to record it for me on my phone.)

There are times when, really, Warren is the funniest person in the world and he can make me laugh in the most intense moments. As I was probably getting too focused on how they would do, I paused for a quick smile when he sent me a *go get 'em* gesture of a thumbs-up, followed by a *sorry* shrug toward his phone—implying he would not get a good video. I shrugged back and returned my attention to my three dogs, who were all set to go.

With only a couple of contestants ahead of us, it felt like we were in the Super Bowl, as I hunkered down with the team, pumping them up, and emphasizing to Evie and Zoey, "You are stars in the Piglet Show, and everyone is going to cheer for you!" When I said "everyone," I gestured to the fifteen or so people who were near us, waiting for their turn. The judges weren't behind a table or anything but actually on the ground next to the different acts.

Something to know about Piglet is that he loves to do his tricks with the other dogs in front of an audience. Warren and I were mystified early on by exactly how he knows there are people watching him. But he does. After a while, it became clear that Piglet not only knows he is in front of people, but he also has an idea of about how many people are there. His incredible nose can differentiate between a few and many people in his vicinity. In certain situations, Piglity will pull back and look uncomfortable.

He also can sense the excitement in the air—whether we are in a classroom, at a presentation, or in this case, in a designated area for the tricks competition. Most of the time the other dogs also rise to the occasion and do very well in front of their audience.

In my own experience, when speaking in front of an audience, or working a room, or, at this stage of the game, livestreaming on social media, I don't get nervous or have stage fright. For most of my life, that comfort and confidence have come from knowing the areas where I have expertise. There's nothing that I love more than talking about pet care, veterinary topics, dog training, animal rescue, adoption, pets with disabilities, animal welfare, and so on.

From the time that Piglet entered our lives, I've had to learn—and am still learning—to express my own personal viewpoints in a balanced way, while maintaining authenticity, when posting and commenting in all media. The power of pink motivated me to raise my game in the process and seize the many opportunities that Piglet's widening platform provided. He meanwhile gave me extra confidence, somehow, maybe just by being a calming force, pushing me to make the most of every public appearance in order to have maximum impact for our cause.

Though I was used to my dogs' confidence, the tricks competition was a new experience of seeing all three—Piglet, Evie, and Zoey— take it up to a higher level. They appeared to know they were going to go into the ring to perform the tricks they had worked hard to perfect. It was ridiculous, but I felt a ripple of nerves as our turn finally came up and I went to set up our "stage" with the hot pink towel and throne for Piggy Lee. The first part of the trick was a group sit, stay, and come.

After setting the dashing Piglet on his pedestal, Evie, all bright-eyed, with her white poodle/terrier coat fluffy and clean, quickly took her place on the left side of Prince Charming. Zoey, chocolate Chihuahua/Yorkie-Maltese, fluffy herself, pranced over to the right side with an extremely intense face that said, *I may look funny and cute, but this is serious stuff, folks*. Scene-stealer that she was, ZoZo sat waiting for me to say something, her ears perked up and rotating like she was a visiting space dog.

After they were in place, I said, "Wait!" and gave Piglet his tap to reinforce what he was already doing. Then I stepped back about ten feet and the three waited attentively for me to call each of them by name. Off to the side, I could see Favorite Dad beaming with pride as the two girl dogs each came to their name when called, while Piglet waited for me to come get him with his tap signal. He performed perfectly, with sweet enthusiasm.

They were hams, hilarious and adorable, milking every moment. As I'd promised, the crowd cheered them on wildly. Next, I instructed them to go back to their stations and "Zoey, sit!" and "Evie, sit!" and then brought Piglet back to his box and gave him his tap to sit. More applause followed, with lots of phone cameras snapping away. We then did "down" with a short "wait" again, and while Zoey and Evie stayed in the "down" position, I called Piglet over with a tap under his chin so he could do an extra little trick by himself, and then finished with them all sitting together, which served as a photo op for everyone who was now curious about the tiny pink dog. As we left the competition ring, each was rewarded with extra treats for doing such an awesome job. After a few more entrants performed their tricks—there were some good ones with multidog acts—I watched the judges conferring briefly. Soon they went through a list of about four awards. Each time an award was announced, "And third prize . . ." I would wait and then feel both disappointment and relief that our name hadn't been called. With each prize except for first having been called, I thought, *Well, this is it*—and held my breath until the winner was announced.

This wasn't the Academy Awards, obviously, but when they said "first prize" and I heard the names of Piglet, Zoey, and Evie, I didn't hide the big smile on my face. I congratulated our three-pack for winning first prize in the tricks competition! Along with the award, the three of them were given the prize of a $25 gift certificate to our local Earth Animal pet supply store.

The day could not have been more perfect. We were able to mill about, greet friends, receive congratulations, and feel the warm embrace of being hometown champs. I met folks who were very interested in how I'd taught Piglet the tap signals, which led to some friendly conversations. All in all, it was a much more satisfying dog festival experience than previous years had been.

In talking about my experience of caring for Piglity, I tried to emphasize that you didn't have to be a vet to adopt a dog with disabilities because guidance from reliable sources was easily accessed through a variety of online and in-person sources. I spoke with one family who was interested in learning about how to work with more than one dog, and I offered recommendations about making sure that when bringing dogs together, they were well matched in size, temperament, and activity level for optimizing success. It's not that the dogs have to be exactly the same; they need to complement one another and bring balance to the group. After hearing about our seven dogs, a woman we met asked, "Who is the alpha dog in Piglet's pack?"

Her husband leaned in, asking, "Is it you?"

I laughed to think of myself that way.

Warren jumped in and offered his insight: "There is no 'alpha' in Piggy's pack. Our philosophy of dog training does not rely on a dominant leader."

His answer was right on the money. Our dog group is particularly even in the distribution of roles, which emerge in different settings and situations.

Before we left, I met a woman who approached me to say, "I follow Piglet on Facebook. Have you ever DNA tested him?" She happened to be starting a new job with a company that did DNA and medical testing for different breeds of dogs.

This was another instance of kismet. I was fairly certain about Piglet's parentage, but the more science the better, I figured. A short time later, she contacted me to arrange getting samples from Piglet and Gina for the company to use them in their research division. They were looking for dogs with a variety of abnormal genetics for their database. I submitted the samples and results came back as expected—Gina was Australian shepherd/border collie mix; Piglet, doxie/Chihuahua mix. No surprises there. However, Annie was also tested, and she was truly an all-inclusive international dog—Chihuahua/poodle mix with a little bit of schnauzer (a terrier) and Pekingese mixed in.

When we were driving home from the dog festival, I couldn't help crowing just a little. "I had so much fun watching the three of them. That was great!" Then I added, "You were a good sport."

Warren joked, "The fact that you had so much fun, it didn't even matter that I didn't have any fun." He became completely serious, and said a few nice things about appreciating how I set the three dogs up to do their best and that I was in good form as the perfectionist that I was. "It's really nice that you won."

"It was a nice reward for all the time I spend with the dogs. I'm pretty happy," I said, feeling about as happy as I get.

"I wish that I could make you that happy." He said it with a straight face.

"I do too," I replied, playing along.

Warren gave me a look. No comeback.

So I said, "Yeah, I'll make a list." The joke was that I would make a list about ways he could make me happy.

We had a good laugh as we shared our successful venture with Piglet and the girls.

❧

Whenever any of my dogs achieves a milestone—like this first time that Piggy and his sisters won the competition on their home turf—I not only share the photos and videos widely with others, but I file them in photo albums on my phone, look at them often, and frequently relive those moments and all the emotions that I had at the time. It's a habit that began with the baby books I made for my three children, then translated to similar chronicles made of my dogs and birds.

Sentimentally recording pretty much every breath in my kids' baby books was a way of life for me. But even when they weren't babies anymore, I kept notebooks for years, writing down memorable milestones, things they accomplished, said, or did. They were right there in my night table, along with my notebooks filled with lists of goals and things to do.

Capturing Piglet's major milestones was right up my alley, not to mention that there were new breakthroughs that showed him defying his limitations every day. He was a living textbook for growth and possibility. He never stopped processing new information or expanding his horizons. There was a step in our living room, for example, that he had to go down to get into the side sunroom. When playing, he would stop short on the floor mat that was in front of the step, avoiding it, until he learned that it wasn't a ten-foot drop. I initially lured him down the six-inch step so he knew it was safe. Then he practiced, using the mat to mark the step, and before long was running and leaping down into the sunroom like a little pink gazelle.

The day when I first taught him to "come" by blowing to him, instead of a tap signal, was historic. Whenever I shared them, the videos and simple observations revealed something people could embrace in themselves—how quirky he is, how he lives in the present moment, happy or annoyed, rambunctious, poised, or so tired he just has to tuck himself away in someone's arms with his tongue sticking out.

The fact that he is who he is and does what he does as a profoundly disabled, tiny dog is never far from my mind—but not because his disabilities are limiting. Not at all. It's because I don't want to downplay his disability, one of the important aspects of a Piglet Mindset—using what you have as your strength and getting past what you don't have. In that way, to defy expectations and attempts by others to limit you then becomes your superpower.

I thought about his adaptive skills every time we drove to New

Haven, where Piglet came with me whenever I attended the Yale Animal Ethics Study Group, which met monthly throughout the school year. Our meetings were held in a small conference room on the lower level of a renovated house. In the beginning, I worried that bringing Piglet, then still a puppy, would be a disruption—even though this was a nice, open-minded group of vets, lawyers, ethicists, and other scientists who met monthly for a midday presentation and discussion.

The first time we arrived at the Yale campus, I was amused at how happy Piglet was to be at yet another college, as if he was prancing—*Oh yeah, I'm an Ivy League dog!*

Once we entered the very small conference room—which barely fit the large conference table with a bunch of chairs around it—I introduced Piglity to the group. Everyone was delighted to have him on board. After all, he presented an ethical situation in his own right: Can a rescue dog with profound disabilities live a good quality, purposeful life?

As always, I was nervous that he'd make a fuss, but he quietly ate his lunch and went to sleep in his soft carrier while I listened closely to the talk and then participated in the discussion. Some of the topics that were tackled that first year included presentations by world-famous professors and experts on everything from "ethical implications of genetic engineering of animals" to the "breeding of wolf-dog hybrids" to "legal rights of animals in cases of abuse and neglect" to "the moral psychology of consumers' attitudes toward cultured or lab-grown meat."

We occasionally had to get up so I could take him outside for a pee, but we both have adapted. For all intents and purposes, Piglet has since become a member of the Yale Animal Ethics Study Group. At every meeting there is at least one new person who gets Piggy's business card and then is interested in his story. Most are surprised by the activism he's leading in educational outreach, both with positive growth mindset and promoting the rescue of animals with disabilities.

It occurred to me on the drive home that Piglet kept defying expectations that others had for him. He didn't recognize those limitations.

It made me think that the beauty of being pink is that you don't have to limit yourself to someone else's expectations. You can be an athlete and a scholar, an activist and an entertainer. You can just be you.

Without anthropomorphizing—something I shouldn't but regularly do—I will say that that one of his favorite things to do is attend conferences. With his adaptive Piggy power, in certain settings something changes in his demeanor. He is more serious, more quiet, and more attuned to my energy and needs. This is what I observed when he and I arrived at the Humane Society of the United States Taking Action for Animals (TAFA) conference, held at the Hyatt Regency in Arlington, Virginia, right across the border of Washington, DC. Piglet acted as if he belonged in the halls of Congress. He loved almost every aspect of mingling with fellow advocates—from our first road trip together, just him and me, to staying in a hotel room for the first time, to meeting several of my friends from the Humane Society Veterinary Medical Association (HSVMA), for which I serve as the Connecticut state representative.

The drive to Arlington was on a Thursday afternoon, so we did hit a fair amount of traffic. It was hot out, and I ended up in a strip mall for Piglet's lunch stop. We had to trek far outside my usual comfort zone to find a pee spot, and when all I could find was a glass-littered patch of grass, I felt bad this was the best I could do. He trusted me to make the right decision, peed quickly, and we hit the road again after that. We ran into even more traffic in downtown Washington, DC, but finally arrived at the Hyatt with plenty of time for Piglet to familiarize himself with the hotel room.

"Oh, it's really nice," I informed him, knowing he was about to find out for himself. He immediately set to work mapping the area. He worked methodically and slowly, moseying around, poking his nose gently into the walls, the bed, the dressers, and the closet. He located his water dish, which of course he promptly dumped. He found his stroller sitting in a corner, which was of great interest because there were cookies in the basket that I then had to move. In his brilliant, compartmentalized brain, he now could see the room, which he considered his home base for the rest of our stay.

Ever since this trip, many hotel rooms later, I'm still amazed at his systematic approach to new environments and situations. That first night, after I unpacked, Piglet and I took off on a long walk along the river before meeting my friends Dr. Barbara Hodges, who is the veterinary advisor to the HSVMA, and Pam Runquist, the HSVMA director. They both live in California, where the HSVMA central offices are located.

Dining at a restaurant with Barbara and Pam—outside on the sidewalk, where we could enjoy the warm summer night and our tasty salads—was one of the only times I had actually sat down to eat out since adopting Piglet. The truth is I didn't miss going out to dine at all. He was sort of an excuse for me to do something else more productive. The good news was that the sweet pink boy didn't mind so much anymore when Warren and I did grab a date night here and there, maybe to attend a concert. He would just hang out in the kitchen with Zoey for a couple of hours.

The trip away gave me perspective on how much life had changed since our Piglet project had begun. As I confessed to my fellow advocates, "I haven't even been going to my yoga classes anymore." Both of them reminded me why it was essential to make time for myself but understood with their own adoptees how that wasn't always possible.

Piggy slept in his stroller the whole time while I ate, as my California colleagues and I discussed future HSVMA events they felt we ought to attend. The main theme for the conference was learning to advocate for animals, with topics that covered advocacy for farm animals, the latest actions being taken on puppy mills, dog-meat markets, protecting endangered wildlife and their habitats, and more. All these issues were of concern to me, but I was most eager to learn what legislative actions were addressing puppy mills and changes for factory-farmed animals.

With a yawn, Piglet poked his nose up, and must have smelled that our dinner was over—his cue to wake up and come out to say hi to his new friends.

From the start of the conference on Friday, it rained for a good part of the weekend. That meant taking Piglet out in the rain and crossing a busy intersection to find him an approved pee spot, which we did numerous times throughout the day.

"Piggy Lee-Lee," I said to him, adding another nickname to his collection, "you're such a good boy to put up with being inside." I would have been more tempted to go on long walks if the weather were nicer, but he was more or less content—as long as I didn't ask him to nap the whole time in his stroller or on my lap. He needed to move around throughout the day. Those limitations forced me to prioritize which lectures I would attend and how much socializing I would be able to do.

If the subject of conversation was about him, not surprisingly, he would become an enthusiastic participant—saying hi to everyone who was interested in learning about who he was and what was so special about him. Even in the ranks of the HSUS, his pink power of attraction drew him an extraordinary amount of attention.

No one commented on how well he was doing in spite of his disabilities. They were mostly all like-minded and just thought he was irresistible. It was a community of people who shared my views, and I could feel the subtle shift of thinking toward acceptance as opposed to seeing him as limited.

Piggy felt that acceptance on some vibrational level, without a doubt. As far as I could tell, he loved meeting all the animal welfare advocate people, but he did seem to think he should be the only dog there. Piglet had his social limits with any dogs other than his familiar Shapiro pack and a couple he knew from the vet hospital—whom he had known as a baby. Piglity had made it clear to us that he didn't like other dogs coming near his stroller—his safety zone, after all. For such a tiny little dog who can't see or hear, he has no trouble knowing when other dogs are near.

On Saturday morning, we arrived at a huge ballroom for a lecture and found seats in the back on the side. Piglet, wrapped in one of his pink blankets, was fast asleep on my lap. The lecture had already started, but a few people were entering. Out of the corner of my eye, I noticed an attendee with a little dog walking by her side who was heading over to where we were planted.

Hoping that she wouldn't sit too close, I saw her slip into the row just behind us, and of course, she sat down in the seat right behind me. Within about five seconds I felt a familiar vibration coming from within the wrapped-up pink package on my lap. Sound asleep, Piglet had detected another canine within range of that powerful pink nose of his. He actually was grumbling and low-growling about the dog that had sat down behind us. I gave Piglet a little tap, letting him know to pipe down, and I moved up a row. Once he was satisfied that there were no other dogs in his personal space, Piggy Lee went right back to sleep.

The evening banquet on Saturday night was quite the gala. There were motivational speeches from the CEO of the HSUS and others who had typically heart-wrenching animal welfare messages to deliver. They served a vegan meal, which is the case at all HSUS functions. Piglet came along, of course, and was kind enough to sleep through most of it in his stroller. There were more than a few double takes when I revealed the habitant of the stroller was a dog and not a baby. Even in this educated assembly, a couple of curious looks were accompanied by comments of "I had to see if that was a dog or a pig there."

As usual, I was very impressed with all the speakers on a wide range of animal welfare topics. But my takeaway from the whole conference was validation of my own project that emphasized the need for more public education about humane issues—starting with school-age children. This was the work we were already doing through Piglet's mission and our educational outreach. I was struck by the fact that in geographical pockets of poverty and illiteracy, especially in the South—where most of my dogs had come from—humane education lagged far behind other, more affluent communities.

Other than the miserable drive home (seven hours in terrible traffic compared to the five hours it took to get there), the trip was a joy for me. It felt extra special to have Piglet along not just as a rescue boy himself but also as an ambassador and advocate for fellow animals. The same subtle but feisty confidence that I'd seen in Piglity on his very first day in our home continued to grow everywhere we went.

OCTOBER 2018
LOWER MANHATTAN

Wihin a year and a half since we'd decided to officially adopt Piglet, we were on the move like never before. By the fall of 2018, the pace had become relentless. Yet the reality is that we were having an adventure and our lives, though somewhat more complicated, were enriched beyond measure as we went along for Piggy's ride.

Not every expedition was logistically easy, I have to confess. One of the most exhausting treks was the one that Piglet and I made to attend a fundraiser on Wall Street. The invitation had come a few weeks earlier, when Piggy and I had attended the first annual Chloe's Fospice Friends fundraiser party. "Fospice" (a blend of foster and hospice) was part of the senior foster dog project of the organization Foster Dogs, Inc. I had met the director, Sarah Brasky, at another dog-related party earlier in the summer.

The organizer of the event, Dorie Herman, whom I finally met at the September fundraiser, was mom to the late Chloe Kardoggian—a teeny brown Chihuahua who had been very popular on Instagram, raising awareness for senior dog adoption. Chloe had died earlier in the year, and the fundraiser was a way to honor her memory. Dorie was there with Kimchi, her new adorable, tiny Chihuahua.

Because the world is always a small place when our beloved nonhuman family members are involved, Dorie's sister Emilie—who lives in Connecticut—would end up becoming a client of mine when she adopted a little apricot poodle, Leo, who was rescued from a dog-meat market in China. Soon after, when Dorie moved to Connecticut too, Kimchi and Dorie's other dog, Cupid, a fluffy little mutt, also became my patients.

At the Fospice Friends fundraiser, I also met Mary and Tom

Fayet from the Bronx. They were there with two of their many dogs—Lexie, a little Maltese who used a front wheel cart, and Candy, also a Maltese, who used a rear wheel cart. At home, Tom and Mary have a whole group of dogs with a variety of orthopedic issues requiring the use of front or back wheels.

Later, when I created a PowerPoint presentation on disabled dogs for a veterinary conference, Mary helped immensely by sending me info and videos of her adorable dog group.

The Fospice party place was small and packed to the brim with people and dogs. Piglet said hi to a few new friends, but he soon became so overwhelmed with the scents of so many dogs that he burrowed into the blanket I was carrying him in and went to sleep. This gave me a chance to mingle and get to know many of the people I would run into at upcoming events. One of our new friends was Franklin, an active, happy Chihuahua mix who used a wheelchair after being born with severe leg deformities. His dog-mom, Kathy Wiz, had adopted him five years earlier from the North Shore Animal League—after losing three of her dogs all in the same year. Kathy exuded kindness and generosity, and had a long history of fostering and a devotion to taking on hard-to-place rescued dogs.

Standing and talking with Kathy, I also met Rick Van Benschoten, the person who belonged to Oscar, a sweet older doxie mix who was paralyzed due to a spinal injury and uses wheels to get around. As Oscar made his way around the party, saying hi to every other dog and person, Rick fell in love with Piglet. So much so that as I was getting ready to leave, Rick turned to me and said, "Melissa, I'd love for you and Piglet to join us at the Wheels on Wall Street event next month."

Even though Piggy Little wasn't a wheelchair dog, the event was to raise awareness for dogs with disabilities—which Piglet definitely was. The fundraiser, sponsored by WagAware, was a benefit for Lovey-Loaves Special Needs Rescue and Sanctuary in Florida, an organization that focuses on paralyzed dogs as well as dogs with congenital limb deformities and amputations.

It was a great cause, and I was happy to attend the daytime event, which required me to plan out our route to get down to Wall Street. Even with my usual superior planning skills, I made some foolish decisions. For starters, I opted to take the train, even though I had to transfer to the subway once we arrived at Grand Central. Driving would have been so much easier, but since I'd decided not to take Piglet's stroller, the train seemed to make more sense. Instead of a carrier, I bundled Piggy up in a little sling and packed his various needs into a light backpack, and off we went. In retrospect, I should have remembered that I didn't like riding the subways at all and that carrying Piglet was too much for my shoulders. Our stroller was his chariot for a reason.

What an ordeal. By the time I got to the dog run on Wall Street, I was exhausted. Instead of a grassy park that I had envisioned, I saw that the dog run I had identified on the map was a paved and fenced area under a roadway. The big gated entryways had heavy swinging doors for safety, intended to keep dogs in. When we went through, we found lots of little dogs running around the various stone benches and decorative sculptures that formed seating areas. Many of the dogs were in wheelchairs, running happily with everyone else. It was very social, and Piglet and I were greeted with smiles. As Piglet began to sniff his way around the space, however, the number of dogs was overwhelming to him and I chose to hold him for the rest of the event.

Some of the faces were familiar from the Chloe's Fospice Friends event, and over the course of the day we made lots of new friends as well—including Cheri and Ward Wells, who run the rescue group LoveyLoaves. Cheri and Ward had brought a few of their dachshunds who used wheels. When I explained that their expertise would be helpful to me for my veterinary talks on disabled dogs, they offered, "Please use us as a resource, anytime."

By now, the sales of Piglet's merchandise were increasingly allowing us to start making meaningful donations to different rescue groups, and we were delighted to be able to add LoveyLoaves to our list. Piglet fans and followers, often from diverse backgrounds, are overwhelmingly devoted animal advocates and are always eager to add a new T-shirt design to their wardrobe, especially with the knowledge that they are directly supporting rescue organizations.

When the Wheels on Wall Street event ended, a large group of us all walked over to South Street Seaport for a late lunch. We all shared dog rescue stories, of course, and Piglet gave a tap-signal demo for everyone to see, including people who were sitting at other tables and walking by. He was in full command, proud and empowered, and I saw vividly that this really was his very own Cinderella story—the saga of the deaf blind pink puppy who grew up to discover that he was part of an inclusive, caring family with friends wherever he went. He was not less than dogs without his disabilities. He was perfect in his pink Piglity ways, imperfections and all—giving permission to others, myself included, to accept ourselves and one another.

When the time came to go home, I started walking back toward the train and then stopped in my tracks and said out loud, "Piggy Lee, let's get a cab. I cannot deal with the subway."

🐾

One of the things that I'd learned quickly once Piglet was given his mission and we knew that fundraising was part of it, is that many of the most worthy causes fall by the wayside due to lack of funding. For years I had considered creating a nonprofit that would provide financial resources for rescuers working on the frontline. Piglet had presented a new opportunity for my long time goal, but I still needed to organize and learn about the process. I thought back to the years when our three kids used the occasions of their music recitals to raise money for important causes. Rachael had started the tradition when her private piano teacher in New York wasn't offering solo recital opportunities. This led us to brainstorm about how we could tap relationships for finding venues and then do outreach to health-related nonprofit organizations. Rachael went on to perform six full concerts over the course of six years in high school and college. Ellie and Daniel joined her for several of these performances, especially the last few, which transformed the effort from Rachael's benefit concerts to the Shapiro family's benefit concerts. They used their hard work and talents to raise thousands of dollars for charitable organizations. These concerts gave all three kids the valuable experience of working hard and giving back and they gave me great preparation for raising money for rescue groups as well as promoting Piglet Mindset educational outreach.

Whenever I praised them for giving of themselves so generously, they all remembered what I'd said to them when they were young: *If you're gonna do nothing, do something . . . for someone.*

As Piglet's Dog-Mom, I was finding that there was more than enough to do for so many, especially, in our case, animals with disabilities and special needs.

As my work became more public, one new concern I had was choosing the right language to speak about disabilities and the individual animals and people who are disabled. I wanted to be respectful, but in researching and consulting with disabilities advocates, and parents of children with a variety of disabilities, I found that there was little agreement about terminology. Ellie helped sort this out for me during her junior year away in England, where she was studying at Oxford. Ellie had attended a lecture given by Haben Girma, a deaf blind lawyer and disability rights advocate whose goals include improving accessibility for people with disabilities through technology.

Ellie explained to me that Haben had responded to a question about why people with disabilities take issue with being called "inspirational." Haben clarified, "That's not accurate. The word is not the problem, it's the fact that so many people use the word in harmful ways that's problematic. I'm honored when people say I've inspired them to take positive action."

Ellie, who probably knew Piglet the best of all my kids, recognized that Haben's approach was similar to what I wanted to communicate to people about how I saw Piglet. In that way Ellie had come around to have a new understanding, acceptance, and appreciation for the focus of Piglet's mission. In fact, the summer before she left for England, Ellie volunteered in a classroom in Bridgeport where Piglet Mindset was being taught.

Around that same time, one of Piggy's top fans—a dog trainer from New York State—wanted to contribute to our educational outreach fund so that I could travel to visit an Alabama elementary school where they were using Piglet Mindset lesson plans. Our generous donor explained that she preferred to donate to a nonprofit for tax purposes. With her encouragement, I agreed that it would make it easier to raise funds to support our own programming and our list of special-needs dog rescues if we became an official 501(c)(3) organization.

With the extraordinary help of my brother-in-law Marc Shapiro, a lawyer, who donated his time to create our corporation, Piglet International Inc., and then helped us apply for and receive 501(c)(3) non-profit status, we were off and running.

None of this turned out to be as daunting as I once might have thought. The lesson from Piglet, as always, was the old adage *You never know until you try.*

Chapter 12

THE PIGLET
MINDSET MOVEMENT

*"These seven dogs are not just lucky but blessed to have you,
Warren, and your family to care for them, to teach them
and to love them. I often close my eyes when I'm looking at
your posts and wonder how in the world Piglet can race
around that back yard without fear and I know without a
doubt it is the complete trust he has in you and your family
to keep him safe. He, and all of your dogs, are living their best
life."*

—Facebook comment from longtime follower (1/29/21)

MARCH 31, 2019
WESTPORT WESTON FAMILY YMCA

One of the things I love most about presenting the Piglet Show is
taking questions afterward. I loved the question from a serious first
grader about "Piglet's sleeping arrangements." I got to tell the whole
story about our bedtime routine and how Zoey, Piglet, and Evie sit on
the bath mat while I brush my teeth, waiting for their bedtime cook-

ies. Another question I heard from young audiences everywhere was, "Why is Piglet pink?"

His pinkness is probably more a result of his breed mix than his being double dapple. But once we've gotten on the subject that lets me talk about what happens to puppies born to two dapple-colored parents, I would explain it as I do to adults, saying, "Piglet is deaf and blind, and he happens to have a white hair coat and a pink nose, all consistent with his being a double dapple. The reason he looks pink is that he has very thin fur on his head, earflaps, and nose, and his undercarriage is completely bald. This thin fur and lack of fur is common in doxies and Chihuahuas. His pink skin coloring shines through, giving him a light pink tinge."

Adults ask similar questions, as well as ones I don't always know how to answer. Such was the case after a Piglet Mindset presentation I gave at an event sponsored by PJ Library at the Westport Weston Family YMCA.

The day had gone really nicely. My parents were there, dressed proudly in their Piglet sweatshirts, along with a handful of their friends and about ninety other people who had come out to hear the talk and meet the tiny pink boy. Half of those in attendance were kids, the other half were adults, and the YMCA meeting room was packed to capacity. During my talk, Piglet snoozed in his stroller, while Zoey, not wanting to be left out, insisted I hold her. Easygoing Evie hung out next to Warren, waiting for the Piglet Show and her name to be called.

After I gave my talk and answered questions, I invited the younger members of the audience to come closer and watch a tap demo with Piglet and his dog sisters. Something about keeping Piglet "offstage" added to the excitement for everyone getting to see him make his entrance, all rested, happy, and eager to show off his skills. Lately, in this period, I had started working with him by sending him signals through my breath. Instead of giving him a tap signal for "come," for example, after he had done "sit" and "stay," I could step back and just blow a stream of breath in his direction and he'd respond.

It was great to have Warren there to answer questions off to the side, as several people were coming forward, crowding around in the hopes of taking a picture with Piggy Lee after the demo, and that can always become overwhelming. But Warren was and is such a diplomat and able to keep everyone engaged and moving, that everyone who wanted a photo got one. Soon the commotion subsided. It was then that a man, along with his very supportive-looking wife, approached me and Piglity—who was snuggled up in my arms.

The middle-age man and his wife introduced themselves and said, "Hello, Piglet!" beaming excitedly at one another as the pink boy inhaled the two of them with a tail wag.

"I just wanted to tell you how much it means for us to hear you give your talk." He explained that there was a question he needed to ask, first prefacing it by saying how they had really been looking forward to finally meeting Piglet. "We started following you on Facebook right after you adopted him, and I want you to know that he has changed my life." He mentioned that he was a veteran and that he frequently had hard days.

The man told me how it had impacted him to see all that Piglet could do—how that had given him motivation in tough times to stay positive and find his own sense of resilience. This gentleman then paused and looked straight into my eyes, asking his important question: "Does Piglet inspire *you*?"

My inclination would have been to smile out of wanting to be polite, but I tried not to do that. I wanted to take his question to heart and not respond superficially or flippantly. Of course I was deeply touched by the positive impact Piglet was able to have on many individuals who knew him only virtually. It never got old hearing that he inspired others to be positive and to find their own resilience, or that he could help them smile whenever they faced unrelenting challenges involving their health, their emotions, difficulties with family and friends, and pets. The stories themselves were very moving—how a little deaf blind pink puppy had helped people change or shifted their attitudes and helped them live more meaningful and productive lives. Yet I frankly never looked at Piglet as an inspiration for myself. It's possible that because I was so connected to my tiny wonder dog, I wanted to avoid saying that I was inspired by myself.

In any case, I answered authentically, in that moment, and said, "No, not really."

Once I said it, I felt bad about having disappointed this man who had asked so sincerely. Maybe it would have been easier to give the desired answer and say, *Yes, I am inspired by Piglet.*

Throughout my life, I have been inspired by people who go above and beyond to advocate and make a difference for other individuals, and who are humble as they do what everyone should be doing without needing recognition. I use their example to model my own generosity and kindness.

So, rather than answering the question "Does Piglet inspire you?" I realized that what I really needed to consider was what Piglet had inspired me to do. Piglet's spunk, his hunger to learn, his challenge to all of us to find a better way to communicate, and his crazy work ethic as he mapped and memorized every bit of his experience were more than impressive. At times he truly brings me to tears with the size of his heart and by the huge impact he has on children and adults every day—at events, on his social media pages, in educational programs, and among people of really different ages and backgrounds. Has he inspired me to action? Without question, he has broadened my vision to think bigger and have higher goals, as to how he and his pack—which includes our family and the various communities he impacts—can make a difference in the lives of that many more animals, particularly those who have disabilities, both by building awareness and promoting their adoption.

Even though I didn't fully answer the man's question at the time, I thanked him for asking it and said I was going to think about it more. What a gift—to look in the mirror and recall different ways I'd changed and grown since the day two years earlier when the upset, screaming foster puppy had barged into our lives, upending them before taking over and changing us in the process.

Piglet has a gift for changing people's thinking about what we can and can't do. He challenges each of us to cultivate a mindset for great possibilities and when faced with obstacles shift our attitude and raise our own expectations. This isn't to say that change is necessarily easy or always of our own making. That was something I knew all too well.

Empty-nest syndrome is real. I have to admit that when our kids were younger, it was much easier keeping to the "two-dog MAX" rule and our "no more animals" rule that we had to put into place when our adopted bird and rodent populations started to swell. Seven dogs? What was I thinking? There's no question that hormones were involved.

When asked about how we would really feel when all three Shapiro kids were out of the house, Warren and I would say that we would be fine—which was true, because with seven dogs and four birds we were going to keep plenty busy. It would be a drastic change, though, as all three, for different reasons, would be far away and not able to just drop in for a visit. Warren and I were committed to having faith that each of them would thrive in their endeavors.

There's no question that it helped having Piglet come along just before Ellie was leaving for college. Life with Piggy Lee had distracted and helped me become emotionally prepared for a successful transition as our kids flew off to distant places and challenging new experiences.

It was hard for me to admit to needing to slow down or to adapt differently to how busy I'd become with work and Piglet's travels. One issue was the sheer physical demands of working as a house-call vet—which often entailed getting on the floor or the ground to be at the same level as my patients. Years of running and cycling had probably taken a toll too. By early 2019, my knees were giving me so much trouble that I had to have knee surgery, which unfortunately didn't fully address all the issues. The recuperation was long, but I had time to do a lot of reflecting on various aspects of my career and family, along with a couple weeks of extra sleep.

For the first days post-op I arranged to have Emily, one of Piglet's vet tech girlfriends from NVH, come in daily to take care of the birds and the dogs while Warren was at work. When Emily arrived one afternoon as Piglet was snuggled with me on the couch, he poked his nose out and suddenly popped up, beside himself, as he realized in an instant that this was his Emily—in his own home! He was in heaven.

While Emily visited with Piglet in all his glory, I had a few minutes to take care of myself. Feeling pretty old at that point, as I brushed my hair, I wasn't surprised to see a few more flecks of gray just in front. All at once I could recall my grandmother, my mom's mom—Dottie or Dot, as I called her—telling me during a visit to Florida, when I was not even forty, "Don't let your hair go gray. You're too young to have gray hair." I had three kids, including a newborn, and no visible gray at the time, and I paused to laugh before telling her, "I'm never going to dye my hair, Grandma. I'm never going to put all those chemicals on my head."

Though I didn't take that advice, my dad's mom, Grandma Freda, gave me advice that I did put to use. She told me the secret to a good marriage and general well-being was "Never go to bed angry. Try to resolve any disagreements before you go to sleep."

This I took to heart for the rest of my life. Whenever it's late and I'm steamed up about something, I think of my grandma and try to resolve whatever it is, the best I can. I'm not always successful at that, but as I've gotten older, I've learned to take things that would normally eat at me in stride.

Ironically, my grandmother Freda and my grandfather Lou had terrible arguments. But I think he made her laugh because he had the best sense of humor of anyone I'd ever met until Warren. Grandpa Lou was a constant source of the most hilarious stories and riveting magic tricks.

My grandmothers were both excellent cooks, with recipes they carried around in their heads that I was intent on getting from them and passing on to my kids. So before either grandmother got too old, I asked them each to write down some of their more beloved recipes—noodle kugel, mandelbrot (Eastern European biscotti), and so on. Occasionally, I would share the recipes with relatives, who would admit to changing them somewhat, which actually made me feel bad—you don't change family history. The only problem with that is occasionally I would ask both of my grandmothers about certain ingredients—"That doesn't seem like a lot of sugar for the kugel, Grandma . . ." and the answer would be, "Oh, I always put more." Hilariously, they both assumed that nobody ever followed a recipe the way it was written anyway.

In this period, as we settled in for the shock of the empty nest, Warren and I had discussions about whether we had done enough to prepare our three kids for the challenges of the real world beyond college. Had we been too protective? With the Shapiro Rules and other ways of guiding our kids, had we passed on the basics we'd developed for being successful in our professional lives? All in all, we felt that we'd emphasized the important things—family, a tough work ethic, a commitment to performing acts of kindness, and celebrating little successes as much as the big ones. We tried to keep a sense of humor and adventure in the household, even if the quarters were somewhat crowded with extra nonhuman family members.

Warren and I both agreed that having a good sense of humor was an important part of our parenting. This was evident in our approach to the Tooth Fairy. It all started when we went to visit our friends, Dr. Howard Hochman, the zoo and avian veterinarian, and his wife, Patty.

One of my kids had just lost a tooth, which brought up the topic of the Tooth Fairy. Patty told me that whenever any one of her kids lost a tooth, she would create a scavenger hunt that would lead to the Tooth Fairy's money reward. Warren and I loved this idea, and decided to take it to the next level.

In the beginning, the clues were just cute and fun. Warren and I would wait until everyone was in bed and then construct a series of messages with clues. I wrote them out on pieces of paper in all caps in large, tidy block letters that didn't look like my handwriting. One clue might say, *Oh, I needed to have a snack!* and that meant to go to the refrigerator. The next note said, *I had to write an email!* and that was a clue to go to the computer. But something got into Warren—who decided that the rest of the world had overly romanticized the Tooth Fairy and that she was really a very unpleasant grumpy old lady. He would have me add funny lines to the clues—they were so hilarious that when the kids woke up in the morning and went on their scavenger hunts, they couldn't wait to read the mean things the Tooth Fairy said about their dad, in her own defense of all the bad things he said about her. In comments addressed to Rachael, the Tooth Fairy insisted:

It's true that tonight, before I came to your house, I did
stop and have a beef burrito, but your father's comments
about my breath and his claims that I was stinking up
the house were uncalled for & personally offensive. So
while I will always love you, your sister, and your brother,
the last person in the world that I would want to be is
your mother. Because, quite frankly, the thought of being
married to your father makes me sick. PS. Go to the BACK
of the water cooler.

Every now and then the Tooth Fairy gave out dental advice:

Take care of your new teeth. Start flossing.

All three kids laughed uproariously at what a villainous yet
quirky character she was. The Tooth Fairy had all kinds of excuses
for being thrown out of the house for being smelly (she was a smoker)
and for not being more creative as time went on:

You were going to get a great scavenger hunt for this tooth,
but your parents (especially your stinkin' father) said they
were tired. Can you believe it? I'm glad you lost the tooth.
You look good . . .

Rachael suspended all disbelief for years. Daniel could never
catch us in the act so he chose to believe too. But especially as Ellie
got wise, we were forced at one point to admit that we had written
some of the notes. Of course, the story became that Warren had to fire
the Tooth Fairy because she was so obnoxious and that was when we
took over.

In hindsight, I realize that my worry about the looming empty
nest might have come from an irrational fear that somehow we
would not get to have family gatherings with hysterical laughter like
that ever again. Apparently, I'm not the only parent who has ever
gone through such unnecessary worry. What I realized quickly once
the three kids started making big moves of their own was that we

would have plenty of occasions to be under the same roof, and to have fun and laugh as we always have. What's more, Warren and I felt very good about having given our three human children the gift of knowing how easy it was to use humor to turn the ordinary into the extraordinary.

The other realization that didn't come until later was that when the kids fly the nest, they still do come back, and they still need and want your love, concern, help, and humor. Rachael had helped pave the way for that recognition back in 2018 when she announced, in a phone call that was prefaced with "Mom, are you sitting down?" (I was, as usual, sitting in the car, driving to go to work), "I'm moving to Germany."

My first reaction was to think back to her college years and how she had spoken often of having the opportunity to live and work in France. A part of me wanted to say, *Germany? What?* but she had always dreamed of learning to speak a foreign language from a completely immersive experience, and after she told me about the job offer, a great one, it made sense.

Europe had already become an increasingly large part of her life, which helped lessen the surprise. For the last year or so, Rachael had been traveling back and forth from New York to Germany to visit her Norwegian girlfriend, Rebekka, a student in humanities and linguistics, and who lived in Germany. So this too made the move make more sense.

It was a challenge to know that Rachael would be so far away, but I comforted myself with the knowledge that we could still talk often on FaceTime. Besides, when your kids start making decisions about who they are, who they love, and how they want to live their lives, those are things you need to celebrate. My other comfort was that Daniel was home living with us after graduating from Manhattan School of Music while looking for work as a professional French horn player; Ellie, a sophomore at Princeton, was a quick two-hour drive away in New Jersey—Piglet's favorite college campus, after all.

In October of 2019, there were more changes. First, Ellie left for England to spend the academic year at Oxford University, a very exciting adventure for her and an opportunity for her to spend more time with Rachael since they were both in Europe. Even so, she was the youngest, growing up to spread her proverbial wings, and I was very emotional about it. Just before she left, a situation had come up where, unusually, she was upset about some ongoing issues with a school project. Ellie is a serious student, a hard worker, and sometimes very hard on herself. At this point, she was feeling overwhelmed. After reminding her that I knew how hard she'd worked and it was better to move on, it occurred to me. "You know"—I paused, knowing she might resist the idea, but then continued—"you really need to develop a Piglet Mindset."

She looked up and nodded, to my shock, saying, "I know! They didn't teach that when I was in elementary school." She laughed and so did I. To my surprise, she then went through the five pillars of growth mindset: "I've got perseverance, empathy, and optimism, but I really need to work on flexibility and resilience!" It made me feel happy that she was so much more aware of what I was doing with Piglet than I'd realized.

The biggest change of all was for Daniel. After months of looking for work in an orchestra—he was not interested in a band—he arrived at a crossroads. Though he had enjoyed a few small horn-playing jobs here and there, his main income came from a pretty awful job cleaning pools. He let us know, with some frustration, "I'm really trying to find another way to support myself." It was at that point that Warren brought up an idea that we'd discussed before but only in passing: "Have you thought about looking for opportunities in the military?"

Daniel listened, but not much happened until, completely coincidentally, he was with a friend who got a text from a Connecticut National Guard recruiter. The friend answered bluntly, "I'm not interested in the Army, I'm a pacifist." This wasn't the first text exchange for the recruiter, a seasoned Army guy and a former bandsman, SFC Joe Colovito, who shot back, "There are a lot of opportunities in the CT Army National Guard, the band for instance!" Daniel saw the text and immediately said, "Tell him I'm interested."

Within two months, we watched as our son's entire life trajec-

tory changed. He was soon playing with the Connecticut National Guard Brass Quintet and preparing to go off to Army basic training in South Carolina.

For weeks, Warren and I readied ourselves to take Daniel to the airport. I wanted to be stoic to show how proud I was. Yet this was a world that Warren and I knew little about. We were worried about how intense basic training was known to be, and the challenges of the physical and mental conditioning required for completing a rigorous program. Would he be overwhelmed? Would he find peers who were also not combat-bound? Would he be safe?

Because he was military, I received special permission to accompany him to the gate, and I tried to be very upbeat and even reserved as I hugged him goodbye, churning inside. As I watched our handsome son walk through the doorway to get onto the plane, I felt proud but crushed. In my mind, I had known the time would come to let him venture out on his own path but had never envisioned sending him off this way.

Before I drove away, Daniel called to say that the plane was delayed for hours. I contemplated going in to stay with him while he waited, but he was with a few others on their way, so I knew he wasn't alone. He didn't arrive in South Carolina until the middle of the night. We heard from him the next day or two, and then the final call before he "shipped" was one of the most humbling experiences I've had. He read a script telling me he wouldn't be talking to me for a while . . . and then he hung up the phone.

There was nothing to do at home but to stay positive and keep busy with lots on my plate, and to take a dose of my own homegrown positive thinking by having a Piglet Mindset. Daniel was going to survive, and so was I, I told myself on a routine basis.

In fact, he not only made it through, he did very well. There was a Facebook group where we could see pictures posted most days, and we saw him there with hundreds of others, doing all the drills just like everyone else. It was a relief to hear from him eventually—letting us know that everything was going well.

We were scheduled to go to the graduation ceremony in South Carolina at the end of December. I had dog and bird sitters lined up and had been getting all of the instructions ready. We were going to drive so we could bring Evie, Zoey, and Piglet. But in the afternoon the day before, I started to feel very sick, very quickly, with that recognizable kidney-stone pain. So instead of packing to go away to see Daniel's army basic training ceremony, I ended up in the hospital with two kidney stones that were not coming out.

We quickly adapted the plan so that I'd stay home while Ellie, back at home for the holiday break, could fly to South Carolina with Warren. The ceremony was beautiful from all reports—and lots of photos—and Daniel looked and seemed amazing, not just in the best shape of his life but with a new poise and stature.

That was exactly how he looked when he came home for two weeks before leaving for the Army School of Music in Virginia Beach. This time our goodbye at the airport was much more relaxed. He had prevailed even with the challenges of basic training, and now, reunited with his French horn, which he carried onto the plane, was off to begin working toward his goal of having a job as a military musician.

It was going to be a change for sure, but knowing Daniel, he would certainly make the most of every opportunity to come his way.

🐾

The question about how Piglet had changed our lives kept resurfacing. Every day I received messages describing how he had helped people face their own challenges. As he gained followers around the world, I realized that a global Inclusion Pack of a very large Piglet Mindset movement was organically taking form.

That was a very heady feeling, but nothing compared to how I felt when I first heard from a journalist at People.com whose name sounded familiar. Somewhere in my list-making and seemingly out-of-reach goals I had said that it would be amazing for Piggy Lee to land on the cover of *People* magazine. The initial article was on People.com, but it did so well that the editors came back and placed it in the print magazine a few weeks later. Piglet was so popular that he was named *People*'s Top Pet Role Model for 2019, which was in the 2019 end-of-the-year edition.

This was our once-upon-a-time one-pound foster project who was now not only a teacher, spokesman, advocate, and philanthropist, but a worldwide ambassador for animals and people with disabilities, and for animals in need of rescue. The primary focus of the online article was our Piglet Mindset inclusion curriculum, which increased our reach to teachers and other educators who didn't know about our online materials and in-person class-visit program. The article brought tens of thousands of new followers to Piglet's social media pages, where most of my animal welfare awareness work takes place.

What made the article even more special and personal was that our journalist, Greta Bjornson, was in fact the daughter of close family friends I'd known most of my life. It was magical.

Following the release of the online *People* article, I received new inquiries for features on online news and media pages for weeks after. I was interviewed on a Chicago news station and a Boston radio show, among many others. I also started getting more and more teacher requests for information about Piglet Mindset educational outreach and school and class visits. New teachers, new ideas, new experiences— our growth mindset curriculum was expanding to new levels.

My Instagram DM inbox was flooded at that point. I mentioned casually to Warren, "I'm probably missing some important messages," and went to clear some of them out. As I was scrolling, I came across a message from a producer who worked at *NBC Nightly News with Lester Holt*. They were interested in recording a Piglet Mindset classroom visit to be featured as a closer for *Nightly News*!

My personality is such that I try not to become overwhelmingly happy about anything. My preference is just to stay in the middle and allow events to play themselves out. Years of goal setting had cultivated that in me. But between *People* and Lester Holt, I was way over my ability to stay in the middle. I found myself feeling great happiness and satisfaction that my story and my program were of interest to mainstream media. The NBC piece to be recorded in Tricia Fregeau's classroom in Plainville, Massachusetts, brought it all full circle—to the birthplace of Piglet Mindset. When I got off the phone, I could barely breathe from disbelief and excitement.

Lukita sputtered and chirped. Dean started to bark, setting off a chorus from most of the others, with Piglet joining in. This was beyond anything anyone could have ever predicted from a one-pound deaf blind pink puppy. I had to give in and celebrate the unexpected impact Piglet had managed to have in so short a time.

Had Piglet, the deaf blind pink puppy, radically changed our lives? Yes, one hundred percent yes. He taught us, all of us, the boundless gifts of allowing unexpected possibilities into our lives.

That's what I felt so strongly on November 8, 2019, when we were able to schedule a visit to the *NBC Nightly News* studio to meet Lester Holt. Piglet was in his little stroller, all bundled up because it was windy and cold as we walked from the Javits Center, where I was attending a veterinary conference, all the way to the Rock—Rockefeller Center!

A part of me was nervous as we approached uncharted territory. As I thought back to how it felt when we attended large events, parties, and fundraisers with Piglet, I'd learned from past experiences how to make sure he was comfortable, and to make sure that others understood and respected his limitations. Piglet is a tiny dog processing a wide world, yet missing the two major senses, hearing and vision. Even though he certainly wanted to be there and enjoyed participating, as I did, he needed a lot of downtime to recharge throughout long-lasting events and activities. On the other hand, when he was doing his Piglet Show, in schools and other venues, or traveling on the train and in his stroller, he was on top of the world—goal- and destination-driven!

These thoughts filled my head as we entered 30 Rock, frankly, because I was worried about what so many people were expecting from their meeting with the tiny deaf blind pink dog. He was often friendly to many, but he was also more interested in doing his tap signals than basking in the smiles and affection other dogs would have been delighted to receive.

I stopped at the NBC check-in area on the ground floor, where the man at the desk made a call up to the *Nightly News* office. We waited for a few minutes for our producer, Kendyl Murtaugh, to come down to meet us.

"Hi, Melissa," Kendyl said with a smile as she stepped out of the elevator to greet me. She also said hi to Piglet, even though she knew he couldn't hear her.

We went up in the same elevator, talking about our previous recording session in Massachusetts, and when the door opened, we rolled out onto the floor where *NBC Nightly News* was produced. After a tour of the broadcast studio, we ended in a large desk-filled production room where there were about twenty producers all working diligently at their computers, but obviously waiting for the pink guest to arrive.

Once out of his stroller, Piglet made the rounds, saying hi to quite a few of his newfound NBC friends, who were now sitting on the floor. He wagged his tail and smelled their breath, as he always does in these situations.

At that point, Lester Holt arrived and the energy shifted. Aware somehow that he was in the presence of an audience that mattered, Piglet lit up and performed with finesse as we went through some of his repertoire. I answered questions and handed out stickers and buttons. Then I put Piglet's pink blanket on a table so he could sit and pose with Lester Holt for some adorable pictures and videos, which we posted on Instagram. Mr. Holt was as gentle, caring, and kind as he comes across on the news.

For a brief moment, I wished that Piglet could have been slightly more like other, "normal" dogs and warmed up to Lester Holt and the others, maybe enjoying being held and snuggled in a more relaxed, personally interactive way. But that was not who Piglity was or is. He was himself, a tiny pink larger-than-life disabled dog loved by everyone who met him.

When I left 30 Rock, with Piggy tucked away in his blanket-lined stroller, I took my time as I walked back to the veterinary conference, letting my life over the past almost three years run through my mind like a slide show. It was all there—my hands-on work with Piglet, the adventures that were to come as a result of his inspirational, motivational, and refreshing story, and the stories and messages from people who were happy, unexpectedly, knowing Piglet and letting him change their lives.

I stopped to eat at a vegan restaurant and even shared a few fries with Piglet, which I rarely do. It was a meditative walk back.

I couldn't help thinking just for a minute what would have happened if there had been no rescue group and Baby Bart had not made it out of the hoarding situation alive. I couldn't help thinking what would have happened if Gloria Andrews hadn't "tricked us" into taking on a one-pound puppy with vision and hearing deficits. More than anything, I couldn't help thinking what would have happened if Warren had said anything other than "okay" when I sent him the picture with the question, *Foster project?*

It wasn't as if he'd really been given a choice in the matter. Before going back into the vet conference, I called Warren to let him know how the NBC visit went. As I gave him a few of the highlights, I thought how he had changed and how much more patient he had become. All those hours of holding Piglity, almost like a human dog bed, must have had a profound calming effect on Favorite Dad. So many of the things that Warren does so well but sometimes takes for granted had become sharpened. Though I'm sure that I acknowledged him before, just in case I had never said it, I ended the call by saying in all sincerity, not very loud, "Thank you, Warren."

Chapter 13

THE MUSIC IS INSIDE

The reward of a thing well done is to have done it.
—Ralph Waldo Emerson,
(The quote I chose to accompany my high school yearbook photo)

MARCH–NOVEMBER 2020

It was early in the morning when we started packing up the car with the "travel team"—Piglet, Evie, and Zoey—to attend the graduation ceremonies at the Army School of Music in Virginia Beach, Virginia, where Daniel had completed his ten weeks of training. The drive ahead of us was about seven and a half hours (without stops), so we had decided to travel down the day before, stay at a hotel on the beach for the night, attend the graduation the next day, and then stay for another night before heading back with Daniel the following morning.

As Warren began setting out dog carriers and taking out our bags, I did a last check of the three remaining Shapiro birds—Betty, Sunny, and Lukita. Climbing the stairs to check on the aging house sparrow Girlitas, who lived in my upstairs office now, I half expected to see Blind Boy Willie up there too but had to remind myself that he had

267

died the previous year. He was the only member of our nonhuman family to leave us since the arrival of Baby Bart, almost three years earlier.

Blind and lame, Willie had been a case study for me in adaptability and resilience. He didn't like leaving his own cage, but he found a way to communicate with Betty (always averse to change but a hilarious character) and Sunny (so named for her love of sunflower seeds). He'd chirp away and they'd chirp back. Whenever I made my nighttime rounds to spend time with the Girlitas and Willie, I'd kneel down in front of his cage, stick my finger in, and let him sit there for a good while. His passing was so sad, yet he left in peace after giving us the gift of his meditative spirit.

After the loss of Stevie, Betty's bonded sister, I knew it would be an adjustment for her to leave The Bird House (making it uninhabited for good) and move inside with Sunny, who was rescued after falling from a nest and had a serious foot injury that prevented her from being released back into the wild. Sunny loved being an office bird, acting as if she could follow the words on my computer as she sat on my shoulder, in my hand, or under my chin. Once Betty arrived, she and Sunny made friends, despite some bantering, and were soon like an old married couple.

Saying goodbye to them, even just for a few days, had a poignancy I couldn't explain. These two were hand-raised by me, at different points, but are bonded to me and to each other. When I turned to go, they both piped up, sensing something maybe, so I turned back and talked-sang to them, telling them I'd be back soon.

As I went back downstairs to make sure our handsome blue parakeet was secure in his spot between the living room and the kitchen, I remembered the loss of Baby Bird and how it took me five months before I could even look at any bird rescue Facebook pages. The first glimpse I took led me to a picture of the most pathetic blue-and-white parakeet, face planted down on newspapers. He had permanently splayed legs that had not been treated when he was young. The woman from the rescue group discouraged me from adopting him because of his severe disabilities. I persisted, persuading her by saying,

"If I were you, I would give him to me. No one will take care of him like I will."

In pain, with his wings clipped, Lukita arrived in terrible shape but I had a plan for his care. He soon began to improve, bond, and became a very happy little bird. He loves to cuddle, chatter away in his foreign language, and fly around the living room in all his blue-feathered glory.

When I went to give him a little goodbye scratch, he bubbled forth with some version of thanks. For a moment, I had to laugh, remembering a time when I wasn't even interested in birds.

We had arranged for dog and bird sitters to come stay with Dean, Gina, Annie, and Susie, "the home team," while we were gone. The four of them and I gathered in the living room as I handed out dog cookies for each, assuring them by name that we would be back soon, and that Nicole and Emily, their loved pet sitters, would be there to take care of them.

"Deanie, here's a cookie," I began with a vigorous rub for our black Lab mix. "Be a good boy and watch out for your sisters."

Leaving the dogs for even a short trip like this was increasingly traumatic for me. Seriously. All the dogs knew what was happening from all the telltale signs—bags being packed, supplies set out, possibly even from overheard conversations—and they all wanted to come with us. I could see their anxiety and worry as they watched Warren and me closely, and I'd invariably leave the house in tears every time we went out of town.

The dogs who knew they were coming (Piglet, Evie, and Zoey) were fine, as was Dean, but the others weren't sure. Gina, who occasionally did get to go, was particularly anxiety-ridden about being left home. I had to be careful not to forget anything, because if I did, and ran back in to get it, Gina would leap into the air as if there were still a chance for her to get to go.

Taking a deep breath, I crouched down to hug her tight, reassuring my sweet white beauty that we'd be back soon, adding softly, "Gina, be nice to Dean, and if he barks too much, that's okay."

Whenever Dean started in on his barking lately, Gina overdid it by barking at him to stop. In advance I gave her a cookie and told her she'd have fun without me because Nicole always takes her out to play with her favorite soccer ball. As stoic as I'd ever seen her, Gina munched on her cookie and gave me the slightest bobbed-tailed wag.

Annie, who often got to come on trips with us whenever we could take four small dogs, just looked at me with the most pleading eyes that penetrated right through me. Since we were already pushing it with three little dogs this time, I felt more tortured than ever looking at our little tan, wiry-haired true melting pot of Chihuahua, poodle, Pekingese, schnauzer (hence her terrier heritage) and more, as she tiptoed over for her cookie. "Anna," I praised her, "you're always a good, sweet girl. Keep an eye on Susie for me." To my surprise, Annie promptly went over to Susie, who had curled up in one of her favorite dog beds.

I knew that our beloved old girl would be fine in our absence and was in good hands with Nicole and Emily, their most favorite vet techs. Yet, as I gave her one last squeeze and ran out to hop in the minivan and get on the road, I couldn't shake the sense that she was at that point in her journey that her time with us was more finite than ever.

As a house-call vet, I understand the aging process in all pets, and know that one of the most important parts of my job is providing in-home end-of-life services for dogs and cats. In offering compassionate guidance to pet parents anticipating the loss of their beloved dog or cat, I sought to let them know that together our job is to do all that we can to maintain quality of life and dignity for their pets. My role is to be there to help with the decision about whether to let them go peacefully. I offer this counsel with a great deal of sincerity and understanding because I know well what they are going through. As an objective professional voice for people who are devastated and afraid of the pain they'll feel when they say goodbye to their treasured pets, I try to be a source of strength when it matters most.

With all that I do for others as their veterinarian, and as rational as I am about letting animals go as their quality of life deteriorates, I am no different from clients I counsel when it comes to losing my own dogs and birds. My understanding of disease processes and

what is likely to happen in specific situations might be at a different level, but the sense of impending loss is as crushing to me as it is to my clients.

Saying little as Warren turned onto the ramp toward the highway, I knew that was where we were with Susie. I'd see her deteriorating, then she'd rally, and then she'd lapse down a few more pegs. My judgment wasn't clouded by my love for her, but dealing with a terminally ill pet was nonetheless emotionally draining. We all felt it, and leaving, even for a couple of days, wasn't easy.

In the course of our drive to Virginia, Warren and I were quiet, listening to classical music in relative silence—with a few minor barks from our three passengers, mostly from ZoZo, who has the least amount of patience for long drives. In that time, I had a sensation of catching my breath and reflecting on unexpected events in our lives, like how Piglet had become a conduit and a connector to so many different communities, from so many different backgrounds. What was it about him that made all this happen?

Sometimes I thought it was just that he was so stinkin' cute. Posing this possibility to Warren, I said, "There's something about the way he looks and moves, even with his unusual-looking eyes that don't see, and his ears that don't hear."

Warren agreed, adding, "He's also very sweet, which people can see."

"He is also a pain in the butt—which is part of who he is as well. He isn't perfect. Of course, you don't have to be perfect to be something special."

But that didn't answer my question about how he made strangers feel like they knew him and connect to each other through him. There was something about the power of empathy, a feeling that I didn't know if Piglet could feel, per se, but that Piglet Mindset taught to children.

In the classrooms and other settings where I'd been meeting more youngsters—from nursery school through high school—I often asked students to close their eyes and imagine what it might feel like to be blind, and then to cover their ears and think about how, without being able to see or hear, they'd manage to communicate with their family and friends. "If you were hungry or had to go to the bathroom, how do you think you'd tell your parents?" Then I'd ask them to imagine what Piglet feels without sight or sound. The ability to feel what someone else feels, even if you aren't limited in the same way, is what helps form a bond between strangers. If you see Piggy Little doing his butt-wiggly, twisty dance and you feel his happiness, you've made a connection that is beyond a mindset but a heartset, and it can make you happy too.

Whatever his drawing power is, I never expected that capturing the antics of the pink boy and his canine siblings—plus some birds and some humans—could have brought together strangers online in such a personal and profound way. While we drove in the car, I scrolled through some of the messages posted on different videos at different points and felt humbled to know that people enjoyed being on our journey with us and found some hope no matter what they were going through:

> This little dog has inspired me to not give up. I suffer from depression and anxiety and not so long ago I thought there was only one way out. But then Piglet came across my page and I saw what this little baby has accomplished and so I got help. Because—if this tiny pink puppy can go through all that he has to, then I can too.

> My son has a lot of health issues and Piglet videos are what he watches now when they are doing blood draws. Thank you for sharing this awesome boy with us.

> Susie has special relationships with all the dogs in her pack. But her loving kindness to Piglet as a puppy who had been rejected by his dog-mom warms my heart. And I know Piggy loves her for it too.

> Piglet has taught me so many things but to sum it all up, he has taught me that life, with all its ups and downs, and all of its highs and lows, is still beautiful. And we are given every single day to enjoy it and live it to the fullest. Thank you Piglet I love you so much!

I teach special ed and whenever my small group needs a happy distraction I'll say, "Let's see what Piglet has been up to." The children are in awe of what he can do. Then after looking at a few posts, spirits are lifted and we get back to work.

This handsome boy helped my aunt pass in a peaceful way. She was in hospice care until this past Friday. For a week I spent day and night with her and I was able to show her pictures and videos of Piglet. I ordered myself a birthday shirt from Piglet but I gave it to her to wear. She fell in love with this precious baby and he made her smile so much in her last few days. She passed wearing her favorite shirt. Her Piglet shirt. Thank you Piglet for sharing your beautiful life with me and my Aunt Shirley. We both love you.

I am so inspired by your pink prince and I've applied to foster a blind cattle dog puppy. Only blind so should be a bit easier right? Poor thing was found wandering alone on a rural road in Tennessee.

I'm in recovery from years of addiction and homelessness and found my boy as a 7-week-old puppy just after losing custody of my first child when I was still homeless. All the love I was losing around me, he replaced. Just one little pink-nosed puppy . . . He's 7 now and my emotional rock—I've been clean almost 6 years, got a beautiful little family and a good life. Not sure I would have made it this far without him.

What all of the attention meant, hopefully, was that Piglity was bringing out good in people and maybe encouraging them to do more for their fellow beings in their corner of the world.

The last year alone had been a whirlwind. There were the PetCon gatherings, where we met fellow canine and other pet influencers.

It was a wild and crazy scene, with fans showing up and wanting to take selfies with their favorite dog celebrities. As fun as it was to hobnob with the rich and famous of the animal world, I much preferred attending such events as the annual meeting of the HSVMA held at the HSUS Animal Care Expo. That was when Piglet took his first airplane ride to New Orleans—which we almost missed due to insane traffic on the way to the airport. We had also traveled out of town to attend the Dog Writers Association of America's award banquets, where a few of my essays won awards.

As I scrolled through many of the photos and videos I myself had posted, I laughed out loud at some of the videos of Piglet at different growth stages with his girlfriend Monica and how euphoric he became around her, getting kissed on both sides of his face. He had this whole audience of people we didn't know but who shared in our appreciation of how he would go pocket diving for treats with all the vet techs.

Some of the comments posted were from "top fans," who responded frequently. Others were from our friends and allied organizations we'd gotten to know since Piggy's arrival. There were shots from the luncheon I gave each year for all of our friends at Norwalk Veterinary Hospital. Then there was a picture of some of the cakes we ordered from Daniela's Little Wish, a nonprofit started by a local immigrant couple when their four-year-old, diagnosed with two rare, life-threatening conditions, made a wish—as she tells it on her Facebook page:

> Hi, my name is Daniela I am a 13-year-old girl who loves
> to bake and decorate birthday cakes or cupcakes for kids
> with severe illnesses and disabilities, or having difficulties in
> their little lives. I realized that I could make a small act
> of contribution in this world. An act of humanity. Do good
> for others.
>
> Do not get me wrong, we are not a wealthy family, my
> parents are very hard working people with big dreams for
> me. I was born here in Stamford, CT, but they want to repay
> in some way to this wonderful country, this beautiful city
> where we live all the benefits that we are having. Some

people ask my parents about if we are not wealthy how we
can afford make cakes for kids and they always said that is
the best way to spend and share our savings, making a kid
smile on their birthday. Nothing is more important than that!!
And that's it!! DANIELA'S LITTLE WISH started. A delicious
cake could calm a sad heart. We are sharing a sweet smile!
Welcome to my cause!! I am baking smiles for kids!!

At almost fourteen, Daniela has spearheaded the search for cures
to rare conditions like hers. She is an ambassador for hope.

There is also our amazing friend Mario, who barely survived his
birth in an ambulance, when he stopped breathing but was saved by a
paramedic. He was left with two debilitating disorders, and much of
his young life was spent recuperating from a series of major surgeries.
Yet he was convinced he had a purpose, and he used his voice to establish an antibullying project called Stand with Mario for Kindness;
its focus is to let children who are bullied know that other kids have
their backs in standing up to bullies. Though Mario never gained
the use of his legs for walking, he developed phenomenal upper-
body strength that gives him mobility on his own terms, and a love
of dancing, which, he says, is how he most finds joy, especially to his
favorite Taylor Swift song, "Shake It Off."

Piglet has his own dance, and it's not because he could hear the
beat of music being played. His moves were not all over the place.
When his crate was in the kitchen, he used to dance around it and
do curlicues at each corner, steps that must have come from a canine
music background deep in his DNA. Someday I predict his twisty and
wiggle-butt moves will become a national dance craze.

For three years, Warren and I never stopped being amazed at our
handsome, pink, tiny man and how he continued to learn, every day.
After mastering the different stages of "go to your bed," he added in
the cutest hesitation as he went forward a few steps, turning back
again to make sure I was following him because he was expecting
a cookie at his destination. That was his poster-boy look—his head
tilted way up and pink ears spread wide like propellers.

In early 2020, Piglet's funky choreography received a compliment from a dance teacher named Debbie Falconer, who went on to comment:

> Please let me know how to order the stickers, bumper
> stickers, and pins! I have adopted the Piglet Mindset
> and brought it to my dance classes I teach in Central
> Massachusetts. I plan to use these when I see RAK's!
> (Random Acts of Kindness). I remind my students each
> week to be kind, courageous, brave and positive. They
> are learning a piece to "You Raise Me Up" and they decided
> to use Piglet as their inspiration. I love Piggy and so do
> my students ❤

After I sent Debbie stickers for her dancers, I heard back from her when she wrote to say how much the kids loved Piglet and how they were using him as their motivator as they prepared for their spring dance competitions. I had hoped that we could make a trek up to Massachusetts to surprise them at one of their competitions—until, of course, they were all canceled because of the pandemic.

We also had to cancel a trip in late March 2020 to go to Alabama—where we'd planned to surprise the class of Joanna Worch with a live and in-person visit from Piglet. It was Joanna Worch who, after discovering Piglet Mindset online, had helped develop some of the concepts for the curriculum. Joanna had coined the phrase "Inclusion Pack" when referring to Piglet's six dog siblings. As a teacher in a school with a diverse student body from economically disadvantaged (high-poverty) backgrounds, Joanna believed that inclusion was essential to creating a group Piglet Mindset. I agreed wholeheartedly. Her input gave me further clues as to why people gravitated to Piggy—he made everyone feel accepted and part of his global Inclusion Pack. In writing about her experiences bringing the story of a pink deaf blind dog into her classroom, Joanna wrote me about her first year:

> In my 23 years of teaching, I have found it most difficult
> to teach tolerance and acceptance in a way that students
> can comprehend. The Piglet Mindset proved to be a way

that students immediately understood the importance of inclusion. Through the eyes of Piglet, they were able to be more accepting of peers they once rejected. All students could accept Piglet's language. I used Piglet's mission to help students learn to not fear others because they are different. Strong relationships were built inside and outside my classroom. They spread the message of Piglet Mindset through their actions and their words.

Joanna had come up with the idea of honoring a Piglet Mindset Ambassador of the Week, a weekly vote by the class to select the one student who exemplified a Piglet Mindset. That student was recognized during the week and on Friday got to wear a Piglet Mindset T-shirt. Joanna wrote me to say how that selection had changed many of the students' overall academic performance and self-esteem. Our trip to Alabama had been timed, in fact, to honor that week's ambassador and give Piglet Mindset T-shirts to the whole class. Ms. Worch is an extraordinary teacher who went on to win Teacher of the Year— an award she credits to Piglet Mindset.

As we made our way to Virginia Beach, we had no idea how serious the Covid-19 situation would become. The last thing we expected was that it would become a pandemic soon to be sweeping across most of the globe. Little was known or understood in early March when we were there for Daniel's graduation. We knew there was a risk, but we didn't realize the depth of the problem as we enjoyed our long drive. In hindsight, we could have gotten sick—not to mention that my parents had come out for one night to attend the graduation with us. My main concern was getting Ellie home from England before flights were completely stopped. Luckily, she was able to get on a flight and arrive home shortly after we did. I was very concerned for Rachael and her soon-to-be-wife, Rebekka, in Germany. They would be fine, hunkering down and working remotely, but it was so upsetting not knowing when we would see Rachael again.

As for Daniel, Warren, and I, along with my parents, we were so fortunate that we were able to celebrate with Daniel, his colleagues, and all of their parents and families, safely, before everything shut down.

When we got to the performance site for the graduation, all the parents and family members were standing outside waiting for the graduating soldiers to march in. It was a dramatic entry that ended in a lineup that allowed parents and guests to take pictures.

Sitting there in the auditorium, there were many moments of wiping tears away as we watched a movie about the military, listened to the large band perform military music with skill and bravado, and then heard performances by small groups of musicians before the formal graduation ceremony.

Afterward, we took some pictures outside with my parents before they left for the long drive home.

"Let's go have lunch," Warren suggested, and invited some of Daniel's friends to come join us. On the way there, Warren looked at me in surprise that I was so happy to be going to a restaurant. Come to think of it, I was surprised too.

It was just fun to go out and meet everyone we'd been hearing about all along and to hear about their different plans postgraduation.

The following morning, before picking Daniel up, we had a chance to get out with the dogs on the vast, empty beach. It was chilly but not too cold for Evie to lead the way, with Zoey following fast. Piggy Lee went for a brief sprint, then did a circular slowdown at a certain point when he got cold and needed to be picked up and wrapped in his blanket. We headed over to the boardwalk, and Piglet decided to lead the way, saying hi to the early risers.

Then we went to get Daniel and headed back home. In the matter of two days, the news was reporting a pending shutdown in California. The world was about to turn upside down.

The pandemic threw a wrench in Daniel's plans to gain employment as a professional musician, as it did for the plans of most everyone. But he felt fortunate to be playing his horn in the Connecticut National Guard Band and Brass Quintet. Despite the challenges ahead, he eventually was able to find a full-time job.

The changes in Daniel were dramatic and unexpected. He had

become interested in joining the Connecticut National Guard because he was excited about playing his horn in the band. Along the way, he took pride in serving his country and being part of the music that rouses the spirits of soldiers and brings gravitas to important events in the state's and nation's history.

In that same spring of 2020, Ellie moved home and adapted rapidly to attending virtual classes for the remainder of her junior year. Since she was home for the summer, Ellie was able to enroll in socially distanced sailing classes, which motivated her to buy a small used sailboat that she kept at our town beach. She and I welcomed time together sailing in the same place I've been sailing and kayaking since I was a child. Her boat, a very old Sunfish, was almost identical to the one I'd owned at the same age. Sailing together—when Warren could stay with the dogs—was an unexpected silver lining of the shutdown. So was having her back in the house.

Even though I was still making outdoor house calls when families needed me to come, I transitioned most of my appointments to seeing patients at Norwalk Veterinary Hospital. The safety protocols for Covid-19 were firmly in place, and we all found it easier and safer that way. In the meantime, Zoom, FaceTime, and other meeting platforms turned out to be ideal for connecting to multiple programs that were teaching Piglet Mindset. In March 2020, I spoke online with a group of about twenty-five students from an elementary school in California. The following month I heard from Debbie Falconer's dance group in Massachusetts; even though competitions were canceled, they wanted me to see them dance.

Not only did I dial in to see them dance, but Piglet was with me to cheer them on. They were incredible! So much of life had been shut down, but they found a way to make it work, and all performed from their own homes via Zoom. We got to watch a grid screen of all the girls dancing to the same music, not together physically, but in sync with one another nonetheless.

I kept telling Piglet what was happening and how excited these dancers were. He sat on my lap quietly as if he were watching, as he commonly does with our virtual Zoom visits.

In April, I received an email from Liz Lawrence, a teacher of deaf students in California, who was initially interested in having one, and then two, of her students have a virtual Piglet meeting. I suggested they first look at the materials on the website to get familiar with Piglet and his mindset. She replied:

> They will know who Piglet is and will have seen some of your videos. We will have talked a little bit about his message and I will help them prepare some questions to ask you. Anything you want to share with them about Piglet, they will be excited to know. They will probably want to know things like how do you get his attention (we tap deaf kids on the shoulder) and does he know any sign language. They will probably also want to know how you got him.

She followed up the next day by adding:

> Both of my students have cochlear implants. The older student uses a combination of sign language and speech. I will interpret for her if she needs me to. The other student is speech only. Our Google Meet platform is also captioned. My older student wrote these questions today after we looked at a video and the power point.
>
> 1. My mom taps me to wake me up. Is this how you wake up Piglet?
> 2. I screamed too when I couldn't hear. (THIS IS TRUE!!) Then, I learned sign language. How does Piglet communicate? Can he see a little bit of sign language from his left eye?
> 3. How old is Piglet now?
> 4. How did the other dogs learn to be patient with Piglet?

"These are excellent questions!" I told the two students when we began our video call. Communication was no problem because the younger student could hear me and Liz signed for the older student to ensure she understood what I was saying.

They loved that I woke him up gently and gradually, just like their parents did for them. And they really liked the "go pee" tap signal.

Without telling us exactly, Piglet seemed to miss the up-close-and-personal interactions of meeting new people that he enjoyed in our prepandemic life. We tried to take longer walks and have more outings in the car, not just for him but for all the dogs. During this time, his pages were bombarded with posts from more and more people who told us that Piglet and his Inclusion Pack had helped them through their toughest days. We might not be able to put our fingers on what it is, but somehow Piggy Little lets us live in the moment and savor it, allowing us to let go of the harder burdens, at least for a short while—and feel the joy that comes from not having to fix the whole world, only to hopefully make it a little bit better.

JANUARY 2021
PIGLET'S VIRTUAL BIRTHDAY PARTY

When it comes to humans, I feel about birthdays the way I feel about weddings. Not my favorite thing. That doesn't apply to our dogs, however. We regularly celebrate their "gotcha days" to mark their official adoption days as members of the Shapiro family. We also celebrate their birthday zones—as has been the case for Piglity, who turned four years old sometime toward the end of January 2021.

We organized a fundraiser for our nonprofit, Piglet International Inc., that included a Zoom gathering complete with goodie bags full of Piglet face masks, stickers, and other party favors for VIP ticket purchasers. Piggy and his entire Inclusion Pack performed the Piglet Show to wild applause from all those watching near and far.

When I told Rachael about the party, she said, "I wouldn't miss it for the world, Mom!" and connected from Germany about two in the morning her time. She told me not to worry, as she was up working anyway. Such is the life of a private equity investor. Talk about unexpected.

During the whole Zoom party, Rachael managed to make every

guest feel that they were a VIP, all while wiping her tears of pride over her pink baby brother's growth and accomplishment. Rachael is one of the most outgoing, gregarious young women I've ever met. She is so sweet to everyone and always has been. At the age of three, she came with us to a vet hospital party where she mingled on her own when we first arrived. Within a few minutes of being there, she took Warren by the hand and gave him a tour of the party, introducing him to each person by name!

Here she was, recently married to Rebekka, building a life together, becoming fluent in German—so that she was able to converse with her Oma, Warren's mom, in her grandmother's native language. Rachael still managed to show up to make everyone who loved Piglet feel included in his birthday celebration. It hadn't hit me until that day how deeply I missed her presence, so much so that when Warren and I said goodbye to her, we all became a bit tearful. We felt so happy for Rachael, and grateful that Daniel was moving along his path as a professional musician and serving his country, and proud of Ellie for her extraordinary discipline and focus. I wasn't sure how to process the many rites of passages we were all experiencing—in our own lives and in the world. Yet one thing I realized was that maybe expectation is really not all it's cracked up to be.

On the Zoom call that day, we were also honored to have Monica with us. I thought back to a recent visit to NVH when she had swept Piggy Little into her arms and he tried to put his nose under her mask—just making sure he could smell the cilantro. Monica began to sing and dance with him that day, and as always, Piglet's tail spun, and his body wiggled to her unheard tune. Once when I asked her what language she was speaking to Piglet, she said, "Oh, every language. Made-up, too."

Monica loved telling the story about the time her daughter Amanda had worn her Piglet T-shirt to school and one of her teachers said, "Oh, I love Piglet!"

Amanda announced, "My mom is Piglet's girlfriend."

The teacher stepped back, paused, and then asked incredulously, "Your mom is Monica?" She couldn't believe one of her students was the daughter of the famous Piglet's girlfriend from the videos.

On that recent visit to NVH everyone wanted to know how Susie was doing. Dr. Duffy leaned his head out to listen for my answer. I shrugged, saying she was hanging in there. There was an audible sigh of relief. Without Susie, things would have been very different in the Shapiro household. She was the unassuming mastermind, the dog who'd broken the "two-dog MAX" barrier that had eventually led to Piglet.

After his birthday party was over, Piggy Lee was exhausted, as were the rest of the six-pack and certainly his Favorite Dad and Dog-Mom. There was no rest in store yet. I was working on PowerPoint presentations for a veterinary conference and developing my new Vet School for Kids, a program for children who are interested in veterinary medicine and all aspects of pet care. Not to mention that I had a book to finish writing. It wasn't exactly how I'd expected to spend the night after a busy day preparing for and celebrating Piggy's fourth birthday, but not much these days has been going the way most of us ever expected.

Living life with an open heart and letting it surprise you now and then keeps everything interesting. The one thing I refuse to let go, though, is my need for routine.

Everyone depends on their routine—on normalcy—especially in volatile times. Mine is one that I've cultivated with birds, children, and dogs for years and years. My morning wake-up and late-night bedtime rituals are the bookends of my day.

On this night, as most, I had a chance to reflect on the day, on the past, and on the future. The bedtime birdie routine was something I started with Baby Bird, a meditative time even though I didn't actively meditate. She had a magnetic calming effect that helped in the transition from an active day to a relaxing sleep. Of course, "relaxing sleep" is a relative term!

After finishing my work late in the evening, I began the birdie good night, I went in to give Betty and Sunny tiny pieces of mango, loving the feel of their beaks taking fruit from my hands.

When I told them at last to go in—and they listened, making their way into their cages to their sleeping perches—I paused, feeling so thankful for my tiny brown feathered friends.

Whispering, I said, "Good night, Sunny. Good night, Betty," but heard nothing because the two Girlitas were already in birdie dreamland. Next I gave one more good night to Lukita downstairs and moved on to getting the dogs ready for bed.

As always, I took everyone out in two groups for a pee, after checking to make sure there were no signs of a racoon, fox, or coyote lurking about. Once everybody was back inside, we all moved into our small kitchen. Sweet Gina went quickly to her spot right below the kitchen sink, drooling on the floor as she anticipated her bedtime snack.

This night I gave out a few rounds of cookies, using the opportunity to get Susie to eat a few extra treats before we all went upstairs.

We fussed with Susie to eat more at night because going to sleep with an empty stomach predisposes her to reflux. Soon we had quite the gourmet eating affair going, which I knew Warren didn't care for; he doesn't like the dogs insisting on eating treats before they go to sleep. For me, though, it is one more place to count heads and be sure everyone is in the house safely before I go to sleep. They look forward to their bedtime snack, like a late night social gathering.

As everyone started the ascent up to our bedroom, Gina went back to lie down on her living room dog bed. She doesn't like to go up the stairs but would be mortified if she were left alone downstairs for the night. It took a few seconds to convince her to join us and, with Piglet cradled in my left arm, I ushered everyone up to our bedroom. By that point, Annie was already asleep, curled up next to Warren in our bed. Susie, Dean, and Gina found their respective dog beds on the floor in the same spots where they sleep every night.

Zoey, Piglet, and Evie came into the bathroom with me as I brushed my teeth. Zoey still uses a pee pad most nights and then, sorry to say, needs a cookie. So these three got one added little treat before we finally were ready to go to sleep. That is, right after Piglet finished getting his teeth brushed, which, his grunts reminded me, he does not like.

"Piggy, you're a very small dog, and food gets caught very far back in your mouth behind your last molars. This will keep your teeth in good shape." It helped to clean the area at night before he got into bed.

Whatever worries, hopes, joys or regrets had been in my mind earlier, they no longer were in my head. I loved the contentment that filled the mostly sleeping room.

Evie headed over to the fleece blanket covering her Pottery Barn chair. Once she jumped up onto the chair, she paused for me to kiss her head, and then began to dig herself a sleeping nest. Zoey and Piggy at last let me pick them up to get into bed with me. I did my usual gymnastics routine, holding the two of them at the same time, plugging in my phone, and eventually working my way into bed with a bit of a leap. I didn't want them to wake Warren up, so I quickly stuffed them under my blanket, where they both curled up into little balls. Zoey was in her spot on my left side and Piggy put himself right on top of me, where he would stay for at least a few hours. He first had to dig a hole in my shirt before doing a few circles and finally curling into just the right tucked-in ball. Moving in stealth, Zoey left my side for Warren's, and I whispered to her, "You are not my dog anymore."

In moments, she returned, reassuring me that she was, in fact, my tiny chocolate lapdog.

Piggy did one more turn around, curled into the tightest little ball right on top of me, and gave his final, emphatic sigh, confirming that he was at last set for the night.

I waited in the dark for a bit, making sure everyone was asleep before putting my glasses on the night table—a signal to myself that the day was officially over and it was time to finally close my eyes. Under my breath, I whispered, "Good night" and "Sleep tight."

Nobody made a sound.

EPILOGUE

From Piglet's Favorite Dad

Melissa is not a particularly philosophical person. She doesn't reflect (much) on what her motivations or beliefs are that give way to her behaviors, habits, goals, and accomplishments. She sees problems and looks for solutions. The closest thing she has to a philosophy is her commitment to action, her daily routines, and setting (and achieving) goals. Once she sets a goal—any goal, but in this case, it was giving Piglet a happy and meaningful life—she will spare no effort in achieving it. Having said that, reflecting on the "why" of our journey with the pink man is not something that comes naturally to her.

From the time that I met her on a bike ride thirty years ago, I was struck by her immense drive and focus (okay, in addition to the fact that she looked spectacular in formfitting Lycra). I noted at the time that she was the *most* disciplined person I'd ever known. In addition, she does love animals, if you can believe it, more than anyone I've ever met. Not because she loves more, but because she has made it a goal that guides her every single action and behavior in life. This is not to take away from the scores of people who love their dogs and the many other kind, devoted, empathetic people who have rescued and cared for disabled dogs, some even more severely impacted than Piggy. But few of them are veterinarians. And none of them are Melissa. The intensity of her drive combined with the depth of her commitment is what makes her unique.

Having said all that about how terrific she is, she doesn't do "I am feeling this way because" very well. So writing this book was, I think, a particular challenge for someone like her: a "doer" more than a "reflector." But the struggle was worth it! In the process of telling Piglet's story, our story, I think she found a great deal of insight into not only what she does but *why* she does it.

Piglet has changed us significantly by treating us to his unbridled compassion, gratitude, and love. Yes, he is amazingly cute, and I think his many fans appreciate that holding him is an experience unlike any other. He doesn't just love you; if he likes you (and he can be indifferent to some people), in most cases he *adores* you. Is this part of his lacking two of his primary senses? Is it just because dachshunds and Chihuahuas are this way? Hard to say, but I think not. Like Melissa, he is hyperfocused on his goals; he is the ultimate "in the moment" little guy. As a tiny puppy, in order for him not to be isolated, he had to be totally committed to being connected to his human and canine family. So out of his sweet desire to be connected, he developed his own version of a growth mindset.

Our little Susie was suffering from end-stage kidney failure during the latter months of the writing of this book. Losing her was devastating when the time came. Still, it's part of the circle of life, I think, that Piglet got the opportunity to repay Susie for the love and acceptance she showed him when he was a tiny puppy with some kindness of his own. No one taught him this. This is the Piglet Mindset. It is not a result of him articulating his philosophy, it's because he is *living* it! When he played with Susie as she got weaker, he was noticeably restrained and gentle. He understood that she didn't feel well all the time. But he still wanted to be connected with her and she with him, and they figured out a way.

Being connected and making connections is really a theme in Piggy's life. Being born deaf and blind, he was pretty isolated at birth. Through his initial connection with us, Monica, his big dog sister Susie, his pack, his friends at Norwalk Vet, and then his legions of fans, he has connected to literally millions of people worldwide. This is the power of compassion. This is the power of kindness and inclusion. This is Piglet's mission.

For Melissa, Piglet is the culmination of a lifetime of love, caring, and self-sacrifice devoted to the well-being of animals and their people. I often hear her say, "Warren, you are the light of my life" (okay, I just made that up). Seriously, for her, to be a veterinarian and to do this work is her life's passion.

Piggy has facilitated Melissa, and me, taking a giant leap forward in appreciating all of life's joys as well as sorrows through a growth mindset. We love him for this and for who he is, and we hope that our story has touched you, encouraged you, and hopefully changed you, even just a bit, as it has us. Perhaps to care a little more, stress a little less, try something you thought was too hard for you to do, or to just make that extra effort to stay connected. Take a moment to invest 100 percent of yourself in a precious moment and do a little wiggle-butt dance (if not in real life, at least in your mind) to celebrate something you did well, even if it wasn't perfect.

With much love and gratitude,
Warren Shapiro
March 2021, Westport, Connecticut

ACKNOWLEDGMENTS

Writing a book has been on my list of long-term goals, but it was never something that I thought would actually happen. This unexpected opportunity to share stories from my life and career with animals, and specifically with Piglet, is really the ultimate reward for saying "yes" just one more time.

Achieving the reality of a completed book would never have happened without so many devoted individuals who have played roles behind the scenes and in them. Let me extend sincere gratitude to everyone who has shown so much enthusiasm for Piglet himself and for your commitment to bringing his story to a broad, welcoming audience around the world.

My heartfelt thanks go to my editor, Leah Miller, for your clear and steadfast vision, for your patience and fortitude. Your insight, dedication, and enthusiasm for all aspects of Piglet have served to guide this project through. Thank you to my agent, Kristyn Keene Benton, and to the rest of the team at ICM for top-notch guidance, support, and advocacy at every step of the writing and marketing process.

I'm most thankful to have worked with writer Mim Eichler Rivas, whose passion for our story magically transformed our seemingly endless phone conversations and email exchanges into a compelling, emotional narrative structure. It has been a pleasure collaborating with such a talented creative writer and observing how you dove into our lives, pulling out what seemed like ancient history to reveal significant events, hilarious memories, and experiences that landed on the page.

Thank you to Melanie Iglesias Pérez and Emma Taussig from Atria, and Catherine Shook from ICM, for keeping track of scheduling and logistics throughout the process. And to Megan Rudloff, my Atria publicist, and Maudee Genao in Atria marketing, for your tireless efforts in bringing this book into the public eye.

And thank you to all the other important Team Piglet members at Atria—Libby McGuire, Lindsay Sagnette, Dana Trocker, Lisa Sciambra, Karlyn Hixson, Nicole Bond, Paige Lytle, Sarah Wright, and Dana Sloan—for your belief in this project and for being the best possible publishing home I could have asked for.

Thank you to my good friend and photographer Joan Carruthers and to your husband, Paul Nebor, for your unlimited patience and willingness to go to all lengths to produce the most beautiful pictures of my family. This includes our extraordinary back-cover photo that showcases all seven dogs lined up next to each other with our sweet Susie front and center—one of my all-time favorite photos.

Thank you is an understatement when I think of Ms. Tricia Fregeau, third grade teacher in Plainville, Massachusetts, and her brilliant, innovative insights that resulted in the creation of Piglet Mindset. Thank you to Joanna Worch for creating the Piglet Mindset Ambassador of the Week program with your second-graders at Foley Elementary School in Alabama. And to all the other teachers, school administrators, guidance counselors, dance coaches, and Girl Scouts leaders who have brought Piglet Mindset into your schools and other organizations, I can't thank you enough for your collaboration.

I must acknowledge Ms. Sue Anderson Limeri for planting the seed that led to our officially becoming a nonprofit. Many thanks as well to my good friends and clients, Jacques and Wendy Bouthillier, for your encouragement and support. I am grateful to Gary and Barbara Brandt, and to Don and Rina McCouch for your early and generous support of Piglet's educational efforts. And thank you to my brother-in-law, Marc Shapiro, and to Jill Block for donating your professional time to incorporate and then achieve 501(c)(3) status for Piglet International Inc.

Thank you to our merchandise fundraising partners at Bonfire, especially our rep Heather Smith, for creating Piglet merchandise that has made its way around the entire world and for designing and generously donating our Piglet logo to our nonprofit. We are most grateful to our neighbor and friend, Katrin Lewertoff, for donating her legal skills and time in trademarking our nonprofit educational and other services.

We want to acknowledge our animal-loving friends at The Dodo for publishing viral videos that put Piglet's story in front of millions of viewers all around the world. Thank you to *People* magazine and to journalist Greta Bjornsen for publishing an amazing People.com article that elevated global awareness of Piglet's mission. Further gratitude goes to Lester Holt, Kristen Dahlgren, and Kendyl Murtaugh at *NBC Nightly News* for the beautiful segment show-casing our Piglet Mindset educational program.

Without my colleagues and friends who devote themselves to animal rescue in general, I wouldn't have had a book to write. I am forever grateful to Dr. Gloria Andrews of Colbert Veterinary Rescue Services, Holly Chasin of The Little Pink Shelter, Susan Inman of the Charleston Dog Shelter, and Morgan Sokolow Gall of Pet Match-maker Rescue for your devotion to dog rescue and for bringing us our current group of rescued dogs.

Gloria Andrews deserves multiple mentions for first rescuing and caring for Baby Bart, who became Piglet. We can't imagine our life without him. Further acknowledgments go to Jim Kilgos of Amazing Aussies Lethal White Rescue of Arizona and to Allison Holloway of Pawsavers Rescue for sharing your expertise in caring for deaf and blind dogs as I took on the challenge of caring for Gina and Piglet.

To our online Piglet Mindset community—Connie Evans, Jake Wojciechowski, Debbie Falconer, Sue Anderson Limeri, Christine Arm-strong, Mara Susskind, and literally hundreds of thousands of others, thank you for your enthusiastic support, confidence, heartfelt com-ments, and encouragement on each and every post. I am grateful for such a positive platform that allows me to advocate for pets and people with disabilities and other animal welfare–related causes, and for bringing Piglet Mindset to children and adults all around the world.

I am indebted to Dr. Charlie Duffy and Dr. Janice Duffy, cherished friends and closest veterinary colleagues, for allowing me to call your hospital, Norwalk Veterinary Hospital, the base for my house-call practice for more than twenty-three years. More veterinarians I wish to thank are: Dr. Nina Shouldberg for your care and guidance with Piglet's allergies, Dr. Camilla Colberg, Dr. Lisa Major, and Dr. Alistair Chapnick, colleagues with whom I have enjoyed working over the years. The technicians, kennel staff, and office staff at Norwalk Vet make me feel at home when I call or bring my own patients in for care. They are: Monica Pagan, Emily Zadravecz, Jessica Paradise, Mallory Caviola, Nora Guzewicz, Ruth Vera, Charlie Duffy, Zack Duffy, Liam Duffy, Alex Pagan, Armando Pagan, Hannah Geisler, Gina Carbone, Samantha McGehee, Doreen Bouab, Sam Soltesz, Oneida Pagan, Kaitlin Caviola, Dawn Grover, Amanda Pagan, Sarah Pagan, Deana Plucker, Ginny Hammons, Patrick Moore, Linda Fakundiny, Liz Harris, Kevin Burns, and many others over the years. The veterinarians and other staff welcome my dogs when they come in with care and compassion whether they are sick or just there for a social visit. My little Piglet feels like he is visiting family when he enters "the back" treatment area at NVH.

On the bird front, I can't express enough gratitude to Dara Reid of Wildlife in Crisis and to the late Dr. Howard Hochman and his wife, Patty Hochman, for their generous support and life-saving help and guidance with all my birds and my kids over the past twenty years. I also want to acknowledge the many bird-rescue enthusiasts and all of the like-minded bird lovers who helped make the Facebook page I began a resource for sharing advice in caring for house sparrows.

An additional mention and deep thank-you and appreciation of course goes to Monica Pagan for her extra special connection to Piglet, which began on March 4, 2017, when I literally could not get the one-pound pink puppy to stop screaming. Piglet adores Monica but he is not the only dog who thinks she is his BFF girlfriend. That's because Monica treats all dogs, cats, birds, and other creatures that come into her care with the same compassionate care she gives to Piggy. And the same goes for Emily Zadravecz, who in addition to being a friend and a tech at Norwalk Vet, has also been my bird and dog sitter for the past fifteen years.

I'm forever grateful to longtime house-call clients Erica Merrill, Amy Kamisher, Leanna Lawter, Nancy Risman, Donna Cifatte, Jake and Liz Glaser, Sharon Pounds, Alicia Chaput, Ken Littlefield, Beverly DellaCorte, and many, many others, who have trusted me with the care of your beloved pets. Your friendship is greatly appreciated, as is your support of my veterinary practice—which has given me the most enjoyable and fulfilling dream job that rarely feels like work.

Thank you to Dr. Barbara Hodges and Pam Runquist from the HSVMA for giving me the opportunity to be an active part of the animal welfare movement. And to the HSUS for modeling how to advocate and lobby in an effective, measured way. Further thanks to Dr. Adam Christman of DVM360 for accepting and promoting my veterinary presentations about pets with disabilities, and Piglet Mindset, through DVM360 Fetch conferences and platform.

Let me thank all my teachers and mentors, particularly Dr. Mark Peterson and others at the Animal Medical Center for setting me on my veterinary path with confidence. At Purdue, I flourished thanks to Dr. Skip Jackson, Dr. James Carter, Dr. Gordon Coppoc, and Dr. Elsa Janle of the veterinary physiology department—who oversaw my work in the diabetes lab that led to my adopting my beautiful dog April. Big thanks to all my veterinary college classmates, including Debbie Harber, Rachael Jones, Peter Smith, and Ames Ziegra. I am so fortunate to have journeyed along with my good friend Sue Kopp (with whom I got to graduate on two occasions—from Norwalk High School and the Purdue Vet School). Now we meet up again at the Yale animal bioethics study group.

Informing my success early on were good friends such as Laura Genduso, college roommate and study partner, and best friends Sally and Kevin Korsh, Lorraine Ring, Ann and Phil Glover, Drs.

Peter Smith and Louise LeBoeuf, Ann and Tom McCormick, Dr. Maryanne Scott and Harold Scott, Dr. Chris Gong, and Dr. Robin McFerrin.

Further acknowledgments belong to the gifted music teachers who played such significant roles in the development of the Shapiro children's musical lives. Thank you to Daniel's French horn teachers, Bob Brewer and Andy Spearman; to Rachael's first piano teacher, the late Norine Harris; and to Ellie's violin teacher at Julliard, Ann Setzer.

It is worth repeating that I love and am forever thankful to my parents, Arline and Harold Foodman, for your unyielding devotion to your kids and grandchildren. You have been there at every moment as my number one supporters even when you must have thought I was nuts. I want to express my gratitude to Warren's late mother and father, for their love and support, and in particular for their hands-on help when our kids were very young.

Warren's dad, Harold Shapiro, passed away years ago. He had become very fond of our dogs—even after not caring much for dogs when his kids were young. We recently lost Warren's dear mom, Ruth Shapiro. She loved hearing about and following her grandchildren and granddogs. We miss both of them.

It is no exaggeration to say that there would be no book without the people who live with me and our six dogs and three birds, starting with my three kids, who are very good sports, as they have willingly participated in the writing of this book.

Thank you to Rachael, for your encouragement, insight, and contributions, and for your enthusiastic participation in our social media fundraisers and live sessions. Welcome to Rachael's wife, Rebekka, who became part of our family in October 2020—in the midst of the worldwide pandemic that has prevented us from having a proper celebration. We look forward to making up for lost time.

Daniel's matter-of-fact reporting of events that no one else remembered provided humor as we planned and then added detail to our story. As much as he would rather have been on his way, it was nice to have him at home for the past year and to have him recall events we would have otherwise forgotten.

Ellie has had the most contact with my dog craziness and I appreciate her patient impatience. Pretty much everything we do is Piglet-centered at this point. But as much as she might protest, she loves our dogs, plays with them, takes pictures of them, and contributed thoughtful accounts of events, conversations, and interpretations throughout the process of writing this book that commonly ended in laughter.

And, without a question, this book would never have happened without Warren. How do I thank my husband of thirty years—yes, three decades—for being the ground base for all this craziness? Three kids, countless dogs, birds, and rodents, an unpredictable work schedule, and minivacations that have always included dogs! I don't think he would complain about any of it other than the fact that we haven't taken our honeymoon trip to Hawaii, yet.

Warren has cheerfully (usually) agreed to pretty much everyone and everything. He has a kind heart and a very soft spot for the extra needy ones, just like I do. It's hard to say no when you know you are in a unique position to help. Of course, there were exceptions, but when he came to his senses, he realized that my judgement was best and he should follow it! (I'm kidding—just checking to see if he would read this and he did, in good-humor.)

Throughout the writing process I kept meaning to include a mention of my sweet special ferret, Cindy, who was with me for only six and a half years—through vet school and a few years afterward. Somehow she never made it onto the page but she has been one of the many muses who has hovered over the writing. I loved her to pieces, my CinCin, the tiny kid. She died a few months before I met Warren, so for a long time we joked that "Warren replaced the ferret!"

The true book muse was always sweet Susie, whose memory fills me with gratitude for the loving, gentle, kind tone she set for our dog family. Each dog that entered our home was given a warm welcome by our little Susan. The more the merrier, as far as she was concerned. She loved her Deanie and Annie, but everyone was part of her family. Susie was building Piglet's Inclusion Pack before there was a Piglet.

When Piglet arrived, Susie rose to offer unimaginable levels of compassion to the tiny screaming baby. She didn't hesitate to comfort him, play with him, and nurture him with extraordinary maternal care. Despite being twelve years apart in age, their friendship was mutual. Piglet was very attached to Susie. He would seek her out to play with him, and she in turn would find him and gently invite him to play with her. I am thankful for iPhones because fortunately I have the most adorable videos of Susie sleeping with Piglet, playing with Piglet, and taking walks with him, and of course with all the other dogs as well. Watching her decline during the writing of this book was extremely painful.

Susie died peacefully on April 3, 2021, after nearly a yearlong decline from chronic kidney failure. Knowing her time was limited, we took advantage of every minute we had with her. We took many trips to the beach, her favorite place of all, and took as many pictures and videos as possible. Thank you to all of Piglet's social media friends for attending two different memorials for Susan. We all come from different places but we came together for a heartwarming celebration of her life.

Of course, we must recognize and thank the pink man himself, for being the most positive, connected, precious deaf and blind dog I could ever wish for. Looking back, I have no idea how I ever considered placing him in any home other than ours. I am thankful that I got to be the one to say "yes."

Finally, my humble thanks to animal lovers, rescuers, fosterers, adopters, and humane activists of every stripe, as well as to every supporter and contributor of Piggy Lee's mission. To all of our readers, thank you for your company on this journey and for opening your heart to the unexpected in your life. Please join our online community on Instagram, @pinkpigletpuppy, and Facebook, Piglet, the deaf blind pink puppy. Visit our website, PigletMindset.org to learn about our Piglet Mindset educational program, and consider making a contribution or picking up some Piglity merchandise. You can also take advantage of a bonanza of information and useful resources for pet safety, adoption, inclusion, and more. We hope you'll bring Piglet Mindset educational outreach into your schools and local organizations. We thank you with all of our hearts for your kindness and all you do to make this a safer, pinker, and better world—one in which we will all do more, as exemplified by Piglet and his Inclusion Pack, to "Stay Connected."

ABOUT THE AUTHORS

Melissa Shapiro, DVM, a practicing veterinarian for over thirty years, has been rescuing, healing, and caring for animals since she was a very young child. A graduate of Purdue University College of Veterinary Medicine, Dr. Shapiro completed an internship at the Animal Medical Center in New York City, followed by a residency at the Veterinary Hospital of the University of Pennsylvania.

Dr. Shapiro's Visiting Vet Service provides custom in-home veterinary care to dogs and cats in Fairfield County, Connecticut. Currently her practice focuses on senior pet wellness, illness, palliative care, and dignified, peaceful end-of-life services. Dr. Shapiro works with a number of dog and cat rescue groups and is the Connecticut state representative for the Humane Society Veterinary Medical Association.

Since adopting Piglet, the deaf blind pink puppy who has become a global social media phenomenon, Dr. Shapiro has used her platform to educate, advocate, and inspire others to foster and/or adopt pets looking for loving homes. In person and virtually, the two also raise funds and awareness for pets with disabilities.

Dr. Shapiro is the founder and president of Piglet International Inc., a 501(c)(3) nonprofit organization dedicated to supporting the Piglet Mindset Educational Outreach Program, a free downloadable educational program that uses Piglet's story to teach growth mindset, acceptance, inclusion, empathy, and kindness in classrooms across the United States and the world. Dr. Shapiro lectures extensively and travels widely with Piglet. They address schools, nonprofits, community groups, and organizations representing people with disabilities. Honored by the Dog Writers Association of America for her writing on a various pet care topics, Melissa and Piglet have been featured on *NBC Nightly News* and in *People Magazine*, and in a wide range of local and national media.

Melissa and her husband, Warren, are the proud parents of three children now in their early twenties. Their household in Westport, Connecticut, includes six rescued dogs, three rescued birds, and Piglet, the deaf blind pink puppy.

Mim Eichler Rivas is coauthor with Chris Gardner of the number one *New York Times* bestseller *The Pursuit of Happyness*. Mim's list of more than three dozen acclaimed coauthorships includes the national bestseller *Finding Fish*, with Antwone Fisher. Mim's solo title, *Beautiful Jim Key*, has sold briskly for more than a dozen years and has a feature film in the works.